The Natural Nursery

The Natural Nursery

*The Parent's Guide
to Ecologically Sound, Nontoxic,
Safe, and Healthy Baby Care*

Louis Pottkotter, M.D., F.A.A.P.

CONTEMPORARY
BOOKS

CHICAGO

Library of Congress Cataloging-in-Publication Data

Pottkotter, Louis.
    The natural nursery : a parent's guide to ecologically sound,
nontoxic, safe, and healthy baby care / Louis Pottkotter.
       p.   cm.
    ISBN 0-8092-3766-0
    1. Infants—Care.   2. Pediatric toxicology.   I. Title.
RJ61.P696   1994
649′.122—dc20   94-29783
                                                    CIP

Published by Contemporary Books, Inc.
Two Prudential Plaza, Chicago, Illinois 60601-6790
Manufactured in the United States of America
International Standard Book Number: 0-8092-3766-0
10   9   8   7   6   5   4   3   2   1

Printed on Recycled Paper

This book has been reviewed carefully for accuracy and conforms to the highest standards of medical care for children, but it is designed to supplement—not replace—the direct advice of your child's doctor. You know your child better than anyone else, and you should always follow your own instincts and judgment as to when it's time to call the doctor for assistance. It's always better to err on the side of being overcautious where the health of your child is concerned.

All suggestions and product recommendations in this book are intended for educational purposes only and made without warranty or guarantee, express or implied, and the author and publisher disclaim all liability in connection with the use of this information. The material presented herein is not a substitute for the advice of a personal health-care professional. Always consult a physician before giving any drug or medicine (even one presumed to be safe) to a baby or child.

Dedicated to
Kathleen, Mary, Louis, Vicki, and Larry

Contents

Introduction

Sometimes it seems that nothing is safe anymore. Air pollutants, radon, asbestos, pesticides, artificial food additives, genetically engineered and irradiated food, salmonella and E. coli food poisoning, electromagnetic fields, lead poisoning, contaminated drinking water, and consumer products loaded with toxic chemicals are just a few of the hazards that challenge the health of our children. As a concerned parent you desperately want to protect your child from the dangers lurking everywhere, but making the right choices can be difficult without a trustworthy guide to direct you safely through the labyrinth of toxicity created by modern technology. That's why I decided to write this book. *The Natural Nursery* combines ecology and baby care to give you environmentally sound advice for raising your child in the healthiest manner possible. There are literally hundreds of easy and inexpensive things you can do to avoid the risks of high technology without having to give up modern conveniences, things that will make a critical difference in promoting good health for your child while preserving the planet for future generations.

The Natural Nursery is divided into eight chapters, each an integral piece of the total wellness puzzle. In Chapter 1 you'll learn about breast-feeding, formula feeding, cow's milk, food irradiation, genetically engineered food, toxins in fish and seafood, food poisoning, artificial additives (colors, preservatives, flavors, and sweeteners), and food contaminants (aluminum, dioxins, and PCBs). The advantages and disadvantages of tap water versus bottled drinking water, as well as water filtering devices, are also discussed. The section on pesticides in food even includes a chart that groups the most frequently consumed fruits and vegetables into three color-coded safety categories (green, yellow, red) based on the average number of synthetic chemical pesticides they typically contain. And as an added bonus, startling new discoveries about the toxic pitfalls of organically grown foods are revealed (you won't find this information in the holistic cookbooks).

Chapter 2 presents the pros and cons of cloth diapers versus disposables from an unbiased, scientific point of view. The answer to this dilemma is not as black and white as some environmentalists would have you believe. In fact recent studies have debunked the myth that cloth diapers are the only ecologically correct choice. Secrets for preventing and curing the four most common forms of diaper rash are also outlined.

Chapter 3 points out the best and worst fabrics for baby clothing and bedding, along with the names and toll-free phone numbers of several mail-order catalogs that specialize in selling 100 percent cotton products. Tips for nontoxic laundering are also included.

Chapter 4 outlines baby bath basics, including the names of the mildest and safest cleansing bars, shampoos, lotions, creams, and ointments. There's also a discussion of the ingredients used in skin-care products so that you can decipher labels for yourself (it's a lot easier than you might think). You'll be surprised to learn how many of the ingredients in popular skin-care products for babies are actually leading causes of allergic contact dermatitis—just the opposite of what you've been led to believe by television advertisements.

Chapter 5 is designed to assist you in dealing with illnesses, infections, and other medical problems that are an inevitable part of growing up. When your child is sick, you don't have the time to weed through pages and pages of encyclopedic text to find out what to do. You need answers, and you need them fast. This chapter provides a quick and easy stepwise plan to help you figure out what danger signs to look for, when to call the doctor, and how to make your child feel better in a jiffy. The important topics of circumcision, colic, SIDS, and other issues related specifically to newborns are also discussed.

Chapter 6 is concerned primarily with pollutants inside the home, such as lead, radon, formaldehyde, carbon monoxide, tobacco smoke, asbestos, biological inhalant allergens, and electromagnetic fields. The problem with many of these indoor pollutants is that you can't see them or smell them, but they can damage your child's immune system and cause a variety of symptoms, including headaches, dizziness, nausea, scratchy eyes, sore throat, runny nose, hoarseness, coughing, and breathing difficulties. In fact some of the most dangerous volatile organic compounds (VOCs) are heavier than air, which means the highest concentration is near the floor, where crawling babies and toddlers are playing. Chapter 6 also lists the major sources of VOCs along with suggestions for choosing nontoxic building materials, paints, furnishings, appliances, and household cleaning products. Natural, low-toxicity, and earth-friendly brand names are provided. In addition, simple ways to prevent lead poisoning and avoid electromagnetic radiation are discussed in detail. The information in this chapter is applicable particularly to the nursery, where your child will be spending more time than just about anywhere else in the house.

The National Academy of Sciences estimates that, because of legal loopholes and lack of government oversight (sound familiar?), more than 75 percent of the ingredients found in pesticides for the home, lawn, and garden have not been tested for their capacity to cause cancer, chromosome damage, birth defects, nerve damage, and immune system dysfunction. Chapter 7 outlines the symptoms of pesticide poisoning and provides quick-reference pesticide charts, nonchemical methods of pest control, recipes for bug sprays using homemade ingredients, and least-toxic commercial pesticide brand names.

Playing outdoors can sometimes be hazardous, and Chapter 8 discusses some of the most common problems that can occur, such as sunburn, swimming accidents, and insect bites. Safe and effective insect repellents are also mentioned.

The Appendix provides you with telephone numbers to obtain most of the products recommended throughout the book.

As you can see from this brief introduction, *The Natural Nursery* is designed to help you raise a healthy child in a heavily polluted world. The information is based on solid scientific facts obtained from leading medical sources, tempered by common sense and practicality, and presented in a balanced manner. *The Natural Nursery* is unique in the baby-care genre in that it provides specific answers that work in real situations. It's just what the doctor ordered for intelligent, caring, ecologically oriented parents of the nineties.

Please note that, for convenience and clarity of presentation, masculine and feminine pronouns are used interchangeably throughout this book with no preference given to either gender.

Louis Pottkotter, M.D., F.A.A.P.

1
Feeding
Your Baby

One of the most important responsibilities you have as a parent is to feed your child a nutritious, well-balanced diet, because good health and resistance to disease are directly proportional to the quality of food eaten. This chapter is designed to help you make optimal nutritional choices that will promote wellness and prevent illness. The topics include feeding schedules, breast-feeding, formula feeding, cow's milk, bottles and nipples, drinking water, baby food, pesticides in food, food irradiation, genetically engineered food, toxins in fish and seafood, food poisoning, artificial food additives (colors, preservatives, and flavors), and pollutants in food and water.

FEEDING SCHEDULES

In general, most newborns should be fed "on demand" whenever they're hungry. A baby's appetite normally fluctuates during the course of the day, and you must always be ready to adjust accordingly. For example, she may want to eat every two hours several times in a row, then every three or four hours, and then back again to every two. Moderation and flexibility are the keys to success. Avoid rigid schedules set by the clock, but don't let her use your breast or a bottle like a pacifier to nibble on at the slightest whim. Try to wait at least an hour and a half between feedings if possible.

Feeding schedules can vary a lot depending on your infant's age and metabolism and on whether you use breast milk or formula. From the second week to around the third month, breast-feeding infants usually nurse every two to three hours (eight to twelve feedings a day), and babies taking formula generally eat every three to four hours (six to eight feedings a day) since formula takes a little longer to digest than breast milk. After three months most babies gradually begin to stretch out the time interval between feedings. Keep in mind that your baby's schedule may differ from the average examples just cited, so be flexible.

A feeding should normally take about 20 to 30 minutes, but some babies eat faster and some a little more slowly. Try not to spend more than 40 minutes per feeding session, or your infant may swallow too much air and get a stomachache. Sucking is a very soothing and pleasurable activity for babies, so don't think that your child is still hungry just because she wants to keep sucking after a routine feeding. Instead of overfeeding, try a pacifier. Believe me, if your baby is really hungry, she will fuss or cry until you offer more food.

The amount of breast milk or formula that a baby needs each day depends on her age, weight, and basal metabolic rate (fast, average, slow). During the first six months an infant with an average metabolic rate needs approximately 50 calories per pound of body weight every 24 hours. Since breast milk and infant formula each supply about 20 calories per ounce, this translates into a daily requirement of about 2½ ounces per pound of body weight. For example, a 12-pound baby with an average metabolic rate whose only source of calories is formula or breast milk will typically drink about 30 ounces a day (2½ ounces × 12 pounds = 30 ounces). A fast metabolizer will need more calories and a slow metabolizer less, so be ready to adapt accordingly.

When all is said and done, your baby's monthly weight gain is one of the most reliable indicators of whether you're feeding her too much or too little. The average-size infant should gain between one and two pounds per month for the first six months. A baby who is gaining less than one pound a month is probably not getting enough nourishment. On the other hand, if your infant is packing on more than three pounds a month, there's a good chance you're overfeeding. In either case, check with your doctor.

BREAST-FEEDING
Why Breast-Feed Your Baby?

Breast-feeding offers many advantages and benefits not provided by infant formulas:

- Breast milk is the perfect food designed by nature exclusively for human babies. It's the gold standard all formula manufacturers try to copy. All infant formulas are made from either cow's milk or soy milk, neither of which is equivalent to human breast milk. No matter how much they are modified and processed, cow's milk and soy milk cannot be turned into human milk. Please note, however, that infant formulas are much healthier for babies than regular homogenized cow's milk, because formulas are designed to meet the special nutritional requirements of infants.
- Infant formulas are rather expensive compared to breast-feeding.
- Formula frequently causes constipation, whereas breast milk rarely does. Breast-fed and formula-fed babies have very different bowel movement patterns. The breast-fed infant has five to eight loose, yellow, seedy, and nonpungent stools daily. In contrast, formula-fed babies usually have three or four formed, yellow or brown, pungent stools daily.
- Infant formulas cause more allergies and digestive problems than breast-feeding. In fact breast-feeding seems to lower a baby's risk of developing respiratory, intestinal, and skin allergies, so if your family has a history of asthma, food allergies, or eczema, breast-feeding until your child is at least one year old is strongly recommended.
- According to the American Academy of Pediatrics (AAP), breast milk provides optimal nutrition for infants during the first 6 to 12 months; the only acceptable alternative to breast milk is iron-fortified infant formula. The AAP does not recommend whole cow's milk or low-iron formulas during the first year.
- Breast milk contains a host of immunologically beneficial factors—interferon, antibodies, white blood cells, and the like—that can help babies fight off many viral, bacterial, and fungal infections. It also promotes the growth of "good" intestinal

bacteria, such as lactobacillus and bifidus, which provide essential micronutrients and inhibit the growth of harmful bacteria and yeast.

- Breast-feeding your baby for at least the first three months will help his baby teeth (and his permanent teeth) come in straighter and reduce the possibility of his needing orthodontic braces later in life.
- Breast-feeding is associated with a lower risk of sudden infant death syndrome (SIDS). See Chapter 5 for further information on SIDS prevention.

Although breast-feeding provides a baby with many healthful benefits, there are a few things it cannot do:

- Breast-feeding cannot guarantee your child won't become allergic to some foods in the long run. Studies have shown that for children who have a genetically inherited susceptibility to food allergies breast-feeding only delays the time when their allergies will appear.
- Breast-feeding cannot prevent infant colic (except when colic is caused by a milk allergy). In most instances it's the baby's temperament that causes colic, and breast-feeding cannot change that. (See Chapter 5 for details on colic.)
- Breast-feeding cannot keep a child from catching infectious diseases. It's the degree of exposure to other children and the general public—not the feeding method—that *primarily* determines how frequently a child will catch respiratory and intestinal infections. Infants who are exposed repeatedly to large groups of people (and their germs) at daycare centers, church and temple nurseries, and shopping malls are going to get sick at least two or three times more often than those who stay at home, regardless of the feeding method employed. In other words, all things being equal, a breast-fed baby who regularly attends day care will get sick much more often than a formula-fed baby who stays home and is not exposed to large groups of children.

After considering all of these facts, you need to think about why you have chosen to breast-feed your baby and make sure you're doing it for the right reasons. Never breast-feed out of a misguided sense of duty or obligation, because if you feel unhappy or resentful about it, the baby will sense your displeasure and both of you will come to dread feeding time. Contrary to popular belief, not everyone enjoys the breast-feeding experience, so be honest with yourself from the start and please don't let friends or relatives pressure you into a decision that's wrong for you. Remember, whether or not you breast-feed your baby has absolutely nothing to do with being a good parent. Furthermore, breast-feeding is not a prerequisite for mother-infant bonding. Regardless of the feeding method chosen, a strong bond will always develop between a mother and her baby as long as feeding and play periods are happy, cheerful times full of love, cuddling, and sharing.

Successful Breast-Feeding

Breast-feeding is the most natural activity in the world, but don't despair if it doesn't feel natural at first. We live in a society where breasts are usually covered, and most of us did not grow up seeing our mothers nursing their babies. The good news is that it won't take long for breast-feeding to become second nature. Remember though, that it is a learned skill for both the mother and the infant, and it almost always takes a few days of practice to smooth out the rough edges. So be patient and don't get discouraged. Your diligence will be amply rewarded.

Many good books contain detailed instructions on breast-feeding (such as *The Womanly Art of Breastfeeding* by La Leche League International). Here are the basics for getting started.

Step 1. Wash your hands right before each nursing session to minimize the spread of germs.

Step 2. Experiment with the three basic nursing positions and use the ones that work best for you and your baby:

- Traditional cradle hold: Sit in a comfortable chair; place a pillow or two in your lap to support most of the baby's weight; lay the

baby sideways on top of the pillows, his body positioned diago-
nally across your abdomen and facing you; cradle the back of his
head in the bend of your elbow at breast level and use your
forearm to hold his body snugly against your abdomen.

• Football hold: Sit in bed or in a chair; place a pillow or two at
your side; lay the baby face up on top of the pillows with your
hand tucked under the back of her head and your forearm sup-
porting her body against your side. You literally hold the baby
like a football.

• Side-lying: You and the baby lie down on your side with the
infant facing your chest.

You may find the sitting positions more comfortable if you prop up
your feet on a low stool. The specially designed Nursing-Stool from
Medela (800-435-8316) works quite well.

No matter which positions you use, support most of the infant's
weight with pillows. Do not hold the baby in your arm without support,
because your muscles will tire within minutes, and as your arm droops
the baby will slide out of position and pull the nipple, resulting in
stretched breast ligaments that really hurt.

Step 3. Latching on: The majority of breast-feeding problems stem
from the baby's failing to latch on to the breast properly. The following
suggestions will help prevent most of these problems. Using your free
hand, cup the underside of your breast with your fingers to give it some
lift and place the tip of your thumb at the 12 o'clock position on your
areola (the circle of dark skin around the nipple). With your thumb and
index finger curved in the shape of a C and lined up along the outer
edge of your areola, gently squeeze the areola so the nipple extends
forward in a pointed fashion; softly stroke your nipple across the
infant's lips to stimulate her sucking reflex. When your baby's mouth
opens as wide as a big yawn, place your entire nipple and at least one
inch of the areola well inside her mouth. If necessary, use your finger
to pull the baby's chin down to open her mouth wider. As the baby
sucks, you should feel her gums press up and down on the areola, not
on the nipple. Your nipple will extend quite a way into your baby's

mouth if positioned properly, and it will feel comfortable for both of you.

If your breast blocks the baby's nostrils, use your fingers to press down gently on the top of your breast to clear the airway, but don't press too hard, or you may block your milk ducts. Be sure the infant faces your breast straight on, because allowing her head to twist sideways while the nipple is in her mouth can not only hurt your breast but also make it harder for her to swallow.

For the first few days after delivery many newborns are so sleepy they won't latch on to the breast properly. Sometimes you can wake up a sleepyhead by tickling his feet, burping him, changing his diaper, or wiping a cool washcloth across his forehead or cheeks. This frustrating situation will improve slowly, day by day, as the baby becomes more alert, so don't panic and don't blame yourself. Just give it a little time.

Step 4. Alternate sides and rotate positions every five minutes. The reason this is so important is that the surface of a baby's tongue is actually quite rough, almost like an emery board, and if you let your infant suck on the same part of the nipple and areola at every nursing session, her tongue can file away the top layer of your skin and cause painful abrasions and bleeding. So every five minutes during a feeding, switch sides from one breast to the other and rotate the baby's nursing position a quarter turn to prevent constant friction on the same area of the nipple and areola. Spending equal amounts of time in the cradle hold and the football hold positions automatically rotates the stress points on the nipples.

Be very careful when removing the baby from the breast. If your infant is sucking vigorously when it's time to switch sides, slide your finger into the corner of her mouth and between the gums to break the suction first.

Take a few seconds to see if your baby wants to burp each time you switch sides. A healthy baby can completely empty each breast in about 10 to 15 minutes.

Stimulation of Milk Flow

During the first few days after delivery, your breasts produce a yellowish milk, called *colostrum*, which is loaded with essential nutrients and infection-fighting antibodies. After about two weeks of nursing, your breast milk will become whiter and richer as it matures, but don't expect it to look as white or be as thick as regular homogenized cow's milk.

Almost every new nursing mother worries about whether she's going to produce enough milk for her baby. Actually the baby's nursing style is what really determines how fast the milk comes in. If your baby nurses vigorously like a piglet right from the start, your milk will probably gush in on the third or fourth day. On the other hand, if your infant is a sleepyhead, it may take a week or two to stimulate an adequate flow of milk. In either case, try to relax and be patient because the more you worry, the harder it is for the pituitary gland to produce the two essential milk hormones (prolactin and oxytocin).

Prolactin activates the mammary glands to produce milk, and oxytocin ejects the milk out of the glands and propels it to the nipples. When oxytocin triggers the milk ejection reflex (or letdown as it is sometimes called), the nipples become erect, the breasts tingle, and milk drips rapidly or spurts from the nipples. Noisy distractions, lack of confidence, exhaustion, stress, pain, fear, anxiety, or anger will block the release of the milk hormones and prevent an adequate milk ejection reflex. If you experience problems with your letdown, try natural relaxation techniques (such as meditation or biofeedback), get plenty of rest, avoid entertaining visitors and other stress-provoking functions, and arrange to nurse the baby in a quiet, peaceful atmosphere without any distractions or negative thoughts. If all else fails, many obstetricians prescribe a safe and effective synthetic oxytocin nasal spray called Syntocinon to assist milk ejection for two or three days.

Toxic Warning

Many popular baby-care books recommend drinking beer or wine to relax the mother and improve the letdown reflex. *This is very dangerous advice.* Recent scientific studies have shown that when nursing mothers consume alcoholic beverages, their babies drink less milk, and some infants even suffer permanent neurologic impairment.

To boost your milk production naturally during the first few days, encourage your baby to nurse frequently, preferably every two to three hours (8 to 12 feeding sessions a day). Be flexible, avoid rigid schedules, and feed your baby whenever she is hungry, but remember the old saying "moderation in all things." From the second week to around the third month, your baby will probably want to nurse every two to four hours (6 to 12 feeding sessions a day) although some may eat more often and some a little less.

Try to leave the hospital as soon as your doctor gives the OK because it's the worst place to establish successful breast-feeding patterns. Rigid nursery schedules don't correspond to the natural biorhythm and sleep-wake-feeding cycles of newborns, and overworked hospital personnel often don't have time to take infants out for feedings except at the designated intervals. The result is a frustrating mismatch of sleepy babies too drowsy to eat when they're with their mothers and hungry infants crying themselves to sleep in the nursery. One way to avoid this unhappy situation is to request "rooming in," which allows your baby to stay in the room with you all day and night.

Breast-Feeding and Dehydration

During the first few weeks of breast-feeding, insufficient milk production by the mother and poor or ineffective nursing effort by the infant can sometimes cause the baby to become dehydrated. Fortunately, this doesn't happen very often, but it's important for parents to be on the alert for signs of dehydration in their newborn, particularly during those first two weeks, when breast-feeding is just getting started. The danger signs include the following:

• The baby is not gaining weight properly (less than one ounce per day).
• The baby produces fewer than six well-soaked wet diapers and/or fewer than three medium-size bowel movements per day.
• The baby's eyes appear sunken and the mouth is dry (little or no saliva).
• The baby sleeps constantly, never cries, and will barely wake up to nurse for only a few minutes every five to six hours (this is

often mistaken as a sign of a "content" newborn when it's actually an indication of extreme weakness due to dehydration).

If you even remotely suspect that your infant is becoming dehydrated, take him in to see the doctor right away, because a simple weight check and physical exam can determine quickly whether your baby is in danger. If a problem is detected, simple corrective measures can be taken. In fact, to be on the safe side, I recommend that you schedule an appointment to have your baby's weight checked at four or five days of age and again at two weeks. Please note that most newborns lose a few ounces of weight during the first three days after delivery, but by the fifth day the infant should be back up to birth weight and then start gaining at least one ounce a day for the next few months. In addition, a healthy newborn should nurse vigorously for at least 10 minutes every two to four hours and produce at least six well-soaked wet diapers and a minimum of three medium-size bowel movements per 24 hours.

Nutrition for Breast-Feeding Mothers

Breast milk provides approximately 20 calories per ounce, so the number of extra calories required for a nursing mother to "break even" every day depends on how many ounces of breast milk her baby is consuming. For example, an average one-month-old may consume about 25 ounces a day, which translates into 500 calories (25 ounces × 20 calories/ounce), while a four-month-old would average 35 ounces (700 calories) per day. A woman whose body size, metabolism, and daily exercise are in the "average" range will need to eat about 2,500 calories a day while nursing a one-month-old and about 2,700 calories a day nursing a four-month-old.

The kind of food you eat is as important as the number of calories. Please choose fresh or minimally processed natural foods (without artificial colors, flavors, or sweeteners) within the healthy guidelines of a well-balanced diet. Avoid the so-called diet or low-cal foods, which are usually loaded with synthetic ingredients. The long-term effects of "fake fat" and sugar substitutes are unknown and may ultimately prove to be quite harmful to humans. Besides, many people who are overweight gobble down these high-tech unnatural foods like they're going out of style, but they never manage to lose weight and keep it off.

You don't have to give up your favorite foods just because you're breast-feeding, but avoid excess consumption of foods with strong odors, because they may give your milk an unpleasant taste that the baby won't like. And don't overdo chocolate or beverages with caffeine or artificial sweeteners, because these might make the baby nervous and irritable.

All babies cry, get stomachaches, and pass a lot of gas during the first two months, so don't automatically blame your diet for such problems. On the other hand, the food you eat does enter your breast milk as soon as 1 hour after consumption and can remain there for at least 12 hours. Therefore, if the baby rejects your milk, acts fussy, or

> *Don't starve yourself to lose weight if you're breast-feeding. Rapid weight loss causes the body to mobilize toxins stored in fat (such as DDT, dioxins, and PCBs) and transfers them directly into the breast milk. And don't take diet pills, because the medication enters your breast milk and can hurt your baby. If weight reduction is your goal, slightly lowering your normal intake by about 500 calories per day will usually result in a one-pound weight loss per week. Do not try to lose weight any faster than that. According to a study published in the* American Journal of Clinical Nutrition *59: (1994): 833–40, women who are breast-feeding can safely lose about one pound per week without adversely affecting the quantity or quality of their milk.*

has a lot of intestinal gas, it's probably a good idea to review what you have eaten or drunk to see if you can identify a problem food. The most common offenders include milk and dairy products, eggs, caffeine (coffee, tea, cola, chocolate), citrus fruits, tuna fish, sardines, garlic, onions, mustard greens, and cauliflower. To figure out if food is really causing a problem, restrict your diet to bland, nonspicy foods and eliminate milk and dairy products for one week. If the bland diet makes your baby feel a lot better, experiment with your menu by adding one new food every day and noting whether it has any adverse affect. If a certain food seems to make things worse, eliminate it from your diet for a week and then try it again. This careful trial-and-error approach will help you spot problem foods. Of course, always inform your doctor of what you're doing in case special supplements or other modifications to your diet may be necessary.

Questions Frequently Asked About Breast-Feeding

Q: *Does breast size determine the amount of milk produced?*

A: *The size of the breasts has nothing to do with the amount of milk produced. The female breast has hundreds of tiny milk-producing (mammary) glands, which empty into about 20 milk ducts leading to the nipple opening. All women have approximately the same number of mammary glands, regardless of size. Large breasts have more fat tissue, not more milk glands.*

Q: *Will flat or inverted nipples prevent successful breast-feeding?*

A: *Flat or inverted nipples should not discourage a mother from nursing, because in most instances the baby's suckling stimulates the nipple to protrude adequately for normal feeding.*

Q: *Are breast-feeding difficulties passed from one generation to the next?*

A: *Breast-feeding difficulties are not passed from one generation to the next. The fact that your mother or grandmother had an unsuccessful breast-feeding experience does not mean that you will.*

Q: *How can I tell if my baby is getting enough breast milk?*

A: *You know your baby is getting enough milk if she produces at least six well-soaked diapers and three medium-size bowel movements every 24 hours and gains an average of at least one ounce per day for the first few months. If your infant is gaining less than one pound a month, she is not getting enough nourishment, and you should consult your doctor for additional feeding instructions.*

Q: *Should I give my baby "sugar water" (glucose) supplements?*

A: *During the first two days while your milk supply is building up, it's a good idea to offer your baby an ounce or two of plain water—not sugar water—after each nursing session is finished to keep her kidneys well hydrated. Some newborns want only a few sips, while others gulp down an ounce or more. Don't force your baby to drink the water if it causes gagging or if she obviously doesn't want it. You should be able to stop the water supplements by the third day as your milk production increases.*

Q: *Should a breast-fed baby occasionally be fed from a bottle?*

A: *Unless you never plan to leave your baby for more than a few hours during the months you nurse her, you'll have to let her get used to feeding from a bottle filled with expressed breast milk (or infant formula). However, timing is very important here. From about the third day to about the third week of age, try not to offer any bottles, or the baby may develop "nipple confusion" and reject the breast entirely. Then, when your baby is about three weeks old, it's a good idea to start offering a supplemental bottle of formula or breast milk once a day or every other day. It's a fact that sooner or later (no matter how strong your commitment to breast-feeding) your baby is going to need a bottle for one reason or another. If you wait until your infant is over six weeks old before offering her a supplemental bottle, you may have a battle on your hands, because by then she may be so fond of the breast that she furiously rejects a rubber nipple. Then you'll have to be available around the clock for breast-feeding purposes until she's about seven months old and able to drink from a cup. One other advantage to a supplemental bottle is that it gives Dad a chance to participate in the feedings.*

Q: *When do supplemental bottle feedings interfere with nursing?*

A: *Supplemental feedings interfere with nursing when you give more than one bottle a day. Babies are smart, and if they're fed too often from a bottle, they begin to realize that breast-feeding requires a lot of effort, which can lead to breast rejection. In addition, the less often you nurse, the less milk your breasts will produce.*

Q: *Should supplemental bottles contain breast milk or formula?*

A: *The choice of milk to use in supplemental bottles is strictly a matter of preference. Some mothers like to pump or hand-express and store breast milk, while other women find it more convenient to use a commercial infant formula.*

Q: *Nursing was going fine, but suddenly my milk supply seems to have decreased. What can I do?*

A: *Stress, pain, exhaustion, fear, anxiety, anger, or resentment can cause a sharp drop in your milk supply by blocking the release of prolactin and oxytocin from the pituitary gland in your brain. To get back on track, follow these suggestions:*

- *Try to relax and get plenty of rest. Forget about working, shopping, cooking, housework, and entertaining until your milk supply is back to normal. Just tell everyone that your doctor has ordered complete bed rest and no visitors until further notice.*
- *Nurse the baby every two or three hours (8 to 12 times a day). The more often you nurse, the more milk your breasts will produce.*
- *Get into the habit of drinking one glass of liquid after every nursing session to replenish the four to eight ounces of milk consumed by the baby.*

Q: *Does vigorous aerobic exercise affect the breast milk?*

A: *Too-vigorous exercise can cause a temporary buildup of excess lactic acid in the breast milk for an hour or two after the exercise. This is not harmful to a nursing infant, but lactic acid does impart a sour taste to the milk, and your baby may reject it. If you are experiencing this problem, consider slowing down your exercise routine, because lactic acid buildup means you have gone from beneficial "aerobic" exercise (which burns primarily fat) into anaerobic exercise (which burns sugar).*

Q: *When is the best time to wean babies from the breast?*

A: *You should breast-feed your baby as long as you both enjoy the experience. Most babies tend to wean themselves naturally at 9 to 12 months of age, but it's OK to stop nursing earlier or later. Weaning should be done gradually by dropping one nursing session every five to seven days over a period of weeks—not abruptly.*

Breast-Feeding and the Working Mother

A few years ago combining breast-feeding and a career outside the home was almost unheard of. Today returning to work no longer means automatically weaning your baby, but you'll need a lot of motivation, planning, moral support, and a good sense of humor.

Timing when you go back to work is the single most important factor in how well your breast-feeding experience turns out. Mothers who can wait until their babies are at least four months old before going back have a much higher rate of success because their breast milk supply is well established and they've gained the extra experience and confidence needed to handle the breast-feeding problems that are bound to crop up from time to time.

The second most important factor in combining employment with breast-feeding is deciding whether you're going to work part-time or full-time. Mothers who work fewer than 20 hours per week are much more likely to have a successful breast-feeding experience than those who put in 40 or more hours per week.

The third factor is child care. If your company provides a daycare facility on-site, or if you can find a nice commercial daycare center located within minutes of work, you can continue to nurse your baby at lunch and at coffee breaks during the day. On the other hand, if neither option is available, you'll have to replace breast-feeding sessions with bottle feedings during the time you'll be at work, which means you'll have to decide whether to use expressed breast milk or infant formula in the supplemental bottles. You can pump or hand-express breast milk two or three times a day during breaks at work and then store the milk in a refrigerator or cooler case so that it will be available for your baby on the following day. On the other hand, if you prefer to supplement with an infant formula, you'll want to avoid painful breast engorgement by gradually weaning your baby to bottle feedings about two weeks before you plan to go back. For example, if you're going to work from 9:00 to 5:00, start feeding the baby with a bottle at around 11:00 A.M. each day for one week. Then, after you both get used to the new schedule, substitute an additional bottle feeding in the afternoon, around 3:00 P.M. On days when you go to work, the baby can nurse first thing in the morning, bottle-feed at 11:00 A.M. and 3:00 P.M., and nurse again as frequently as possible in the evening and at night. On weekends and holidays you can breast-feed your baby throughout the day to help boost your milk supply.

Now let's talk about the "real" world. The sad fact is that most women who work outside the home have to go back full-time after only four to eight weeks of maternity leave. This means that specific and reasonable ground rules must be negotiated in advance with your husband and your employer. Nursing takes energy, and doing everything yourself might be more than your body can handle. Dad will have to take care of half the household chores, and the boss will have to be willing to compromise on missed days due to unavoidable childhood illnesses. Don't let yourself slip into the role of supermom, the tireless wonder who holds down a full-time job while trying single-handedly to take perfect care of a house, husband, and baby. And don't let those television programs showing career women who "have it all together" make you feel inadequate. The truth is, most of those women are highly paid professionals who have a full-time nanny and two maids to help them.

Expressing and Storing Breast Milk

Hand Expressing

Milking your breasts by hand is as easy as pie if you follow the instructions detailed here. Choose a time to express your milk when your breasts are at least partially full, such as right after a short nursing session, when there's a long stretch in between feedings, or in the morning—rather than the late afternoon or evening when your supply is usually lower.

Step 1. Wash your hands, and then gently wipe your nipples with a cotton ball and clean tap water.

Step 2. Activate your milk ejection reflex right before you're ready to start expressing. Breast milk won't come out fast enough unless you trigger a good letdown first. One method that often works is to sit in a comfortable chair, relax, and think about your baby actually nursing while you lightly stroke or gently massage your nipples. Another way is to let your baby nurse on one side while you collect the milk that's dripping or spurting from the other side. Or, some women find that a warm shower or bath stimulates their milk to flow. Use the method that works best for you. As soon as your letdown reflex is properly activated, go on to step 3.

Step 3. Picture your areola (the circle of dark skin around the nipple) as the face of a clock. Place your thumb at the 12 o'clock position along the outer edge of your areola, and cup the underside of your breast with your index and middle fingers at the 6 o'clock position about one inch from the nipple. To collect the milk, hold a wide-mouth cup or bowl close to the nipple, and lean forward slightly so that the nipple points downward toward the container. (Or, you can use a hand expression funnel such as the one designed by Medela, Inc., to collect breast milk.) Gently compress and roll your thumb and finger pads forward toward the nipple, release, and repeat with a steady back-and-forth "milking" movement, just as if the baby were nursing. Don't squeeze or pull directly on the nipple itself. Repeat the milking maneuver 10 times, and then rotate the position of your thumb and fingers a quarter turn to the 3 o'clock/9 o'clock position and perform the same maneuver. Keep rotating a quarter turn after every 10 squeezes. Work on your right breast for about 5 minutes, and then switch to the left breast.

Alternate sides every 5 minutes for about 20 minutes or until the milk stops flowing in a stream (whichever comes first). It should not take more than 20 minutes total time to finish both sides. If the milking maneuver produces only a trickle of milk instead of a squirt or spray from the nipples, you should stop for the time being; because either your breasts are temporarily empty or your letdown is not properly activated.

Breast Pumps

If you decide to use a breast pump, the key to success is to activate your letdown reflex first, using the same techniques suggested in the previous section on hand expressing. Be sure the breast pump suction cup fits correctly so the pressure is actually exerted on the areola, not on the nipple itself. Don't let the funnel rub back and forth against the nipple because the friction will cause an abrasion. Again, alternate sides every 5 minutes, and don't take more than 20 minutes total time to finish both sides. All parts of the pump that come into direct contact with the milk should be washed and rinsed thoroughly after each use.

There are four basic breast pumps, each one having its own advantages and disadvantages:

Plastic cylinder or piston-type breast pump. The piston-type pump is fast, portable, comfortable, effective, and easy to keep clean. For an average price range of $20–$30, it's an excellent choice. The best brand-name pump is the Medela Manualectric Breastpump (model 50001), which is sold through hospitals and pharmacies, or you can order it directly from Medela, Inc., (800-435-8316). Medela is less likely to injure the nipples than most other brands, and it's dishwasher-safe. Other good brand names sold at pharmacies include Ross Deluxe, Comfort Plus, and Marshall Kaneson.

The main disadvantage of the piston-type pump is that it requires a fair amount of muscular effort and may tire your arm. And holding the pump incorrectly (palm down and elbow flipped up and away from your side) can cause tenderness of the elbow (similar to a tennis elbow). To prevent this, be sure to hold the pump with your palm up, and keep your elbow positioned right next to your side while pumping.

Automatic electric breast pump. The automatic electric breast pump is fast, comfortable, effortless, and easy to keep clean. Its mode of action is very smooth, simulating the nursing rhythm better than any other breast pump. The two best brands are made by Medela (800-435-8316) and Ameda/Egnell (800-323-8750).

Medela, Inc., offers a wide selection of automatic electric pumps, including the heavy-duty hospital model; the portable Lactina Electric Plus model with a special power pack for operation by electricity, battery, or car lighter; and the minielectric battery-operated model. Please note that most other brands of small battery-operated pumps tend to have a rough mode of action that injures the nipples.

It's also worth noting that Medela sells a highly recommended attachment called a double-pumping kit that allows you to pump both breasts simultaneously and finish a pumping session in just 10–15 minutes. In addition, double pumping increases prolactin levels and thus helps to maintain an adequate milk supply. This is particularly beneficial for moms who are planning to pump and store breast milk at work.

The only drawback to automatic electric pumps is the purchase price. However, many hospitals and pharmacies rent them for about $2.00/day, and some La Leche League groups even offer free rental (La Leche phone numbers are listed in the white pages, or call 1-800-LA-LECHE).

Lloyd B breast pump. The Lloyd B breast pump is fast, portable, effective, and easy to keep clean. It costs about $40. You'll definitely give your forearm muscles a good workout trying to squeeze the awkward handle on this pump.

Rubber bulb or "bicycle horn" breast pump. Never use this type of pump! It's slow, rough, awkward, and uncomfortable. It can injure the nipples, and the rubber bulb harbors germs and bacteria that contaminate the milk.

Storing Breast Milk

If you plan to use the milk within 24 to 48 hours after collection, refrigerate it at approximately 38° F. On the other hand, if you're not going to use the milk right away, chill it first in the refrigerator and then freeze it right after that. For best results try these suggestions:

- Store about four ounces in each bottle to avoid waste and facilitate thawing later on.
- Leave some extra room at the top of the bottle (at least two inches) for the milk to expand as it freezes.
- Put a label with the date on the bottle so the stock can be rotated properly.

Glass containers are best for *refrigerating* expressed breast milk. For *freezing* breast milk, however, hard plastic baby bottles are best because (a) glass may break and (b) disposable plastic nursers often contain toxic "plasticizer" chemicals that may leach into the milk. For more information, see the section "Bottles and Nipples."

Breast milk is not pasteurized, so it contains bacteria that make it spoil much more quickly than pasteurized store-bought milk. That's why *refrigerated* breast milk should be used 48 hours after it's collected. In contrast, *frozen* breast milk will keep for about three months in a regular freezer set at 0° F and up to six months in a deep freeze where the temperature is maintained continuously below 0° F. Always discard the milk beyond these dates.

Do not under any circumstances feed your baby breast milk obtained from anyone other than yourself. Many dangerous (and potentially fatal) viruses can be transmitted to infants through breast milk (such as AIDS or HIV, hepatitis B virus, and cytomegalovirus/CMV) even though the donor appears perfectly healthy.

Thawing Breast Milk

The best way to thaw frozen breast milk is to transfer it from the freezer to the refrigerator 24 hours before you plan to use it. On the other hand, if you're in a hurry, you can either rotate the bottle of frozen milk under a stream of warm running water or put the bottle in a bowl of warm tap water for about 15 minutes. Prior to feeding, give the bottle a good shake to emulsify the fat. Breast milk does not have to be warmed before being fed to the baby. Room temperature or slightly cooler is just fine.

Caution: Once thawed, breast milk can be refrigerated at 38° F for up to 24 hours, but *never refreeze it* and *do not leave it at room temperature for more than 30 minutes, or it will spoil.* The bacterial growth doubles every 20 minutes at room temperature.

It is not safe to thaw or warm breast milk in a microwave oven. When breast milk is heated in a microwave to 100° F, it loses many nutrients and much of its natural anti-infection properties. And with microwave heating there's always the danger of producing hidden pockets of milk hot enough to scald the inside of the baby's mouth, throat, and esophagus. In fact the milk may be extremely hot even though the outside of the container feels cool to the touch. In addition, heating a bottle of milk in the microwave can cause it to explode and spray scalding liquid on innocent bystanders. Therefore, since there's no reason to warm the milk in the first place, I strongly advise against microwave heating. (See "Formula Preparation Tips" for more details on microwave heating.)

Common Breast-Feeding Problems

Sore Nipples

To keep your nipples from becoming bruised, chafed, cracked, sore, and tender, follow these suggestions right from the start:

- The real keys to preventing sore nipples are to alternate breasts every 5 minutes, rotate positions, be sure the baby's gums are pressing on the areola (not the nipple), limit feedings to 40 minutes, and break the suction before removing the baby from your breast—all described in steps 3 and 4 under "Successful Breast-Feeding."
- Don't use alcohol or soap of any kind on your nipples or areolas, because they remove the natural protective oils from the skin.
- The baby's saliva contains digestive enzymes that can irritate the skin, so as soon as each nursing session is finished, use plain tap water and a cotton ball to gently wipe off your nipples and areolas. Breast milk contains natural substances that promote skin healing, so after wiping away the saliva, express a few drops of milk, gently apply the milk to the nipples and areolas, and air-dry.
- Most commercial breast creams contain lanolin obtained from wool fat. Unfortunately, recent analyses of lanolin performed by the FDA demonstrated a total of 16 different pesticides in various lanolin creams. The study also found that at the highest concentrations the amount of pesticides ingested by an infant could actually exceed the acceptable daily intake currently set by the Environmental Protection Agency (EPA). Using lanolin breast

cream for a few days probably doesn't pose too great a risk, but the long-term effects of chronic pesticide exposure on the immature immune system and liver of an infant are unknown, so stop the applications once the skin heals (usually in just a couple of days). It's worth noting that Medela (800-435-8316) sells a lanolin breast cream that has had almost all of the pesticides removed.

- Keep your nipples as dry as possible: (a) Lower the flaps of your nursing bra several times a day to let the skin air-dry. (b) Use a soft nursing bra without plastic liners, because plastic traps heat and moisture. (c) Use soft, disposable nursing pads and change them frequently.

  Do not use an electric hair dryer to dry the nipples and areolas. The high-velocity flow of hot air may chap the skin. And a lot of the older dryers contain toxic asbestos fibers, which are hazardous to breathe. Furthermore, a hair dryer produces a strong electromagnetic field (EMF) that may be quite harmful. (See Chapter 6 for details on EMFs.)

- Don't nurse the baby while wearing rubber nipple shields, because your infant will get used to the smell and texture of the rubber and will refuse to suck on your bare nipple later on. On the other hand, if your nipples are cracked or sore, it's OK to wear hard plastic nipple shields or breast shells between nursing sessions to prevent the nipples from rubbing against the bra. You can order these from Medela (800-435-8316).

- If you use a breast pump to express your milk, be sure the suction cup fits correctly so the pressure is actually exerted on the areola, not on the nipple. Don't let the funnel rub back and forth against the nipple, because the friction will cause an abrasion. And avoid overly vigorous or high-pressure pumping.

  If your nipples become extremely sore and start to crack and bleed, continue the regimen for preventing sore nipples and follow these additional suggestions:

- Start each nursing session on the side that is less sore. Then alternate breasts and rotate the feeding position every 5 minutes for up to a maximum of 10 minutes on each side. At this point, if your baby isn't satisfied, offer a few ounces of formula from a bottle. If your nipples are extremely sore and bruised, don't nurse more often than once every 3 hours. If your baby wants more frequent feedings, supplement a few ounces of formula in between.

- Extra-strength acetaminophen (Tylenol or Panadol) is a good choice for the relief of pain if necessary.

Breast Engorgement and Swelling

Sometimes the breast milk really gushes in on the third or fourth day after delivery, and both breasts become swollen, lumpy, and painful because they're producing more milk than your baby can drink. The engorgement and discomfort will subside within a few days, but in the meantime, encourage your baby to nurse as frequently as possible and follow these suggestions:

- If your nipples are so swollen that the baby can't latch on properly, either pump or hand-express just enough milk (usually a few teaspoons) to soften the areola so it can fit inside the infant's mouth. Don't overdo it; the more milk you express, the more your breasts are going to produce. Nipple stimulation signals your breasts to produce extra milk, so if you're really engorged, a trick that often works is to take a warm shower or bath; the warm water may trigger your letdown reflex without stimulating the nipples, and the breast milk will drip out automatically to relieve some of the pressure and discomfort.
- Wear a soft, snug nursing bra 24 hours a day to gently bind the breasts and prevent unrestrained swelling.
- Extra-strength acetaminophen (Tylenol or Panadol) is a good choice for the relief of pain if necessary.

Mastitis

Mastitis is an infection inside the breast tissue. It starts suddenly with flulike symptoms such as fever, chills, and aching muscles, and then part of one breast becomes red, swollen, painful, hot, and tender.

Mastitis makes you feel very sick and usually doesn't occur until you've been nursing for at least two weeks. In contrast, breast engorgement causes both breasts to swell, makes you feel uncomfortable but not sick, and normally occurs when your milk first comes in or when you abruptly skip several feeding sessions in a row.

If you develop mastitis, you'll need a prescription antibiotic that is effective against staphylococcal bacteria yet safe to take while nursing a baby. Tegopen, Keflex, Ceclor, and Duricef are good choices for persons who are not allergic to penicillin or cephalosporin antibiotics. If you are allergic to penicillin or cephalosporins, erythromycin is probably the best alternative.

Bed rest is absolutely essential. Forget about work, housework, shopping, cooking, and entertaining until you have completely recovered. Just tell everyone that your doctor has ordered complete bed rest and accept no visitors until further notice. It will usually take two to three days to recover.

Pesticides and Pollutants in Breast Milk
Pesticides, Dioxins, and Polychlorinated Biphenyls (PCBs)

When lactation begins, the mother's fat cells release stored lipids to be used for producing breast milk. Along with the lipids, however, fat-soluble pesticides and pollutants that have been stored in the mother's fat tissue over the years are also discharged into the breast milk. That's why recent studies by the World Health Organization have found that some samples of breast milk contain significant amounts of dioxins, PCBs, and pesticides (such as DDT, DDE, dieldrin, chlordane, heptachlor).

Over a period of several months a nursing mother may eventually unload into her breast milk up to 20 percent (or more) of her lifetime accumulation of environmental pollutants. In fact getting rid of these toxic chemicals is one of the main reasons why breast-feeding significantly lowers a woman's risk of developing breast cancer. Unfortunately, the nursing baby absorbs the contaminants from the breast milk and stores them in his fat tissue, brain, thyroid, adrenals, and liver. The long-term health effects of these toxic bioaccumulations are unknown, but experts agree that in most instances the benefits of breast-feeding outweigh the risks. Therefore, don't let this somewhat distressing information discourage you from breast-feeding. Instead, think of it as a positive learning experience that will motivate you to prudently avoid environmental pollutants in the future. Remember, toxins are pumped into breast milk in direct proportion to the environmental pollutant exposure of the mother. If your exposure has been consistently low in the past and remains low while nursing, the chances are good that your breast milk will not contain dangerous amounts of dioxins or other fat-soluble pollutants. On the other hand, mothers who smoke cigarettes and/or regularly eat seafood from the Great Lakes or other polluted waterways generally have unacceptably high levels of contaminants in their breast milk and should consider a commercial infant formula for their babies instead of breast-feeding. Also note that rapid weight loss (more than one pound per week) can cause fat cells to unload their toxic contents into breast milk. For further information, see "Aluminum, Dioxins, and PCBs in Food, Water, and Consumer Products" later in this chapter.

Alcoholic Beverages

Alcohol (beer, wine, or liquor) enters breast milk as quickly as it enters your bloodstream and affects the baby's brain just as it does yours, so it's best not to drink any alcoholic beverages at all as long as you intend to breast-feed. Recent scientific studies have found that mothers who drink small to moderate amounts of alcohol while nursing run the risk of causing permanent brain damage and hyperactivity in their children. Many popular baby-care books advise nursing mothers to have a glass of wine or beer to help increase their milk production, but this advice is woefully out of date and just plain wrong. Do not nurse your baby for a minimum of four hours after consumption of any alcohol or if you feel even the slightest bit woozy.

Silicone Breast Implants

Women who have silicone breast implants leach silicones (polydimethyl siloxanes) into their breast milk. According to a study published in the *Journal of the American Medical Association* 271: (January 19,

1994): 213–16, six out of eight babies who drank silicone-tainted breast milk developed swallowing problems. Until a final conclusion is reached on this issue, if you have silicone breast implants, ask your doctor for advice about whether to breast-feed.

Taking Medicine and Breast-Feeding

Almost any medicine or drug can enter the breast milk and cause potentially serious side effects in your baby, so try not to take any medication unless it's absolutely necessary. This section will give you a general idea about what's safe and what isn't, but always consult your doctor for specific recommendations in this area.

When several alternative medications are available to treat a particular problem, choose the one that has the lowest concentration in breast milk and the least risk of side effects in the baby. Ask your doctor when the medicine can be expected to reach its peak blood level and try to schedule the medication so that nursing periods coincide with the medicine's lowest level in your bloodstream. For example, if a drug's concentration tends to be highest 30 to 60 minutes after administration, take the medicine right after a nursing session so it can peak and drop before the next feeding.

Whenever you're taking medicine while breast-feeding, monitor your infant closely for any unusual symptoms or side effects, such as drowsiness, irritability, loss of appetite, hyperactivity, sleep disturbances, vomiting, diarrhea, constipation, or skin rashes.

The following chart is a color-coded rating system for prescription and nonprescription drugs.

Green Light means "usually compatible with breast-feeding."

Yellow Light means "generally compatible with breast-feeding, but use with caution."

Red Light means "not compatible with breast-feeding."

Please note that space limitations do not permit an all-inclusive listing, and a medicine's omission from this chart is not meant to imply that it is not transferred into breast milk or that it does not have an effect on the nursing baby. For detailed information on all prescription drugs sold in the United States, consult the *Physicians' Desk Reference* (available at most libraries and bookstores).

DRUGS AND BREAST-FEEDING
Medicine for Pain, Headaches, Fever
Green Light
acetaminophen (Tylenol, Panadol)

Yellow Light
codeine (Tylenol 3, Phenaphen 3)
aspirin (Bayer, Bufferin)
ibuprofen (Motrin, Advil, Nuprin)
   Caution: A nursing mother should not take aspirin or ibuprofen if her infant is either jaundiced or under one month old.

Red Light
ergotamine (Cafergot)
methysergide (Sansert)

Antibiotics
Green Light
penicillins (penicillin, Ampicillin, Amoxicillin, Tegopen)
cephalosporins (Keflex, Ceclor, Duricef)

Yellow Light
erythromycin (Ilosone, E.E.S., E-Mycin, PCE, ERYC, and others)
sulfa (Gantrisin, Septra, Bactrim)
   Caution: A nursing mother should not take sulfa antibiotics if her infant is jaundiced, under one month old, or suffering from a hereditary blood disorder such as G6PD.

Red Light
griseofulvin (Grifulvin V)
chloramphenicol (Chloromycetin)
metronidazole (Flagyl)
isoniazid (INH, Laniazid, Rifamate, Tubizid)

Antihistamines, Decongestants, Cold Remedies
If possible, try to stay away from all antihistamines, decongestants, and cold remedies since they can cause potentially serious side effects in babies, such as disorientation, hyperactivity, irritability, insomnia, drowsiness, loss of appetite, irregular heartbeats, high blood pressure, allergic reactions, difficult urination, and/or constipation.

Toxic Warning

Reports are now linking sudden death in adults to the "nonsedating" class of antihistamines (Seldane, Hismanal), primarily when these drugs are used either in larger-than-recommended doses or in conjunction with erythromycin, Nizoral, or other oral antifungal agents. Even though the chance of such a catastrophic event occurring is quite small, it seems unwise to take the chance when there are safer antihistamines on the market.

Diarrhea Medicine

Green Light
Diasorb
Kaopectate
Donnagel

Yellow Light
Pepto-Bismol (contains an aspirinlike ingredient that can cause the same undesirable side effects as aspirin)

Laxatives

Green Light
milk of magnesia (Haley's M-O, Phillips')
psyllium seed fiber (Metamucil, etc.)
Maltsupex
Dialose
Colace

Red Light
The following laxatives may give your baby diarrhea and stomach cramps, so don't use them if you're breast-feeding:
castor oil
casanthranol
cascara
Doxidan
Dorbane; Dorbantyl
Dialose Plus
Peri-Colace
phenolphthalein (Ex-Lax, Correctol, Feen-A-Mint)

Diet Pills
Red Light

The stimulants used in diet pills (Acutrim, Dexatrim, Dietac, and the like) can cause irritability, hyperactivity, loss of appetite, or high blood pressure in anyone, including infants, so do not use any diet pills if you're breast-feeding.

Mind-Altering Drugs
Red Light

Mind-altering drugs, whether they're prescription or illegal, enter the breast milk and can cause permanent brain damage or even death in babies. The following list includes the most commonly abused substances, but there are many others just as deadly. So if you use any mind-altering drugs at all, do not breast-feed your child under any circumstances. Incidentally, many of these drugs stay in your breast milk for days after you use them just once.

Narcotics: heroin
Stimulants: amphetamines, Dexedrine, Desoxyn, Ritalin
Tranquilizers/Sedatives: Miltown, Equanil, Nembutal, Seconal
Hallucinogenics: LSD, PCP
Cocaine
Marijuana

FORMULA AND COW'S MILK

According to the American Academy of Pediatrics, for the first 12 months the only acceptable alternative to breast milk is an iron-fortified infant formula. Low-iron formulas and regular cow's milk should not be used during the first year of life.

In situations where parents choose not to breast-feed, commercial infant formulas are recommended until the baby is at least one year old. Feeding schedules and formula preparation tips are provided in this section.

How Much Formula
Do Babies Need Each Day?

The amount of formula a baby needs each day was explained earlier in this chapter. Remember that the precise amount depends on many factors, including the baby's age, weight, and basic metabolic rate, so you have to be very flexible and always consult your doctor when in doubt. The following chart provides a rough guideline for the amount of formula an average-size, full-term baby with an average appetite and metabolism would be expected to drink every 24 hours, but always ask your doctor to be sure what's best for your infant.

Baby's Age	Average Number of Ounces Taken Per 24 Hours
1–2 weeks	2–3 ounces every 3–4 hours
3–4 weeks	3–4 ounces every 3–4 hours
1–2 months	4–5 ounces every 3–4 hours
2–3 months	5–6 ounces every 4–5 hours
3–4 months	6–7 ounces every 4–5 hours
4–5 months	7–8 ounces every 4–6 hours

According to most pediatric nutritionists, once babies reach the point where they need more than 40 ounces of formula a day to meet their caloric requirements (this usually occurs when babies are four to six months old and weigh about 16 pounds), it's healthier for the additional calories to come from age-appropriate baby foods.

Cow's Milk–Based Formulas

Similac, Gerber, Enfamil, and SMA are collectively referred to as the cow's milk–based infant formulas, because their protein (whey and casein) comes from cow's milk. The carbohydrate is primarily lactose sugar, and the fat comes from vegetable oils (soy, corn, coconut, palm, sunflower, and/or safflower). Please note that infants need plenty of saturated fats in their diets for proper growth, so don't be alarmed when you see coconut oil or palm oil in the list of ingredients on the formula label. During the manufacturing process the protein, fat, carbohydrate, sodium (salt), potassium, chloride, calcium, and phosphorus are carefully adjusted to levels that meet the unique nutritional requirements of growing babies. Essential vitamins and other nutrients are also added.

All cow's milk–based infant formulas stack up pretty much the same nutritionally, but I generally recommend Similac over all the other national brands, because Ross Laboratories takes every possible precaution to avoid using milk from cows treated with recombinant bovine growth hormone (see the section "Cow's Milk" for details on rBGH).

> *Preparing homemade infant formula using evaporated cow's milk (PET or Carnation, for example) is asking for trouble. All of the painstaking work that goes into making the national-brand formulas cannot be duplicated at home. If you decide not to breast-feed, stick with commercial infant formulas for the first 12 months.*

Hypoallergenic Formulas

For babies who are allergic to both cow's milk protein and soy protein, a hypoallergenic formula may be necessary. Alimentum and Nutramigen are two excellent brands readily available at most supermarkets and pharmacies.

"Iron-Fortified" vs. "Low-Iron" Formulas

"Iron-fortified" formula is strongly recommended over "low-iron" because iron fortification prevents iron-deficiency anemia. Recent studies indicate that iron deficiency in early childhood may lead to significant delays in mental development. If the formula label says "low-iron," it is not iron-fortified.

Contrary to popular belief, iron fortification rarely, if ever, causes constipation, diarrhea, or spitting up. And please note that the iron in fortified infant cereals is not sufficient to meet the iron requirements of babies who are fed low-iron formulas or regular cow's milk.

The hospital nursery will probably give you a formula gift pack to take home when you leave the hospital. These so-called gifts are simply free samples donated to the hospital by the formula companies for advertisement purposes. They are not necessarily endorsed by the hospital or your doctor, so don't feel you have to keep using one particular brand just because you started out with it in the hospital. If the formula you start with causes spitting up or other digestive problems, ask your doctor about switching to another brand.

Soy Formulas

Isomil, Gerber Soy, Nursoy, ProSobee, and I-Soyalac are collectively referred to as the soy-based infant formulas because their protein comes from soybeans, not from animal sources. They use vegetable oils (soy, corn, coconut, sunflower, and/or safflower) for their fat and nonlactose carbohydrate sources (sucrose [table sugar], corn syrup, and/or tapioca dextrins). All soy formulas are iron-fortified; there are no low-iron versions.

Most nutritional experts recommend cow's milk–based infant formulas over the soy-based ones because cow's milk protein is more nutritious than soy protein. However, about 5 percent of babies will ultimately develop cow's milk protein allergy or lactose sugar intolerance, and for them a soy formula is usually an acceptable substitute.

Ready-to-Feed Liquid vs. Concentrated Liquid vs. Powder Formula

When diluted properly with water, concentrated liquid and powder formulas are nutritionally equivalent to "ready-to-feed." The main differences are in the areas of convenience, expense, and flavor. Ready-to-feed liquid formula is slightly more expensive, but since you don't have to add water, you'll save preparation time and avoid possible mistakes in dilution. In addition, when you're out running errands, or at other special times, the eight-ounce cans of ready-to-feed liquid are very handy. The powder formula is the most economical, the hardest to mix, and the least flavorful. In fact, once they've gotten used to drink-

ing ready-to-serve or concentrated liquid, some babies find the powdered version displeasing to their taste buds and may flatly reject it. If
you're nursing and supplementing formula only once every few days,
however, the powder is a good choice because you can mix just enough
for one bottle at a time.

Toxic Warning

If you use the concentrated liquid or powder formula,
always add the exact amount of water recommended
on the package label. Formula that is diluted too
much causes malnutrition, and formula that is too
concentrated can cause kidney overload, diarrhea,
seizures (convulsions), and potentially fatal blood
electrolyte (salt) imbalances.

Formula Preparation Tips

Unopened cans of formula can be stored at room temperature until the
expiration date, but once opened, the formula must be refrigerated and
used within 48 hours. Also, any formula that remains in the bottle after
your baby is finished drinking is contaminated with germs and should
be discarded.

When it comes to sterilization of formula, bottles, and nipples,
follow your doctor's advice. However, many experts feel that sterilization is not necessary as long as (a) the formula is a ready-to-feed liquid,
which is sterilized at the factory; (b) the preparation utensils, bottles,
and nipples are washed thoroughly with clean water from a municipal
source approved by the local health department; and (c) the formula is
properly refrigerated prior to use. On the other hand, almost everyone
agrees that sterilization is necessary if the formula is going to be left
unrefrigerated for more than 30 minutes or if the formula requires
dilution with tap water, especially if the safety of the water supply is
uncertain, such as might be the case if you get your water from a private
well.

Cold formula does not cause colic or digestion problems. Frankly, babies don't care whether their formula is served warm or cold, but if it makes you feel better, remove the chill by either setting the bottle of formula in a bowl of warm water for about five minutes or running warm tap water along the outside of the bottle for a minute or two while rotating it to distribute the warmth evenly. These old-fashioned methods of warming formula may take a few minutes longer, but they're a lot safer than microwaving. And don't forget, if you do warm the formula, always shake a few drops on your wrist to be sure it isn't too hot before offering it to your baby. In case you overheat it, you can add cold formula from the refrigerator to lower the temperature back to lukewarm.

I do not recommend microwave heating, especially since there's no reason to warm the formula in the first place. Microwave ovens are fast and convenient, but there are too many dangers associated with their use:

- The outside of the bottle may seem cool to the touch, but there may be hidden pockets of hot liquid that can scald the baby's mouth, throat, and esophagus. That's why it's so important to mix or stir the formula after heating and then test a small portion before feeding it to the baby.
- Microwaving food or liquids in a closed container (or one not specifically designed for microwaves, such as a disposable plastic nurser) can cause a rapid buildup of steam and pressure, resulting in an explosion that sprays scalding liquid on you or your baby.
- Plastic containers—bowls, trays, bottles, disposable plastic nursers—often leach toxic plasticizer chemicals into the formula during the heating process. To avoid this pitfall, use glass or Corning Ware containers that are approved for use in microwave ovens.
- Microwave heating destroys some of the vitamins in the formula.

If you decide to use a microwave oven to warm formula, please follow these precautions:

1. Heat only formula that has been refrigerated. Do not heat formula that is already at room temperature.

2. Use only microwave-safe containers and avoid excessive heating times. Place four to eight ounces of formula in an uncovered glass or Corning Ware bowl designed specifically for use in a microwave oven. Using full power, heat four ounces for no more than 20 seconds and eight ounces for no more than 30 seconds. Remove the bowl from the microwave, stir the formula to distribute the warmth, and then test a few drops. It should be lukewarm. In case of overheating, add an ounce or two of cold formula from the refrigerator to lower the temperature to lukewarm. Finally, pour the formula into a bottle, attach the nipple assembly, and feed.

Lead Poisoning from Infant Formula

Because of strict regulations governing the manufacturing process, ready-to-feed infant formula does not present any risk of lead poisoning. On the other hand, when powder or concentrated liquid formula is reconstituted with tap water that has a lead concentration of 15 micrograms or more per liter (15 parts per billion), the result can be lead poisoning and brain damage. The "Drinking Water" section of this chapter and the "Lead Poisoning" section of Chapter 6 have all of the details, but here are a few basic precautions to take if you decide to use tap water (instead of bottled drinking water) for mixing with formula:

- Tap water first drawn in the morning has the highest lead content because it sits in pipes overnight, so flush the lead and other toxic metals out of the pipes by simply letting the tap water run for two minutes before collecting it to prepare the formula.
- Use water from the cold side of the tap since the hot side contains much higher amounts of lead and other toxic heavy metals.
- Infant formula labels recommend boiling water for five minutes before adding it to the formula, but as the steam evaporates, the toxic metals are left behind and become more concentrated in the remaining water. In addition, boiling water in a lead-based, copper-clad, or aluminum kettle allows these toxic metals to leach into the water.

Formula Feeding Tips

- Cuddle and talk softly to your baby during feedings. Give your child as much loving face-to-face interaction while bottle-feeding as you would if you were nursing.
- If your baby swallows air, the air goes right into the intestine and can cause painful gas cramps. To minimize air swallowing, tilt or angle the bottle so that the nipple is always filled with milk and hold your infant in a semiupright position during feedings.
- Never leave your child alone with a propped bottle. Some babies don't know when it's time to come up for air. They'll keep drinking until they become so breathless that they gasp and choke on the formula. Also, sucking on a bottle while lying flat can lead to an ear infection.
- Encourage (but don't force) your baby to take a breather and burp after every ounce or two. Try not to let him guzzle down a whole bottle without taking a break every few minutes.
- Avoid overfeeding. Never make a baby finish a bottle if he doesn't want to. It's smarter to waste a few ounces than to force an infant to drink so much he vomits or gets a stomachache. And remember that crying does not always mean your baby is hungry. Don't use a formula bottle as if it were a pacifier.
- Rinse out the bottle and nipple as soon as the feeding is over, because milk is a lot harder to remove once it dries.
- Don't get into the bad habit of letting your child sleep with a bottle or carry it around all day, especially after his teeth start coming in, because constant sipping on formula or juice between regular feedings strips away tooth enamel and can lead to serious tooth decay.

Cow's Milk

For an American symbol of goodness almost as sacred as Mom's apple pie, cow's milk has been taking quite a beating from all sides lately. Is cow's milk getting a bum rap? Let's examine the pros and cons one at a time, and then you be the judge.

Cow's Milk Is For Calves

Nature designed regular cow's milk for calves, not human babies. Homogenized cow's milk lacks many essential vitamins and nutrients (especially zinc, iron, linoleic acid, and vitamins C and E) that infants need, and it also contains too much protein, sodium chloride (salt), potassium, calcium, and phosphorus. As mentioned previously, however, cow's milk used in infant formula is specially modified during the manufacturing process; essential vitamins and nutrients are added, and excess protein, sodium, chloride, potassium, calcium, and phosphorus are reduced to levels that meet the unique nutritional requirements of growing babies.

Cow's Milk Can Trigger Allergies

Feeding regular cow's milk to infants can cause food allergies and/or iron-deficiency anemia. The immature digestive system of babies under one year of age allows undigested milk proteins to be absorbed across the intestinal lining and interact with the fledgling immune system. Most of the time no harm is done, but about 5 percent of children are genetically predisposed to cow's milk allergy and will develop an inappropriate allergic response. After the first 12 months, a baby's intestinal lining matures and becomes much less permeable to allergy-causing dietary proteins.

A moderate to severe cow's milk protein allergy will provoke one or more of the following symptoms: nausea, vomiting, diarrhea, colic, gas, cramps, blood or mucus in the stools, eczema, hives, itching, swelling of the lips or eyes, runny nose, frequent ear infections, labored breathing, wheezing, or coughing. On the other hand, if the allergy is relatively mild, you probably won't even be aware of it, but blood may be lost through the stools in sufficient amounts to cause iron-deficiency anemia.

Saturated Fat and Cholesterol

Cow's milk does contain saturated fat and cholesterol, but so does breast milk, and besides, adequate amounts of dietary fat (such as the kind found in cow's milk) are essential for normal brain growth in young children. That's why youngsters under four years old should not be fed skim milk or low-fat milk (less than 2 percent).

Lactose Intolerance

Cow's milk sugar is primarily lactose, which can be a problem for some people. If a child lacks the intestinal enzyme (lactase) required to break lactose down into its two component sugars (glucose and galactose), the lactose will not be digested properly. The result is a condition called *lactose intolerance*, which causes a variety of digestive symptoms, such as gas, cramps, and diarrhea. Keep in mind, however, that the primary sugar in breast milk is also lactose. Furthermore, only about 10 percent of children actually experience symptoms of lactose intolerance when they drink cow's milk.

Cow's Milk May Contain rBGH

Recombinant bovine growth hormone (rBGH), or recombinant bovine somatotropin (rBST) as it's sometimes called, is a genetically bioengineered hormone that can make cows produce 10–20 percent more milk. According to the FDA, rBGH injections increase the frequency of

- mastitis (infection of the udder), which discharges pus into the milk and requires the regular use of potent antibiotics that contaminate the milk,
- painful bone lesions in the feet, knees, and legs,
- indigestion, off-feed, bloat, and diarrhea,
- reproductive problems,
- cystic ovaries.

Because of all the side effects rBGH causes in cows, there are serious concerns about the potential health problems it may cause in humans. The milk from cows treated with rBGH (rBST) contains increased amounts of a hormone called insulinlike growth factor-1 (IGF-1). In fact, it's the release of IGF-1, which is triggered by rBGH, that actually stimulates the cow's udder to produce more milk. IGF-1 works by promoting rapid cell growth. IGF-1 in cow's milk is not completely destroyed by pasteurization or digestion, and some of it is absorbed across the intestinal wall. And since IGF-1 in cows is chemically identical to the IGF-1 produced by humans, it should come as no surprise that it can have the same effect on human breast tissue that it has on bovine udders. Furthermore, exposure to excessive amounts of IGF-1 may sensitize the breast tissue of female infants and make them more susceptible to the cancer-promoting effects of estrogenlike pesticides later in life. It is also possible that IGF-1 will be found to promote the development of colon cancer. Unfortunately, no long-term studies have been done to determine if the consumption of excess IGF-1 in rBGH-treated milk or infant formula might possibly cause childhood cancers, abnormal growth in children, or future reproductive problems.

What benefits do consumers get in exchange for accepting milk that may contain more pus, dangerous antibiotics, and a tumor-promoting hormone? None at all. In fact, Consumers Union estimates that it will cost taxpayers an additional $200 million per year in government price supports for surplus milk.

In view of the many unanswered questions concerning the safety of rBGH (rBST), my advice is to totally avoid dairy products, infant formulas, and meat from cows treated with rBGH. In addition, call the Pure Food Campaign (800-253-0681 or 202-775-1132) and request their list of companies who have pledged in writing not to use rBGH dairy products. And please note that certified organic dairy products do not come from rBGH-treated cows.

The following companies will not accept milk or dairy products from cows treated with rBGH: Similac infant formula, Alta-Dena Certified Dairy, A&P food stores, Ben and Jerry's, Cabot Creamery, Colombo, Hunt-Wesson, Swiss Miss Foods, and Vermont Butter and Cheese Company.

While not demanding legal certification, the following companies have at least requested that dairy farmers not send them milk from cows treated with rBGH: Carnation and SMA infant formulas, Borden's, Baskin-Robbins, and Kroger.

The following companies do accept milk from cows treated with rBGH: Enfamil and Gerber infant formulas, Kraft, Land O'Lakes, Dannon, Haagen-Daz, and McDonald's.

Cow's Milk and Antibiotics

Many dairy farmers routinely treat their herds with antibiotics (such as penicillin, sulfa, tetracycline), which then contaminate the milk. In fact over 50 percent of randomly selected milk samples test positive for antibiotics, and many of these drugs can cause allergic reactions in susceptible people who unknowingly consume even trace amounts of them. The other problem is that routinely feeding animals antibiotics causes them to develop antibiotic-resistant bacteria (E. coli, salmonella, or campylobacter, for example), which can be quite harmful (or even fatal in some cases) when they infect humans.

Pesticides and Cow's Milk

The milk-fat portion of cow's milk contains trace amounts of synthetic pesticides, dioxins, and PCBs, but human breast milk typically contains higher levels of these chemical pollutants, making this the only category where cow's milk has an advantage over breast milk. In spite of the pollutants, however, breast milk is still healthier for infants overall. See "Pesticides and Pollutants in Breast Milk" in this chapter for details.

Cow's milk–based infant formulas (such as Similac) contain less fat-soluble chemical pollutants than whole cow's milk or breast milk because the milk-fat is removed from the formula and replaced with vegetable oil.

Certified organic dairy products usually do not contain detectable synthetic pesticides.

Cow's Milk Is Rich in Calcium

Cow's milk is an extremely rich source of bioavailable calcium that the body can readily absorb and use.

The recommended daily intake for calcium is based on age: 0–6 months, 400 milligrams; 6–12 months, 600 milligrams; and 1–10 years, 800–1,000 milligrams. Each of the following dairy products provides approximately 300 milligrams of calcium per indicated serving size:

1 cup (8 ounces) whole cow's milk
2½ cups (20 ounces) milk-based infant formula
2 ounces cheese
7 ounces low-fat or nonfat yogurt
2 cups low-fat cottage cheese
1½ cups ice cream

What about nondairy sources of calcium? Each of the following single servings typically contains approximately 250–350 milligrams of calcium:

½ cup almonds   1 cup tofu (soybean curd)
2 cups soy-based infant formula   2 cups collard greens
2 cups spinach   2 cups turnip greens
3 cups broccoli   3 cups green beans
3 cups kale

Unfortunately, there are two major obstacles to obtaining calcium from nondairy sources. First, children would have to eat a large quantity of nondairy calcium foods to match the equivalent amount of calcium in just 1 cup of milk. How many kids are going to eat 1 cup of tofu for breakfast, 3 cups of broccoli for lunch, and 2 cups of spinach for dinner? Not many, believe me. So the idea of providing children with dietary calcium strictly through nondairy food sources is simply not realistic. But there's an even greater problem. The bioavailability of calcium from dairy and nondairy sources is not equivalent. Certain fruits and vegetables contain high levels of phytates and oxalates, which are natural compounds that block the absorption of calcium. In other words, the body cannot absorb the calcium in vegetables nearly as well as it absorbs the calcium from dairy sources.

For children over one year old, calcium-fortified orange juice can be an excellent calcium source, providing about 300 milligrams of bioavailable calcium per cup. The only problem is that most brands don't taste very good.

Toxic Warning

Please note that calcium supplements derived from dolomite, bonemeal, oyster shells, or natural source calcium carbonate (chalk) often contain high levels of lead and other toxic substances. See "Lead Poisoning" in Chapter 6 for details.

Vitamin D

Vitamin D is essential for proper bone growth and calcium metabolism. Without enough vitamin D, children will develop calcium deficiency and rickets (softening of the bones). Too much dietary vitamin D, on the other hand, can cause dangerously high levels of calcium in the blood and eventually lead to bone loss and kidney failure. The Daily Value (DV) or RDA for vitamin D for children and adults is 400 international units (IUs).

Fortified cow's milk and infant formula are supposed to contain approximately 400 IUs of vitamin D per quart, which would ordinarily make them excellent dietary sources of this vitamin. However, recent laboratory analyses of fortified milk samples from the United States and Canada revealed that 25 percent contained unacceptably high levels of vitamin D, and 50 percent did not have enough (14 percent actually had undetectable levels). To be on the safe side, contact the dairy processing plant listed on the label of the brand you are using and ask how often its milk is tested for vitamin D by an independent lab.

Human breast milk contains 50–150 IUs of vitamin D per quart, depending on the nutritional status of the mother and the amount of sunlight she receives every day.

Most multivitamin supplements for children contain 400 IUs of vitamin D per daily recommended dose.

When exposed to direct sunlight, human skin produces vitamin D. That's why it's called the *sunshine vitamin*. Normally it takes only about 15 minutes per day of direct sun exposure for the body to produce enough vitamin D, assuming the sun is of adequate intensity (mid-morning or late afternoon) and strikes an adequate amount of skin (face, neck, arms, hands).

A child who either takes the recommended dose of a multivitamin every day or drinks infant formula or milk fortified with vitamin D usually maintains adequate body levels of vitamin D without any direct sun exposure. On the other hand, an infant who is exclusively breast-fed and does not take a vitamin D supplement requires about 15 minutes of direct sunshine daily to maintain adequate levels. During the winter months in northern latitudes of the United States and Canada, the sun is too weak to stimulate enough production of vitamin D, so exclusively breast-fed babies in these areas often require a vitamin D supplement. Ask your doctor to be sure.

The Bottom Line

Cow's milk is not perfect (no single food is), but its benefits, especially bioavailable calcium, far outweigh its risks for most children. Like everything else in life, however, moderation is the key, so don't let babies under 12 months consume more than 40 ounces of milk-based formula per day, and limit children over one year old to no more than 24 ounces of cow's milk per day.

Toxic Warning

Please note that pasteurization is absolutely essential to prevent the spread of foodborne infectious diseases, such as listeriosis and brucellosis. *Never drink raw, unpasteurized milk of any kind under any circumstances.*

BOTTLES AND NIPPLES

Glass baby bottles are highly recommended for routine everyday use, because they are nontoxic and recyclable; the only drawback of glass is that it can break.

Hard plastic bottles work great for storing breast milk, and they won't break when dropped on the floor, but plastic bottles are not generally recommended for several reasons:

- Plastic production uses up finite natural resources.
- Some plastics are not recyclable.
- Most plastics contain plasticizer chemicals to maintain flexibility. In general, the softer and more flexible the plastic bottle, the more plasticizers it contains. Unfortunately, plasticizers can leach into the liquid or food, making it smell and taste like plastic. Some plasticizers cause cancer (and there may be other

adverse health problems that we don't know about yet), so if you decide to use plastic bottles, choose *hard* plastic ones. And, before you buy a plastic bottle, place it near your nose and give it a good "sniff test." Reject any that smell of plastic.

For the toxicological and ecological reasons just cited, disposable plastic nursers are not recommended for routine everyday use. However, using them occasionally probably won't do much harm, as long as you don't store milk or juice in them for more than an hour.

Rubber nipples and pacifiers contain small amounts of carcinogenic chemicals called *nitrosamines*. However, the average level of nitrosamines found in nipples today is much lower than it was just a few years ago. In fact a recent study in the *Canadian Journal of Public Health* (1988; 79: 443–46) found that about two-thirds of the rubber nipples and pacifiers tested had no detectable nitrosamines, and the remaining one-third had levels well below the maximum permitted by government regulations.

Before letting your baby use a new rubber nipple or pacifier for the first time, perform a simple onetime treatment to lower the nitrosamine level: boil the nipples in water for five minutes, remove with tongs, and then rinse them off immediately in cool running tap water. Of course, be sure to discard the water, which now contains traces of nitrosamines.

You'll have to experiment with different brands (Nuk, Gerber, EvenFlo, Playtex, and the like) and shapes (standard, natural-action, orthodontic) to find the one your baby likes best. If you use an orthodontic nipple, be sure to place it in your infant's mouth with the hole facing up so the liquid disperses across the roof of the mouth instead of squirting down the throat. And, contrary to the somewhat misleading name, orthodontic nipples won't prevent crooked teeth or future trips to the orthodontist.

It's a good idea to test the nipple before each feeding. Simply turn the bottle upside down—but don't shake it—and observe how fast the milk drips out. There should be about one drop of liquid every second or two. If the milk comes out in a stream, discard the nipple; it might cause your baby to swallow too much at once and choke.

DRINKING WATER
Tap Water

Household tap water may contain a variety of toxic contaminants, but the main ones to be concerned about are:

- metals such as aluminum, arsenic, barium, cadmium, chromium, copper, iron, lead, mercury, nickel, selenium, and silver
- nitrates
- chlorine
- fluoride
- pesticides including insecticides, fungicides, and herbicides
- dioxins and polychlorinated biphenyls (PCBs)
- radium and radon
- volatile organic compounds (VOCs) such as benzene, toluene, xylenes, petroleum by-products, chloroform, trihalomethanes (THMs), vinyl chloride, carbon tetrachloride, trichloroethylene (TCE), tetrachloroethylene (perchloroethylene), and many others
- microbes such as viruses, coliform bacteria, algae, mold, fungi, and intestinal parasites like *Giardia* and *Cryptosporidium*

Lead
Lead contamination of drinking water can cause many serious health problems. See the section "Lead Poisoning" in Chapter 6 for details and prevention strategies.

Nitrates
In babies under nine months of age, excessive nitrate consumption converts a substantial portion of oxygen-carrying hemoglobin into methemoglobin. Methemoglobin blocks the delivery of oxygen to the tissues and thereby causes cellular asphyxiation. The signs and symptoms of methemoglobinemia correlate directly with the percentage of methemoglobin in the blood. When 10–20 percent of the total hemoglobin in the blood is methemoglobin, the skin, lips, ears, and nose

turn blue with shades of chocolate-brown or slate-gray. As the percent-age of methemoglobin increases to 25–45 percent, additional symptoms of asphyxia appear, including headache, disorientation, dizziness, fa-tigue, weakness, irritability, lethargy, fainting, nausea, vomiting, short-ness of breath, rapid or labored breathing, and a fast heartbeat.

Major sources of nitrates include drinking water (especially from rural wells) and certain vegetables. The EPA has established a maxi-mum nitrate contaminant level of 10 parts per million for public drink-ing water. For further information regarding nitrates in baby foods, see the discussion of strained vegetables later in this chapter.

Chlorine

Chlorination is the primary method used by most U.S. cities to disinfect public water supplies and thereby prevent water-borne infections such as diarrhea, dysentery, hepatitis, cholera, and typhoid. Unfortunately, chlorine reacts with dissolved organic debris (leaves, grass, wood, and the like) and produces toxic and carcinogenic VOCs called trihalome-thanes, such as chloroform. (Please note that chlorinated surface water usually contains much higher levels of trihalomethanes than ground-water.) The EPA has set 100 micrograms per liter (100 parts per billion) as the maximum allowable concentration for trihalomethanes (THMs) in drinking water, but some public health experts say that this level should be much lower.

Although chlorination prevents microbial contamination of public water supplies, studies have shown that drinking chlorinated water on a regular basis increases the risk of developing chronic health problems (especially bladder cancer). To circumvent this problem, many experts recommend using nonchlorinated premium bottled water (see brand-name recommendations later in this chapter) for everyday drinking, cooking, and infant formula preparation.

Significant absorption of chloroform, trihalomethanes (THMs), and other VOCs occurs through the skin and lungs during routine daily exposures to chlorinated water, such as showers, baths, cooking, wash-ing clothes, and washing dishes. For example, the absorption of THMs and VOCs during a typical 10-minute shower is equivalent to drinking 2 quarts of the same water. To minimize your family's risk, have your tap water tested as suggested later in this chapter. If the level of chloro-form and total trihalomethanes is higher than 50 micrograms per liter (50 parts per billion), I would do three things. First, limit bathing time to just a few minutes; this one precaution will drastically reduce your family's exposure. Second, run a bathroom exhaust fan (vented to the outdoors) whenever the bathroom is in use, especially during showers or baths; this will reduce inhalation exposure by up to 33 percent. And third, encourage your water district to reduce the THMs voluntarily; if they're uncooperative, contact your state water board or the Environmental Protection Agency and tell them you're having a water quality problem.

Please note that the *chloride* level in a water analysis report is not the same thing as the *chlorine* level. To get a rough idea of the chlorine level of your tap water, all you need is a $5.00 chlorine and pH test kit like the kind commonly used for testing the water in swimming pools. The optimal chlorine level in municipal tap water is 0.5–1.0 milligram per liter (parts per million), and the optimal pH is 7–8. If the chlorine level of your tap water is higher than 1 part per million (ppm), I would find another source of drinking water and follow the suggestions mentioned above for THMs. In addition, a pH level below 7 should alert you to the possibility that the acidity of the water may be leaching toxic amounts of copper and other metals from the pipes into the tap water.

Fluoride

Although it's never been proved conclusively, the American Dental Association (ADA) contends that adding fluoride to drinking water prevents cavities. (Keep in mind, however, that the ADA also says that silver-mercury fillings are harmless in spite of overwhelming scientific evidence to the contrary.) One thing is sure: when children ingest too much fluoride their permanent teeth develop unsightly brown and yellow spots, a condition known as fluorosis. And a recent study published in the *Journal of the American Medical Association* 268 (August 12, 1992): 746–48 found that drinking water fluoridated at levels of one milligram per liter (one part per million) or higher makes bones brittle and significantly increases the risk of hip fractures in the elderly.

The experts will be arguing over the safety of water fluoridation

100 years from now, so what can you do in the meantime? Call your local water district office to find out how much fluoride is added to your drinking water, or have your home tap water tested as suggested later in this chapter. If the fluoride level is higher than one part per million (one milligram per liter), you should find another source of drinking water.

Safety Tips for Tap Water Use

If you use tap water for drinking, cooking, or mixing with infant formula, take it from the cold side of the tap. Water from the hot side of the tap should never be used for drinking, cooking, or infant formula preparation, because it contains much higher amounts of lead and other toxic heavy metals compared to the cold side of the tap. When you need hot water, use cold tap water and warm it on the stove. If you have a single-lever faucet, be sure the handle is turned all the way to the cold side so that hot water doesn't mix with it.

Tap water first drawn in the morning has the highest lead and toxic heavy metal content because it has been sitting in the pipes for hours. Let the water run for two minutes each morning (or whenever the faucet has not been used for three hours or longer) to flush the toxic metals out of the pipes before collecting it for food or beverages. This may seem wasteful to an ecological parent, but a little wasted water is better than serious neurologic damage from metal toxicity. Besides, you can easily make up for the water wasted by reducing your yard watering or car washing. Or use the first draw for watering houseplants.

Do not boil tap water for routine drinking purposes unless you believe it to be contaminated with microbes such as bacteria or parasites. Boiling water for five minutes disinfects it (and evaporates some of the chlorine and VOCs), but as the steam evaporates, it leaves behind the toxic metals (such as lead, arsenic, and aluminum). Boiling tap water for just five minutes triples its concentration of lead and other metals. See "Lead Poisoning" in Chapter 6 for further suggestions on reducing lead in tap water.

Visible Problems or Unusual
Tastes and Odors in Tap Water

Visible problems or unusual tastes and odors can serve as an early warning that a contaminant is present in your tap water. For example:

- Stains on plumbing fixtures, appliances, dishes, and laundry, including red or brown stains (iron), green or blue stains (copper), and black stains (manganese).
- Reddish-brown slime on fixtures indicates iron bacteria.
- Off-color water—red or rusty color (iron), brown or yellow color (iron, tannic acids), and black color (manganese, hydrogen sulfide).
- Soap residue, scale, and lime deposits on plumbing fixtures, appliances, and dishes are usually the result of hard water and/ or high total dissolved solids.

Please note that water analysis reports normally list the total hardness and total dissolved solids of the water. The total dissolved solids are primarily the salts, minerals (especially calcium carbonate), and metals dissolved in the water. Total hardness is defined generally as the sum of the calcium and magnesium ions in the water, or to be more specific, it is the sum of the calcium concentration (mg per liter) multiplied by 2.497, plus the magnesium concentration (mg per liter) multiplied by 4.118. In other words, total hardness + (2.497 × calcium) + (4.118 × magnesium).

For example, if a water analysis shows the calcium is 50 milligrams per liter, and the magnesium is 8 milligrams per liter, the total hardness of the water is approximately 158 milligrams per liter. A total hardness of 0–60 milligrams per liter is considered "soft" water, 61–120 milligrams per liter is "moderate," and anything above 121 milligrams per liter is "hard" water. Water that contains more than 85 milligrams per liter (parts per million) of calcium carbonate or more than 100 milligrams per liter (parts per million) total dissolved solids is also considered hard water.

• Cloudy water (turbidity) may be caused by hard water, high total dissolved solids, or visible particles (dirt, sand, silt, clay, and other particulate matter).

Please note that if the sediment filters at the water company are not removing visible particles, they may not be removing parasite cysts either.

• Unusual odor: rotten egg odor (hydrogen sulfide), bleach-like odor (chlorine), septic or musty odor (coliform bacteria), gasoline or petroleum-based solvent odors.
• Unusual taste: metallic taste (copper, iron, lead, zinc), salty taste (sodium chloride, hard water, high total dissolved solids), bitter taste (hard water, high total dissolved solids).

It's worth noting that water may become salty or bitter tasting when the total dissolved solids exceed 400 milligrams per liter (parts per million).

Testing Your Tap Water

Every home (regardless of where you live) should have its water tested once a year for bacterial growth, lead, mercury, cadmium, arsenic, aluminum, radon, nitrates, fluoride, VOCs, chloroform, and total trihalomethanes. It's especially important to test tap water that has any of the visible problems or unusual tastes and odors described earlier in this chapter or if the water comes from a private well. Laboratory testing is the only way to be sure your family's drinking water is safe. Water can pick up pollutants from water mains, service pipes, or the household plumbing, and just because it tests safe one year does not mean that it will remain safe in the future.

If your tap water is supplied by a city or municipal system, the quickest (and cheapest) way to get a general idea of the quality of your home tap water is to call your local water district office (its phone number usually appears on the water bill each month) and request a copy of its most recent comprehensive water contaminant analysis report. Contaminants in your tap water should be lower than half of the maximum allowable contaminant levels established by the Safe Drinking Water Act. (A list of the maximum allowable contaminant levels is usually available through your local municipal water district office, or call the EPA Safe Drinking Water hot line at 800-426-4791 and ask for a copy of the EPA's National Drinking Water Regulations.)

After reading the report, ask the water district to test a sample of water from your home tap (some districts provide this as a free service) to be sure contaminants are not finding their way into your water at some point along the distribution line to your home faucet. The levels of coliform bacteria, radon, lead, mercury, copper, cadmium, nitrates, arsenic, aluminum, fluoride, VOCs, chloroform, and total trihalomethanes should be well below the maximum allowable limits set by the EPA. If your local water district is uncooperative (or if you get your water from a private well), have your home tap water tested by an independent laboratory. Your city, county, or state health department or water agency can recommend a qualified water testing lab in your area, or you can contact the EPA Safe Drinking Water hot line (800-426-4791) for questions concerning water quality. It's also worth noting the names of two excellent national testing labs: WaterTest Corporation of America (800-426-8378) and National Testing Laboratories (800-458-3330). Both will test your water for important metals, inorganics, VOCs, and coliform bacteria. For a small additional fee, they will also check for pesticide contamination.

Bottled Drinking Water

Municipal tap water is cheap and convenient, but it's no bargain if it damages your family's health. If your home tap water analysis indicates significant problems, or if your tap water comes from heavily polluted lakes (such as the Great Lakes) or rivers (the Mississippi or the Hudson, for example), the best alternative is a premium bottled drinking water. A much less desirable option would be a water filtration system (see the following section for details).

More than 100 different brands of bottled drinking water are on the market, but many of them are much lower in quality than city tap water. As a matter of fact, some expensive bottled brands are actually drawn from municipal tap water sources and then filtered to remove the chlorine and improve the taste; several brands actually have trihalomethane (THM) levels that exceed the 100 parts per billion limit set by the EPA for municipal drinking water. That's why, if you decide to use bottled drinking water, you should buy a premium brand that is naturally pure and thoroughly tested for contaminants at the source. Mountain Valley Spring Water and Evian are two of the very best brands of bottled drinking water. They're not fluoridated, not chlorinated, and have no detectable VOCs, chloroform, trihalomethanes (THMs), or pesticides. In addition, neither has detectable levels of aluminum, lead, arsenic, copper, cadmium, mercury, or radon.

Mountain Valley beats all EPA requirements and goes several steps further by testing for pesticides and VOCs that the government doesn't even regulate. Mountain Valley Spring Water is bottled by the Mountain Valley Spring Company (800-643-1501) at the source, the pristine Hot Springs National Park in Arkansas. No other brand (except for Evian) subjects its water to so many tests for purity. In addition, Mountain Valley has distributors in many cities across the country that will deliver the water to your home at no extra charge (call its toll-free number for further information).

Although Evian is a high-quality drinking water, my first choice is Mountain Valley Spring water because it is produced in the United States and available in glass bottles. Glass bottles are the best containers for bottled drinking water because they are recyclable and nontoxic. Second choice would be firm plastic bottles that are recyclable and chemically stable enough not to leach plasticizers into the water. One of the safest and most stable plastics is PETE (which stands for polyethylene terephthalate). It's easy to identify PETE plastic bottles. Simply look on the bottom of the container for a code number 1 stamped inside a triangular symbol with the letters PETE (or PET) next to it.

Soft, flimsy plastic bottles or containers are usually made of chemically unstable plastic that leaches toxic plasticizers—chemicals added to plastic to keep it flexible—into the water. The softer the plastic, the

more likely it is to leach plasticizers. Never drink any bottled water that
has a plastic or metallic taste or smell.

Because most bottled water is not chlorinated, it's usually a good
idea to refrigerate the bottle after it's been opened to prevent bacterial
contamination. Also, never use water from the coin-operated water
filter machines found in many supermarkets; the water that comes from
these machines does not have enough chlorine to inhibit bacterial
growth, and when you put nonchlorinated water into nonsterile containers, you're asking for bacterial overgrowth and illness.

Distilled Water

I do not recommend drinking or cooking with distilled water because
it lacks health-promoting minerals, it may contain VOCs that can be
hazardous to your health, and distilled water is often sold in flimsy
plastic containers that are more likely to be contaminated with toxic
plasticizer chemicals.

Water Filters

Most experts strongly advise against using home tap water filtering
devices, because the water could end up with more contaminants than
it had originally if the filters are not properly installed and maintained
exactly according to the manufacturer's specifications. Of course, in
situations where serious pollutants are found in your tap water and the
problem cannot be corrected by the municipal water company, a water
filtering device may become necessary. If so, always have your tap
water tested first since the type of equipment you're going to need will
depend on the specific contaminants that require removal (no one
device can remove them all). And be sure that the home water filtering
system you choose is approved by National Sanitation Foundation
International (313-769-8010), a nonprofit organization that specializes
in testing water filtering devices to verify that they meet manufacturers'
claims. Call NSF and ask for a copy of their informative brochure
Determining the Quality of Your Drinking Water, and NSF Listings of
water treatment units.

The three most frequently used home water treatment devices are sediment filters, activated carbon filters, and reverse osmosis units. Each one is capable of removing a specific group of contaminants. (Please note that the small, cheap water filters that fit on the end of the faucet or shower head will not even be discussed because they are woefully inadequate and also harbor bacteria and algae.)

Sediment Filters

Sediment filters are designed to remove or reduce the following substances: parasite cysts, iron (ferrous) compounds, and dirt, sand, silt, clay, and other particulate matter. Sediment filters will not remove most metals, salts, minerals, nitrates, radon, or radium, and they are not useful for correcting problems due to hard water or high total dissolved solids.

Sediment filters usually have a micron rating according to the size particles they can remove: Class I (particles less than 1 micron or submicron), Class II (particles 1–5 microns or extra fine), Class III (particles 5–15 microns or medium fine), Class IV (particles 15–30 microns or fine), Class V (particles 30–50 microns or medium coarse), and Class VI (particles over 50 microns or coarse).

A Class IV or V filter is usually adequate for most home applications, except in situations where parasites are a concern. *Giardia* cysts are approximately 8–15 microns in size and would thus require a Class III filter, while a Class II filter would be necessary to remove *Cryptosporidium* cysts, which are only 4–6 microns in size.

For best results, sediment filters should usually be installed on the main water line as it enters the home.

Activated Carbon Filters

Activated carbon filters are designed to remove or reduce the following substances: chlorine, PCBs, radon, tannic acids, many VOCs (including chloroform and THMs), and many pesticides (such as endrin, lindane, methoxychlor, toxaphene, 2,4-D, and the like).

Activated carbon filters will not remove most metals, salts, or minerals (such as calcium carbonate or magnesium), so they are not useful for correcting problems due to hard water or high total dissolved solids. In addition, activated carbon filters do not remove nitrates or bacteria. Please note that some carbon filters will remove lead; check with the manufacturer to be sure.

Activated carbon filters usually have a chlorine reduction rating: Class I filters remove 75 percent or more of the chlorine; Class II filters remove 50–75 percent of the chlorine; and Class III filters remove 25–50 percent of the chlorine.

The major drawback to using activated carbon filters is that they remove the chlorine, and nonchlorinated tap water traveling from the filter to the faucet can then become heavily contaminated with disease-causing bacteria and algae. Some manufacturers try to reduce the microbial overgrowth problem by adding metallic silver to their carbon filters, but all that does is replace chlorine with a metal contaminant that can also cause health problems. Furthermore, solid block carbon filters are held together by glue, which can sometimes leach into the water.

For best results, activated carbon filters should be installed under the sink or at the point of use on the cold water line.

Reverse Osmosis Filters

Reverse osmosis filters are designed to remove or reduce the following substances: metals (such as aluminum, arsenic, barium, cadmium, chromium, copper, iron, lead, manganese, mercury, silver, and zinc), minerals (such as calcium carbonate and magnesium), sodium, potassium, chloride, bicarbonate, fluoride, nitrates, sulfates, radium, dirt, sand, silt, clay, and other particulate matter, and parasite cysts. Reverse osmosis filters will not remove VOCs, chloroform, THMs, chlorine, radon, or pesticides.

Reverse osmosis units are expensive ($500–$1,000), slow (depending on the type of semipermeable membrane used, maximum output is 5–20 gallons per 24 hours), and waste a lot of water (the production of 1 good gallon of water often requires wasting 4 gallons down the drain). Some bacteria even get through the membrane and contaminate the water downstream. Furthermore, water without minerals tastes flat.

For best results, reverse osmosis filters should be installed under the sink or at the point of use on the cold water line.

Water Supplements for Babies

Healthy babies normally do not need water supplements on a routine basis, because breast milk and infant formulas have a water content of approximately 88 percent, which is generally sufficient to maintain adequate hydration. On the other hand, it's OK to offer your child an ounce or two of plain water several times a day if desired, especially during the summer months. And a sip of water after a feeding can sometimes bring up a nice burp or stop the hiccups.

BABY FOOD

Your baby's rate of growth, stage of development, age, weight, and daily formula or breast milk consumption must all be taken into account when deciding to start baby food. It's generally time to introduce solid foods when your baby is five to six months old, weighs 16 pounds, or drinks more than 40 ounces of formula or breast milk per day (whichever comes first).

There are several reasons why these three milestones have been chosen as good starting points for introducing solid foods. First, introducing solid foods too early can occasionally lead to food allergies; it can also cause a breast-feeding infant to nurse less, resulting in a drop in milk production. Second, the average baby reaches 16 pounds between the fourth and sixth month, and since most babies need approximately 50 calories per pound of body weight to maintain optimal growth, an infant who weighs 16 pounds requires at least 800 calories per day ($16 \times 50 = 800$), which is about 40 ounces of formula or breast milk at 20 calories per ounce. Third, according to most pediatric nutritionists, when a baby needs more than 40 ounces of formula or breast milk a day to meet his or her caloric requirement, it's healthier for the additional calories to come from baby food. And fourth, the maximum achievable breast milk production for most women is about 40 ounces per day. (Please note that an infant with a very fast metabolism may need to start baby food before the fourth month, but always ask your doctor first.)

Introducing Solid Food

When introducing a new food to your baby, offer it at least once a day for four or five days in a row. When you start a new food, be on the lookout for signs of an adverse reaction, such as spitting up, vomiting, diarrhea, gas, stomach cramps, constipation, hives, eczema, diaper rash, runny nose, coughing, or wheezing. If you suspect a food is causing a problem, consult your baby's doctor. During the trial period for the new item, continue to give your child any of the other foods that you've tested previously and found to be well tolerated. Don't experiment with more than one new item at a time; this way you'll know which food is the culprit if a reaction occurs.

Cereal

At the appropriate age (usually five or six months), start with Gerber instant rice, oatmeal, or barley cereal. Place 2 tablespoons of cereal in a bowl and then stir in ¼ cup of infant formula, breast milk, or water. Serve as is or warm. Offer your baby 2 or 3 teaspoons at first and then increase the amount by 1 teaspoon each day, up to 8–12 teaspoons per serving twice a day if desired. As your baby gets used to the cereal, you can thicken the mixture to 3 tablespoons of cereal per ¼ cup of liquid if you want to. (Cereal mixed with breast milk may look a little watery because enzymes in the breast milk tend to predigest the starch in the cereal, but that's normal.)

Strained Fruit

After your five- or six-month-old has been eating cereal for two or three weeks, you can try strained applesauce, bananas, and pears, being careful to introduce them one at a time. Start with 4 or 5 teaspoons of a strained fruit per meal, two or three times a day if desired, and gradually work your way up. Some babies enjoy having strained fruit added to their cereal for flavor.

Strained Vegetables

At six or seven months, try strained carrots, squash, and sweet potatoes, being careful to introduce them one at a time. Start with 4 or 5 teaspoons of a strained vegetable per meal, twice a day if desired, and gradually work your way up. Many parents feel an intense need to make their child eat vegetables, and if the child refuses (which many do), mealtime becomes a real battleground. While it's true that vegetables are nutritious, they're not so important that you have to make them a major issue. If your child accepts vegetables without a fuss, great; if not, she can usually compensate by eating fruit and taking the recommended dose of an age-appropriate multivitamin. Even the most stubborn children will eventually learn to enjoy eating vegetables if you go slow and don't force them.

> **Toxic Warning**
> Several baby food vegetables (spinach, green beans, and beets) contain very high levels of nitrates. As explained in the section on drinking water, excessive nitrate consumption by infants under nine months of age can cause a disorder called methemoglobinemia, in which the tissues are deprived of vital oxygen. The EPA has established a maximum nitrate contaminant level of 10 parts per million (ppm) for public drinking water, so it may surprise you to learn that the concentration of nitrates in a typical jar of strained spinach is approximately 150 ppm, in green beans about 300 ppm, and in beets a whopping 2,000 ppm. (One four-oz. jar of strained beets contains an amount of nitrates roughly equivalent to 20 quarts of water containing 10 ppm nitrates.) Therefore, avoid feeding spinach, green beans, and beets to babies under nine months of age.

Strained Meat

At seven or eight months strained chicken, turkey, or beef can be offered, along with a strained vegetable, at lunch and dinner. (A strained fruit makes a tasty dessert.) Start with 5 or 6 teaspoons of a strained meat per serving, twice a day if desired, and gradually work your way up. If your baby doesn't like the taste of strained meat by itself, you can improve the flavor by stirring in a few teaspoons of strained sweet potatoes, carrots, bananas, or applesauce.

A Note for Vegetarians

Many modern families choose not to eat meat for humanitarian or health reasons. If you are among them, be sure to supplement your child's vegetarian diet with an age-appropriate multivitamin once a day to prevent a vitamin deficiency (especially B_{12}) and consult your doctor or a certified nutritionist for information on preparing vegetarian meals that provide all of the essential amino acids in proper proportions.

Fruit Juice Alert

Fruit juices tend to cause spitting up, acid indigestion, intestinal gas, cramps, and/or diarrhea in babies. Therefore, I strongly suggest waiting until your child is at least seven or eight months old before you offer any fruit juice. When you do start fruit juices, follow these suggestions:

- Always dilute infant fruit juice with an equal amount of plain water because undiluted juice has a tendency to cause digestive problems.
- If fruit juice causes spitting up, heartburn, gas, cramps, diarrhea, or other digestive problems, stop serving it for the time being.
- Orange, lemon, lime, grapefruit, and pineapple fruit juices are notorious for causing allergies and digestive problems in babies, so avoid them during the entire first year.
- Apple, prune, pear, peach, grape, and cherry juices contain a sugar called *sorbitol* that can sometimes trigger abdominal pain, bloating, and/or diarrhea; if your baby develops any of these digestive problems, you should consider reducing the intake of these particular juices or avoiding them altogether to see if the symptoms go away. (Prune juice has the highest sorbitol content, which accounts for its well-known laxative effect.)

Food Allergy Alert

The immature digestive system of babies under one year of age allows undigested food proteins to be absorbed across the intestinal lining and interact with the fledgling immune system. Most of the time the immune system samples the allergenic (allergy-causing) substances and rapidly forms appropriate antibodies to block them (a process called *tolerance*), and no harm is done. However, in children genetically predisposed to food allergies (about 5 percent of the general population), tolerance is slow to develop, and the result can be an inappropriate allergic response to certain foods that lasts for months or even years. Fortunately the majority of children with food allergies will outgrow the problem as soon as their intestinal tract and immune system mature, usually between 12 and 36 months of age.

Symptoms of Food Allergy

The symptoms of a food allergy may appear within 15 minutes after eating or drinking the allergenic item, or the onset may be more gradual and take from 12 to 24 hours before becoming apparent. A food allergy can cause almost any symptom (or symptom complex) imaginable, but the following list includes some of the more common ones: nausea, vomiting, diarrhea, colic, gas, cramps, blood or mucus in the stools, eczema, hives, itching, swelling of the lips or eyes, runny nose, frequent ear infections, labored breathing, wheezing, or coughing.

A severe food allergy can cause anaphylactic shock, a rare but potentially fatal allergic reaction in which the throat and windpipe swell shut, the heart beats very fast, the blood pressure drops precipitously, and the child collapses. Medical assistance must be obtained immediately (dial 911 in most areas).

Food allergies can also cause symptoms that you would not ordinarily think of as an allergic reaction, including an intense craving for the food to which the person is allergic, Jekyll-and-Hyde behavior or mood swings, hyperactivity or difficulty paying attention, unexplained fatigue, ears turning bright red shortly after eating the allergenic food, and microscopic blood loss in the stools sufficient to cause iron-deficiency anemia.

LOW-ALLERGY (HYPOALLERGENIC) FOODS

Any food can cause an allergy, but the following foods are the ones least likely to trigger allergic reactions and are therefore generally good choices for babies during their first year:

Cereals: rice, oatmeal, barley
Fruits: apples, applesauce, bananas, pears, peaches
Vegetables: carrots, squash, sweet potatoes, white potatoes
Meats: chicken, turkey, beef

HIGH-ALLERGY FOODS

The following foods are the ones that most commonly provoke allergic reactions in babies under 12 months of age, so avoid them during the first year:

Eggs (Egg allergy occurs in about 4 percent of babies.)
Fish and shellfish (Fish allergy occurs in about 4 percent of babies.)
Cow's milk (Milk allergy occurs in about 3 percent of babies.)
Tree nuts (such as pecans or walnuts), nut butters, peanuts, peanut butter
Citrus fruits: oranges, lemon, limes, grapefruits
Strawberries
Pineapples
Tomatoes
Chocolate

Please note that onions, peppers, garlic, spinach, beets, turnips, radishes, collard greens, cauliflower, cabbage, lettuce, and celery are notorious for causing nonallergic digestive problems in babies under 12 months of age, so avoid them during the first year.

Some nutritionists believe that refined cane sugar can cause undesirable reactions in children, such as hyperactivity, attention deficit disorder, a craving for sugary foods, or frequent colds and ear infections. Try to avoid excess refined sugar in your child's daily diet.

Honey, Corn Syrup, and Botulism

Some batches of honey and corn syrup contain the spores of botulism bacteria (*Clostridium botulinum*). If a baby under one year of age swallows botulism spores, the bacteria can germinate and grow inside his immature intestines and produce toxins that cause muscle paralysis. The first symptom of infant botulism is usually severe constipation; as the paralysis spreads, the baby becomes very limp and floppy, unable to lift his head or move his arms or legs. Additional symptoms include a weak cry, difficulty sucking and swallowing, droopy eyelids, and loss of facial expressions. Left untreated, botulism eventually paralyzes the muscles required for breathing. If your baby develops any symptoms of botulism, have the doctor examine him immediately. The diagnosis is confirmed by the identification of botulism toxins and *Clostridium botulinum* bacteria in the stool.

Until your child is at least one year old, do not give him honey or corn syrup (such as Karo). By 12 months of age the average child's digestive system is usually mature enough to handle the spores without any problem.

What about cooking with honey or corn syrup for children less than one year old? This practice cannot be recommended, because botulism spores are very resistant to heat, and baking alone is not sufficient to kill them. It generally takes a pressure cooker set at 15 pounds (245° F) for 30 minutes to kill botulism spores, keeping in mind that time-temperature-pressure requirements may vary with the item being cooked. The botulism toxin (but not the spores themselves) is destroyed by boiling for 10 minutes.

Helpful Hints for Feeding Your Baby Solid Food

• Food can be a choking hazard, so do not give the following items to children under four years old: nuts, popcorn, bony fish, celery, raw vegetables, hard candy, or gum. And, if you let your child have meat sticks, frankfurters, or grapes, you must cut them into tiny bits so small they can't lodge in the windpipe.

Also, until your child has at least four molars (usually at 14–18 months) and knows how to chew, you'll have to mash, mince, or puree table food to a smooth consistency. A blender or food processor makes it easy. If your baby always gags on a certain item, or if that item appears in the bowel movements as undigested chunks, mince the food into even smaller pieces or eliminate it from the menu for a while.

To prevent choking, always hold your child in an upright sitting position when feeding solid food. Adult supervision during the entire meal is essential. Using an infant-size spoon, try to place the food toward the middle of your baby's tongue rather than on the tip, so that he instinctively swallows it.

- Always test the food yourself to be sure it has a pleasant taste before giving it to the baby, but do not share the same spoon, because saliva contains viruses and bacteria. And don't spoon-feed your child directly from the jar the food is stored in unless you know she'll finish all of it; her own saliva, left behind, will contaminate any unused portion of food. It's more sanitary to spoon the desired amount of food out of the jar and into a serving dish first.
- During their meals, most babies like a swallow of milk or water after every few spoonfuls to help them wash down the food.
- Always keep commercially prepared baby food refrigerated after opening. Once opened, a jar of baby food will keep for only two days in the refrigerator, so don't open more than a few jars at a time.
- Discard home-cooked fruits and vegetables that have been stored in the refrigerator for more than 48 hours. To avoid waste, try not to prepare more food than your baby can eat in a day.

Warming Baby Food

Some parents do not warm baby food at all; others warm everything. I think most fruits taste best chilled, while cereals, vegetables, and meats are usually more flavorful served at room temperature or lukewarm.

Warning

Never heat baby food in the jar it comes in (the glass is not heat-tempered), or in any container that has a restricted opening or cap, because it might crack or explode.

Conventional Heating

Conventional heating methods, as opposed to microwave heating, are preferred. Spoon the desired amount of food into a glass bowl designed for heating (Pyrex or Corning Ware, for example) and set it in a pan of warm water on top of the range, stirring frequently to distribute the heat evenly. A baby dish with a warm water compartment underneath also works. Always test the food yourself to be sure it isn't too hot before giving it to the baby, but don't share the same spoon, because saliva contains germs.

Microwave Heating

Microwaves are fast and convenient, and I know it's hard to resist using them, but they alter the molecular structure and chemical composition of food in potentially harmful ways not fully understood, so I do not recommend the microwave heating of baby food. For now, there are just too many unanswered safety questions. However, if you decide to use a microwave in spite of my warning, please follow these precautions:

- Spoon out the desired amount of food into an open bowl or serving dish specifically designed for use in a microwave oven, and do not heat it for longer than 10 seconds.
- After warming the food, stir it well to evenly distribute the warmth and break up the "hot spots."
- Always test the food yourself to be sure it isn't hot before giving it to the baby, but don't share the same spoon.
- Always use conventional heating methods for cooking raw meat, because microwave heating may not kill all of the disease-

causing germs (such as salmonella in poultry, E. coli in beef, or trichinella in pork).

- Some microwave packages of heat-and-serve foods (popcorn, french fries, pizzas, and fish, for instance) have a built-in heat-susceptor, a piece of plastic with a metal coating designed to absorb microwaves and brown or "crisp" the food somewhat like a conventional oven would. The problem is that the plastic and metal become so hot they leach into the food and could be health hazards, so avoid all packaging that uses heat susceptors.

Homemade vs. Commercial Baby Food

Trying to decide whether to use homemade or ready-to-serve commercial baby food can be difficult. Here are a few of the pros and cons:

- Homemade baby food almost always tastes better, usually a lot better, than commercial varieties. (Gerber cereals and fruits are pretty tasty, but when it comes to vegetables and meats, homemade wins by a mile.) In fact your baby may develop such a preference for homemade that he rejects the store-bought versions.
- Homemade baby food is usually more nutritious than ready-to-serve brands. For instance, it contains no added sugar or salt and thus educates a child's palate to the naturally subtle and delicious flavor of unprocessed foods. And garden-fresh produce is preferable to the overcooked, pureed commercial versions that often sit in jars for a year or more before being purchased.
- Homemade baby foods (such as mashed bananas, tiny bits of apple or pear, tiny chunks of chicken or turkey) are quite handy when your baby graduates to finger foods at 9–12 months. Homemade baby finger food encourages self-feeding and thus allows baby to eat according to his own inner body signals rather than being forced to comply with the wishes of the parent.
- Homemade baby food costs less than commercial brands.
- Using ready-to-serve commercial baby food is convenient, but

home preparation is not as difficult as one might think. Here are a few hints for preparing fruits and vegetables:

1. For most fresh produce, start with a thorough rinse under cool running water, using a soft scrub brush. Always peel if possible. Do not wash your produce with soap, detergent, or dishwashing liquid, because no matter how hard you try, you cannot completely rinse off the residues, which can be toxic when ingested. And wait to wash produce until right before you're ready to prepare it, because placing damp produce in the refrigerator promotes harmful mold growth.
2. Ripe bananas and avocados are so soft that all you have to do is peel them, mash them with a fork, and then, if desired, add a little breast milk or formula for a smooth consistency.
3. For apples or pears, rinse, peel, and slice into quarters. Discard the core. Place the slices in a saucepan, add water, and cook uncovered over medium-low heat until the fruit is fork-tender. Puree in a blender or food processor. Allow to cool before serving.
4. Firm vegetables such as carrots, potatoes, sweet potatoes, and squash can be boiled, steamed, or baked. Then, when they are fully cooked and soft, you can mash or puree them to a smooth consistency in a blender or food processor, adding a little breast milk or formula if desired. Allow to cool before serving.
5. You can always make extra portions and freeze leftovers for later use. Discard home-cooked fruits and vegetables that have been stored unfrozen in the refrigerator for more than 48 hours.

If You Use Commercial Baby Food

Because a baby's sense of smell and taste are so well developed, the food you offer should have a relatively pleasant aroma and flavor for proper digestion to occur. Of the three national brand-name baby foods, my patients feel that Gerber has the best taste by far, and Gerber doesn't have the aftertaste or cause the heartburn mothers have reported with the other brands. (Another nice thing about Gerber baby food is that the Gerber company goes to great lengths to purchase the highest-quality produce from farms that practice integrated pest management, a system that seeks to reduce or eliminate the use of synthetic pesticides.) Of course, you can and should perform your own taste test right at home and be your own judge. Remember, if it smells and tastes awful to you, it's going to have the same effect on your little baby. Don't force your child to eat something you wouldn't eat.

Try not to use the commercially prepared mixed dinners, because they contain ingredients (tomatoes, onions, peppers, garlic) and additives that can cause digestive problems in babies under a year of age. You can make your own tasty and nutritious vegetable-meat combos by mixing together equal amounts of a strained single-ingredient vegetable and meat in a serving dish.

Don't get into the bad habit of giving your baby commercially prepared desserts, puddings, cobblers, or custards. These infant versions of adult junk food are full of refined cane sugar, which has very little nutritional value. They'll give your child a sweet tooth and spoil his appetite for nutritious foods. Strained fruit is a much healthier choice for dessert. And don't use sweets as a bribe or reward.

At this point you're probably wondering why I haven't mentioned using organic baby foods (fresh or jars) as advocated by nutritional gurus all across the country. The reason is that organically grown food is not necessarily more nutritious or healthier than the conventionally grown varieties. I know this is a radical concept for ecologically oriented persons to deal with at first (it certainly was for me), but as you read the following section, you'll begin to see what I'm talking about.

PESTICIDES IN FOOD

Pesticides are poisonous substances that kill pests, such as insects (insecticides), weeds (herbicides), fungi (fungicides), and rodents (rodenticides). There are two kinds of pesticides in food: natural and synthetic.

Natural Pesticides

Natural pesticides are toxic chemicals produced by plants themselves as a defense against insects, bacteria, fungi, and animals. Examples of natural pesticide chemicals include belladonna alkaloids, caffeic acid, canavanine, catechol, chaconine, estragole, formaldehyde, hydrazine, limonene, nicotine, psoralens, pyrethrins, pyrrolizidine alkaloids, safrole, and solanine. Every variety of plant produces its own unique combination of natural pesticide chemicals. For example, cabbage contains 49 different natural pesticides, lima beans 23, and so on.

The amount of natural pesticides a plant produces is one of the major factors that determines whether it is edible or poisonous. Those that produce large amounts are poisonous and humans have learned not to eat them.

Natural pesticides constitute approximately 2–7 percent of a plant's dry weight with concentrations ranging from 5,000 to 70,000 parts per million depending on the specific variety of plant and whether it was stressed or not during cultivation. In contrast, synthetic pesticide levels are typically less than 1 part per million. Thus, 99.9 percent of the pesticide chemicals found in fruits, vegetables, and grains are natural pesticides produced by the plants themselves. Fortunately, the plants also produce a superabundance of natural anticancer vitamins and antioxidants that offset the negative impact of the pesticides so that on balance the health benefits of eating plenty of fruits and vegetables far outweigh any minor risks. Furthermore, cooking destroys a substantial quantity of the natural pesticides in the produce and thus reduces the toxic potential.

When plants are attacked by pests, they quickly respond by producing higher levels of natural pesticides, sometimes levels so high the plants become acutely toxic to humans. Furthermore, crops that are bred to be naturally resistant to fungi and insects (as a way to reduce the need for synthetic pesticides) are usually big producers of natural pesticide chemicals that can be harmful. For example, plant breeders recently developed a potato that was resistant to insect attack, but it had to be withdrawn from the market because it contained such high levels of the natural neurotoxins solanine and chaconine that people who ate the potatoes got very sick. And a major celery grower introduced a strain of celery that was so highly insect resistant it did not require the usual heavy spraying with synthetic pesticides. Unfortunately, it contained 10 times the normal levels of the natural pesticide psoralen, which caused people who handled it or ate it to break out in a rash when their skin was exposed to sunlight. These two cases illustrate why organically grown produce is not necessarily better for your health than conventionally grown items.

Conventionally Grown Produce and Synthetic Pesticides

The term *conventionally grown* means that synthetic pesticides have been used on the produce. Synthetic pesticides are man-made chemicals applied to plants to protect them against pests. The synthetic pesticides detected most frequently in fresh fruits, vegetables, and grains include *organophosphate insecticides* (acephate, azinphos-methyl, chlorpyrifos, chlorpyrifos-methyl, DDVP, demeton, diazinon, dimethoate, ethion, malathion, methamidophos, mevinphos, parathion, phosmet), *organochlorine insecticides* (DDT, dieldrin, endosulfan, heptachlor, lindane), *carbamate insecticides* (aldicarb, carbaryl), *pyrethroid insecticides* (fenvalerate, permethrin), *herbicides* (2,4-D, atrazine, chlorpropham, DCPA, dicamba, trifluralin), and *fungicides* (benomyl, captan, chlorothalonil, dicloran, EBDCs [Maneb, Mancozeb, Manzeb, Zineb], folpet, hexachlorobenzene, imazalil, iprodione, o-phenylphenol, quintozene, thiabendazole, vinclozolin). Chapter 7 discusses these chemicals in detail.

Many synthetic pesticides are located primarily on the surface of the produce and can be removed somewhat by rinsing with warm water and peeling. In contrast, the *systemic* synthetic pesticides are absorbed into the produce and cannot be removed by washing or peeling. The *systemics* include acephate, aldicarb, chlorpropham, DCPA, demeton, dimethoate, methomyl, methamidophos, and mevinphos.

A "tolerance" is the maximum amount of a pesticide residue that is permitted in or on a food. The Environmental Protection Agency (EPA) sets the legal limits or tolerances for synthetic pesticide residues, and the Food and Drug Administration (FDA) enforces them. Unfortunately, the FDA samples less than 1 percent of the food supply for its synthetic pesticide content, and the routine multiresidue tests employed by the FDA can detect only about half of the approximately 300 synthetic pesticides registered for use in agriculture today. To fill in these gaps, many large supermarket chains have begun contracting independent laboratories to analyze their fresh produce for its pesticide content.

The acute symptoms of exposure to high or moderate levels of pesticides are well known and described in detail in Chapter 7. The long-term health effects of extremely low-level exposure to pesticides in food are largely unknown, however, because they don't cause the abrupt and visible signs of acute poisoning and are therefore much harder to quantify. Most members of the scientific community believe the levels found in our food supply are so minuscule (measured in parts per million) they are virtually harmless, but some warn that even trace amounts can cause cancer, infertility, birth defects, and immune system damage.

Single samples of some fruits and vegetables have been found to contain up to eight different synthetic pesticide residues per item. However, it's the concentration of the pesticides—not the number— that's important. For example, a fruit that contains eight pesticides with a total concentration of only 1 part per million is generally safer than a fruit with only one pesticide at a concentration of 15 parts per million. And it's worth noting that 92 percent of all the conventionally grown fruits and vegetables in the United States have a total synthetic pesticide concentration of less than 1 part per million (in fact, 55 percent are actually less than 0.1 ppm total).

For details on synthetic pesticide residues in food, contact your local FDA branch office and request a free copy of the *Food and Drug Administration (FDA) Pesticide Residue Monitoring Program*. The USDA also publishes a very informative brochure called the *Pesticide Data Program*; call the USDA Agricultural Marketing Service at 202-720-5231 for a free copy. Another excellent source is *Pesticides in Children's Food*, which can be purchased from the Environmental Working Group, 1718 Connecticut Avenue, N.W., Suite 600, Washington, D.C. 20009 (202-667-6982).

How to Reduce Your Exposure
to Pesticides in Produce

You can reduce your family's exposure to natural and synthetic pesticides in food by observing the following guidelines.

Before eating fruits and vegetables, always rinse them thoroughly under clean running water with a soft vegetable scrub brush. Do not use soap, detergent, or dishwashing liquid on produce, because the soap residues do not completely rinse off. Don't wash produce until right before you're ready to prepare it; storing damp produce in the refrigerator encourages harmful mold and fungus growth.

It cannot be emphasized strongly enough that one of the most effective ways to remove pesticide residues is to peel fruits and vegetables whenever possible. While it's true that the outer skin or rind is vitamin rich, it also contains a lot of the synthetic pesticide residues, and given the choice, I'd rather sacrifice some vitamins to avoid the pesticides. Always discard the outer leaves of lettuce, cabbage, kale, endive, and spinach for the same reason.

Cooking fresh vegetables is another way to reduce the amount of natural and synthetic pesticides, as the heat destroys a substantial portion of the toxic chemicals.

Don't buy produce (organic or conventional) that has more than just a minor amount of bruising or insect damage. Cut away and discard all damaged or bruised spots, because they contain toxic material.

Fruits and vegetables should look pleasing to the eye and relatively unblemished, but avoid items that have been cosmetically altered with dyes and waxes to appear absolutely flawless. In other words, try to find a happy medium between ugly produce on the one hand and picture-perfect Hollywood versions on the other, because danger lurks at both extremes.

Waxes are applied to many types of fresh produce: apples, avocados, bell peppers, cantaloupes, citrus fruits, cucumbers, eggplants, melons, peaches, pineapples, pumpkins, squashes, sweet potatoes, and tomatoes. Paraffin (petroleum), shellac (lac bugs), carnauba (palm trees), or vegetable oils are the waxes used most frequently. Many of these same food waxes are also used to polish automobiles and floors. The real danger, however, is that most waxes contain fungicides to retard spoilage during shipping. Fungicide waxes cannot be washed off, but they can be removed very effectively by peeling the produce. Therefore, don't buy waxed fruits or vegetables unless you can peel them. Sometimes you can tell just by looking at the produce that it has been waxed, but in most cases it isn't that obvious; to find out for sure, look on the original shipping crate or box if available (the FDA requires all waxed produce to be labeled with the specific ingredients including the names of the fungicides), or ask the produce manager of your supermarket.

Try to balance your exposure to the different synthetic and natural pesticides by rotating foods on a regular basis so that your family does not eat or drink the same thing (or too much of any one item) day in and day out.

Buy fresh produce in season and grown in the United States. Out-of-season fresh produce is usually imported, which generally means it's been heavily sprayed with pesticides, then picked green and sealed in fungicide wax or gassed with preservatives. It's ironic that many foreign countries buy American-made pesticides that our farmers are not allowed to use, then turn right around and sell their tainted crops back to American consumers. So always ask your grocer about the country of origin of the produce you intend to buy, and stay away from the imported items. (Exceptions: Bananas and mangoes are imported, but they are generally safe to eat since peeling removes most of the synthetic pesticides.)

Although the judicious use of synthetic fungicides is less hazardous to human health than allowing molds and fungi to contaminate the crops with potent mycotoxins, it's certainly preferable to buy fresh produce with the least amount of synthetic fungicides whenever possible. Crops grown in regions of the country where the humidity and rainfall are high typically receive more extensive synthetic fungicide applications than crops grown in dry climates (such as California and the southwestern United States) where there is less need for fungicides. Therefore, fresh fruits and vegetables from California are generally the healthiest choices.

Avoid any produce (conventional or organic) grown with fertilizers derived from either sewage sludge or untreated animal manure.

Organically Grown Produce

The term *organically grown* means that the food is grown without synthetic pesticides or synthetic fertilizers. Organically grown produce can be a healthy choice for your family, but it can also present some unique health hazards (as the following discussion illustrates), so don't automatically assume something is good for you just because it's organically grown!

Poor Quality

The appearance, color, texture, and/or flavor of organically grown produce can often be quite disappointing. Of course the holistic nutritional gurus unflinchingly urge everyone to eat organic as if the absence of synthetic pesticides could somehow make up for the fact that half the time, the fruits and vegetables look like mutants from a science fiction movie. In fact, a significant portion of organically grown produce ends up being thrown in the garbage because of mold growth, spoilage, insect damage, or awful taste. Be very selective when purchasing organically grown produce. Follow your instincts, and don't talk yourself into eating something your senses are rejecting. You know how fruits and vegetables should normally look, feel, smell, and taste. I'm not saying things have to be flawless, but if an item doesn't measure up to a reasonable standard, don't buy it just because it's organically grown.

Manure Fertilizer

Crops fertilized with untreated animal manure may be contaminated with disease-causing viruses, bacteria (salmonella, E. coli, or Listeria, for example), and parasites. These germs can cause severe vomiting, diarrhea, and dehydration in humans. Manure used on crops is supposed to be pretreated or composted to kill disease-causing microorganisms, but if the composting is not done properly, the germs carried in the animal waste may contaminate the food. That's why produce fertilized with manure should be washed thoroughly with plain water (no soap) and a vegetable scrub brush and then peeled or cooked before being eaten.

Natural Pesticides

Normal amounts of natural pesticides in the diet are not considered harmful, but high levels can be hazardous to human health. Organically grown crops that are specially bred for pest resistance or those that have been badly stressed as evidenced by a lot of bruises, insect damage, or mold growth often contain large amounts of natural pesticides. Avoid such produce like the plague!

Mycotoxins

Molds and fungi synthesize their own natural biocides, called *mycotoxins*, to defend themselves against microbial enemies, and because organic farmers do not use synthetic fungicides, their crops sometimes contain higher than normal levels of mycotoxins. To minimize mycotoxin contamination, avoid produce that shows evidence of mold growth, spoilage, or significant bruising.

More than 300 natural mycotoxins have been discovered so far. Some are well-known antibiotics (such as erythromycin, griseofulvin, oxytetracycline, and penicillin) used to cure human infections, but others are either poisonous or carcinogenic (such as citrinin, ochratoxin A, sterigmatocystin, streptozotocin, and aflatoxin). Aflatoxin concentrations as low as 50 parts per billion in the diet can produce liver damage in lab animals, and aflatoxin is known to cause liver cancer in humans. Depending on the method of food storage and precautions taken to prevent fungal growth, aflatoxins may be found in many nuts and grains, such as peanuts, pistachio nuts, almonds, walnuts, pecans, corn, and rice. Aflatoxin contamination is more common in foods grown outside the United States.

Deciding What Produce to Buy

The ongoing debate over the safety of our food has centered for some time on synthetic pesticides. Nearly everyone agrees that the improper use of pesticides is dangerous. The controversy arises over whether the trace amounts of synthetic pesticides found in conventionally grown crops are harmful. Some respected scientists are firmly convinced that low-level exposure to synthetic pesticides in food can cause serious health problems such as cancer, infertility, birth defects, allergies, multiple chemical sensitivity, chronic fatigue, immune system dysfunction, frequent infections, and autoimmune diseases (lupus, multiple sclerosis, and the like).

On the other hand, most scientific and medical authorities believe that when synthetic pesticides are used properly, the risk of causing problems is less than one in a million. In fact, they say, old-fashioned carcinogenicity tests involving high-dose exposures to laboratory mice are invalid and misleading, because if you feed mice hundreds or thousands of times the normal amount of a pesticide every day for two years a lot of them are going to develop cancers that they would normally not have contracted under more realistic conditions. Furthermore, they argue, scientific studies have proved conclusively that eating plenty of fruits and vegetables with all of their anticancer vitamins and antioxidants is one of the most effective ways to lower the risk of cancer and heart disease. (It's estimated that eating five servings per day of conventionally grown fresh fruits and vegetables reduces a person's cancer risk by an average of 50 percent.) Therefore, according to their line of reasoning, synthetic pesticides promote human health by keeping the cost of fruits and vegetables low and thus increasing their consumption. Who's right?

As with any polarized, emotional debate, the truth probably lies somewhere in the middle. Proponents of pesticides underestimate the health and environmental risks too much. On the other hand, some (not all) environmentalists tend to exaggerate the dangers of synthetic pesticides in food way out of proportion to the actual threat. There's no question that federal testing and regulation need to be strengthened and enforced, but it would be unreasonable and unhealthful to ban all synthetic pesticides, because the organic or natural alternatives can sometimes be much worse for your health than the synthetic versions. In my opinion, one of the best options is to purchase conventionally grown produce from supermarkets that have samples of their fresh fruits and vegetables routinely tested by an independent laboratory and certified to be free of synthetic pesticides before being placed on the shelves. This way you avoid the minor risks of synthetic pesticides as well as the drawbacks often associated with organic produce. Another option is to carefully select organically grown fruits and vegetables that are relatively unblemished, are not specially bred for pest resistance, and are not fertilized with untreated animal manure.

Produce Pesticide Chart

If the grocery stores where you live do not test their conventionally grown fruits and vegetables for synthetic pesticides, the following produce pesticide chart will help you predict which items can be expected to have the least pesticide residues. The chart groups conventionally grown domestic produce into three color categories (green, yellow, and red) based on information taken from the 1991, 1992, and 1993 FDA pesticide residue database as well as the supermarket warehouse pesticide residue monitoring program performed by private laboratories for grocery store chains in the United States.

Please note that some fruits and vegetables appear in more than one color-coded category depending on whether they are fresh and peeled, fresh and unpeeled, canned, or commercially processed into juice or sauce. The reason is that washing, peeling, cooking, canning, and commercial heat processing remove a significant amount of the synthetic pesticide chemical residues from the produce. In fact, high-pressure water washes and steam peeling can eliminate almost all of the synthetic pesticides from the surface of the produce. *Systemic* pesticides, however, are absorbed into the plant and cannot be removed by washing or peeling.

Warning

Because of potential digestion problems, allergic reactions, or choking hazards, several of the items (onions or beets, for example) listed in the chart should not be given to children under one year of age even though they may be relatively safe in terms of synthetic pesticide contamination. Use common sense and always check with your doctor first to be sure.

Green Light

This group of conventionally grown domestic produce typically has the lowest total synthetic pesticide concentration, averaging less than 0.5 parts per million:

Fruits	Applesauce, avocados (fresh, peeled), bananas (fresh, peeled), blackberries, blueberries, cantaloupe, coconuts (fresh or canned), dates, figs, kiwifruit, mangoes (fresh, peeled), olives, peaches (canned), pears (canned), pineapples (fresh or canned), pineapple juice, papayas, tangerines, tomatoes (canned), watermelon
Vegetables	Asparagus, beets (canned), black-eyed peas, broccoli, cabbage, carrots (fresh or canned), cauliflower, leeks, navy beans, onions, pinto beans, radishes, sweet peas (fresh or canned), watercress
Nuts	Almonds, chestnuts, hazelnuts, pecans, walnuts, water chestnuts
Other	Corn (fresh or canned), corn bread, corn flakes, corn tortillas, farina, hominy grits, pasta, egg noodles, oats, oatmeal, Cheerios, Rice Krispies, Grape-Nuts Flakes, shredded wheat cereal

Yellow Light

This group of conventionally grown domestic produce typically has a total synthetic pesticide concentration that averages 0.5–1 part per million, so a moderate intake of four or five medium servings a week per item is generally safe:

Fruits	Apples (fresh, peeled), apple juice, apricots, cherries (fresh or canned), cranberries (canned), cranberry juice, grapefruit, grapefruit juice, grapes, grape juice, honeydew, lemons, lemonade, limes, nectarines (fresh, peeled), oranges, orange juice, peaches (fresh, peeled), pears (fresh, peeled), plums (fresh, peeled), prune juice, raspberries

Yellow Light

Vegetables   Beets, cucumbers (fresh, peeled), kale, leeks, lettuce, lima beans, mushrooms, potatoes (fresh, peeled), pumpkin (canned), radishes, rutabagas, soybeans, spinach (canned), winter squash, string beans, sweet potatoes (fresh, peeled), Swiss chard, tomatoes (fresh, peeled), tomato juice, tomato sauce, turnips, yams (fresh, peeled)

Other   Barley, rice, rye

Red Light

This group of conventionally grown domestic produce often has a total synthetic pesticide concentration that exceeds 1 part per million (sometimes as high as 20 parts per million), so it would be prudent to limit consumption to about one or two servings a week per item:

Fruits   Apples (fresh, unpeeled), cranberries (fresh), nectarines (fresh, unpeeled), peaches (fresh, unpeeled), pears (fresh, unpeeled), plums (fresh, unpeeled), prunes, raisins, strawberries

Vegetables   Bell peppers, celery, collards, mustard greens, parsnips, potatoes (fresh, unpeeled), snow/sugar snap peas (fresh), spinach (fresh), summer squash, sweet potatoes (fresh, unpeeled), turnip greens, yams (fresh, unpeeled)

Other   Peanuts, peanut butter

Buying food with minimal pesticide residues is certainly a desirable goal, but try to keep the minor risks of dietary synthetic pesticides in their proper perspective. Tobacco smoke, home and garden pesticide sprays and foggers, radon, asbestos, sun tanning, junk food high in fat and refined cane sugar, fish and seafood from polluted waterways, and foods that are charcoal-broiled, barbecued, or charred are much greater threats to your family's health than eating conventionally grown produce that contains extremely low amounts of synthetic pesticides.

FOOD IRRADIATION

Food irradiation is the process of exposing food to high doses of gamma rays from radioactive cobalt 60 for the purpose of killing germs and thereby extending the shelf life. Proponents of food irradiation say that it can significantly reduce food-borne infectious illnesses, but an FDA review of more than 400 scientific studies on the effects of food irradiation revealed so many safety concerns that most people believe the risks outweigh the few benefits. Here are a few examples:

• Exposing food to gamma radiation breaks natural chemical bonds in the food's proteins, fats, and carbohydrates. These free molecules then recombine in random fashion to form new compounds, never before seen in nature, called *unique radiolytic products.* URPs have not been tested rigorously for their carcinogenic, mutagenic, or teratogenic potential, but the FDA says URPs are probably safe because the levels are in the range of 10–30 parts per million. The fact is that many toxic chemicals are quite hazardous even at levels in the parts per billion range, so if URPs are in fact toxic, even the low level caused by irradiation could be unsafe.

• Several scientific studies have suggested that eating irradiated food can cause chromosomal damage, reduced fertility, miscarriages, metabolic disturbances, weight loss, shortened life span, immune system damage, and cancer. A study published in the *American Journal of Clinical Nutrition* 28 (February 1975): 130–35, found that children who ate irradiated wheat developed significant numbers of premalignant white blood cells. The cells gradually increased, then gradually disappeared after the irradiated wheat was withdrawn, thus establishing a cause-and-effect relationship. None of the children fed the nonirradiated wheat developed any abnormal white blood cells.

• Food irradiation increases the concentration of free radicals linked to premature aging, cancer, and coronary artery disease, and destroys 25 percent or more of a food's natural vitamins and minerals, especially the cancer-fighting antioxidants and the B vitamins.

- Radiation lowers the food's own natural resistance to infection, allowing disease-causing germs to stimulate production of cancer-causing and poisonous substances. It also triggers production of formaldehyde, mutagenic peroxides, and cancer-causing benzene.

Despite all the safety concerns and questions surrounding irradiated food, the government does not require full and complete disclosure on product labels. The Radura logo (an innocent-looking stylized flower) as well as the ominous statement "Treated by irradiation" will be placed on whole foods that have been irradiated, but there is no such requirement for processed or packaged foods that contain irradiated ingredients or for irradiated food prepared in restaurants and cafeterias. So, for example, you won't be able to tell the difference between a strawberry dessert containing irradiated strawberries from one with nonirradiated fruit unless the manager voluntarily discloses the information. Furthermore, no one can tell how often a food has been irradiated and how large a dose of radiation it really received. Irradiation can be used illegally to "freshen" rancid food containing toxic bacterial waste, and you will never even suspect it.

So the FDA has declared food irradiation safe and does not intend to reconsider the matter. This means you'll have to rely on environmental watchdog groups for reliable information. For now, my advice is to avoid all irradiated foods.

GENETICALLY ENGINEERED FOOD

Picture this: tomatoes with flounder genes, potatoes with silkworm genes, and fish and dairy cows with human genes. No, this isn't a page out of Mary Shelley's *Frankenstein*. This is happening right now in American supermarkets thanks to biotechnology companies that have learned to transfer genes among insects, fish, birds, other animals, and plants. The FDA is not going to require any special testing or labeling regulations for gene-spliced foods, but some 1,500 well-known chefs across the United States have decided to boycott these "Frankenfoods." Tampering with the DNA of living creatures solely to improve the flavor or texture of foods is asking for big trouble. My recommendation is to avoid all these freakish concoctions completely.

TOXINS IN FISH AND SEAFOOD

Nutritionists are telling us to eat more fish because of the health-promoting polyunsaturated omega fatty acids they contain, but what the gurus often fail to mention is that many fish are loaded with toxic chemicals (such as chlordane, dioxin, DDT, DDE, and PCBs) and toxic heavy metals (arsenic, lead, mercury, and cadmium). For example, by eating just one fish from the Great Lakes, you can potentially absorb as much PCB as you would from drinking the water and breathing the air around Lake Michigan for 119 years. That's quite a toxic wallop! And when rats were fed salmon from Lake Ontario, they became hyperactive within 20 days and could no longer cope with stress. Their offspring showed the same problems even though they weren't fed the tainted fish. Apparently the chemical toxins were passed to the rat pups through the placenta in utero and then through the breast milk.

The skin, dark meat, and internal organs (especially the liver) of fish have the highest concentration of pollutants and therefore should not be eaten. In general, the most heavily polluted fish are large fish, predators, fish with a long life span, fish with a high fat content, and fish that feed near the bottom of lakes. Fish from the Great Lakes are among the most heavily contaminated with pollutants (dioxin, PCBs, DDT, and the like) and should be avoided completely. In one epidemiological study, women who ate fish from Lake Michigan three times a month for six years or more prior to pregnancy were statistically more likely to give birth to babies with low birth weight, small head circumference, short-term memory difficulties, and coordination problems. The Michigan Department of Public Health and a chapter of the Michigan State Medical Society have in fact warned the following groups to avoid eating fish from the Great Lakes: pregnant women, nursing mothers, women who intend to have children, and children under age 15. More specifics on the relative contamination levels are in the "Pollutants in Fish and Seafood" chart.

POLLUTANTS IN FISH AND SEAFOOD

Least Contaminated	Most Contaminated
Deep-ocean fish caught more than 3 miles offshore	Freshwater fish caught in lakes and ponds, saltwater fish caught in big-city bays and harbors
Deep-ocean fish from Canada and Iceland, New Zealand, Central America, South America	
cod from North Atlantic	freshwater bass
flounder	striped bass
haddock	bluefish
orange roughy	carp
Pacific salmon	catfish
pollack	caviar
red snapper	chub
scallops	cod
sea bass	croaker
shrimp	herring
sole	lobster
	mackerel
	freshwater perch
	ocean perch
	pike
	salmon (especially Great Lakes)
	shark
	swordfish
	trout (sea, lake, and rainbow)*
	walleye

*Trout from pristine high-mountain lakes and streams are usually not very polluted.
These fish accumulate toxic mercury: halibut, marlin, northern pike, shark, striped bass, swordfish, tuna, and walleye.

Here are a few additional safety tips when buying seafood:

- Seafood that smells too "fishy" or has a strong ammonia odor indicates that it is past its prime or has not been refrigerated properly.
- When buying fresh fish, beware of fillets stacked several layers high on a single layer of ice; those on top are not going to be chilled enough to prevent bacterial overgrowth. The eyes of whole fish should be clear and bulging, not cloudy or sunken; the flesh should also spring back quickly when you press it with your finger.
- Never buy cooked seafood that has been lying next to raw seafood. Germs on the raw food could very easily have contaminated the cooked food, which will probably not be reheated to high enough temperatures to kill the germs prior to eating it.
- Before you purchase any fish or seafood, always ask the supermarket or restaurant manager where the fish was caught.

FOOD POISONING FROM MEAT, POULTRY, AND FISH

Contamination of meat, poultry, and fish with bacteria and parasites is a much more serious threat to your family's health than the theoretical one-in-a-million cancer risk from the pesticides they contain. Every year about six million Americans get infections (and a few even die) from the food they eat. The bacteria and parasites most commonly implicated in food poisoning are listeria in cheese and dairy products, E. coli in beef and hamburgers, trichinella in pork, worms and parasites in fish, and salmonella and campylobacter in fish and poultry. It's estimated that 80 percent of poultry and 50 percent of the fish sold in U.S. supermarkets are contaminated with bacteria that can cause food poisoning. Furthermore, raw or undercooked shrimp, crabs, clams, and oysters may even be contaminated with bacteria that can cause cholera.

The symptoms of food poisoning usually appear within 1–24 hours of eating the contaminated item and commonly include one or more of the following: fever, nausea, vomiting, painful abdominal (stomach) cramps, bloating, gas, diarrhea, dehydration, and blood or mucus in the stools. Always call your doctor for advice if you suspect a family member has food poisoning, because medicating with certain antidiarrhea drugs (such as Lomotil or Imodium) could, in this instance, make things a lot worse by trapping the toxins inside the body instead of allowing the diarrhea to flush them out.

The following food handling, storage, and cooking tips will reduce your risk of food poisoning from meat, poultry, eggs, and fish:

- When you're at the supermarket, buy perishable foods like meat, poultry, eggs, and fish last and then get them home and into the refrigerator as quickly as possible, because food poisoning bacteria multiply quickly at room temperature.
- Store eggs in the refrigerator, preferably in their original container. Don't wash the eggs before storage, because you'll remove the protective coating applied to the shell at the processing plant. It is, however, a good idea to rinse an egg with plain water right before you open it to find hidden cracks. Discard any eggs with cracks in the shell or blood in the yolk.

  Cook eggs thoroughly until both the yolk and white are firm, not runny, because the eggs could be infected with salmonella even if they look and smell fine. (Salmonella bacteria are transmitted from infected laying hens directly into the egg before the shell forms.) Avoid eating foods containing raw eggs, such as hollandaise sauces, Caesar salad dressing, eggnog, Orange Julius, homemade mayonnaise, cake icing, and meringue. Restaurants that serve items containing raw eggs are supposed to use pasteurized eggs that are free of disease-causing bacteria. Always ask your waiter to be sure. Unfortunately, the general public does not have ready access to pasteurized eggs for home use; very few supermarkets stock them because they have such a short shelf life, but it wouldn't hurt to ask the store manager. (Excess consumption of raw eggs can also lead to a deficiency of biotin, an essential B vitamin.)
- Don't let your child lick a bowl of batter or icing containing raw eggs.

• All raw meat products—beef, pork, poultry, fish, and shellfish—must be thoroughly cooked (preferably well done) all the way through until all the pink is gone and the juices run clear. The internal temperature of the meat should reach at least 160° F. Never under any circumstances allow any family members to eat raw, rare, or undercooked meat. After meat is cooked, put it on a clean plate and either eat it right away or cover it and refrigerate or freeze it until it is time to eat. Refrigerate leftovers within two hours. Do not cook raw meat in a slow cooker or a microwave oven, because uneven heating may not be adequate to kill all of the germs and spores that may be present.

• To prevent food spoilage, set the refrigerator temperature at 38° F and the freezer section at 0° F or below. Keep raw meat refrigerated or frozen at all times. Don't leave uncooked meat in the refrigerator for more than two days; any raw meat that you think will not be consumed within two days should be frozen as soon as you bring it home from the supermarket.

Thaw frozen meat overnight by transferring it from the freezer to the refrigerator or simply cook it directly from the frozen state. Never leave raw meat on a kitchen table or countertop to defrost, because the outer surface of the meat will quickly build up a high bacterial count. Never thaw and refreeze meat.

• Keep raw and cooked foods separate. Be very careful when handling raw meat (and its drippings) to prevent bacterial cross-contamination of food and other items in the kitchen preparation area and refrigerator. Store raw meat on a plate or in a plastic bag to keep the juices from dripping on other foods. Consider anything touched by raw meat or its juices to be contaminated with potentially dangerous bacteria or parasites.

Wear powder-free disposable plastic gloves (such as Magla Skin-Eez, 800-247-5281) when handling raw meat and be sure to wash your hands thoroughly with soap and water after touching raw meat. All countertops, containers, utensils, cutting boards, and plates that have been in direct contact with raw meat or its juice must be washed thoroughly with hot, soapy water (preferably in an automatic dishwasher with heat cycle) before they can be used again. Use paper towels to clean contaminated food preparation surfaces and discard the towels immediately. Sponges are not recommended because they trap bacteria and cross-contaminate subsequent items or surfaces you wipe.

- Do not stuff poultry. It's safer to cook dressing in a separate pan.
- Milk and dairy products must be pasteurized. Never eat unpasteurized dairy products under any circumstances. Avoid cheese or dairy products from foreign countries; their sanitation standards are usually even worse than ours.
- Never eat any food that has a peculiar or unfamiliar odor, color, or taste.

For further details on the safe handling and storage of food products, contact the U.S. Department of Agriculture's Meat and Poultry hot line at 800-535-4555.

ARTIFICIAL ADDITIVES IN FOOD AND BEVERAGES

The number of synthetic chemicals added to food and beverages is staggering. Most of them are synthesized from coal tar or petroleums, and most are harmful. The artificial additives include colors, preservatives, and flavors. According to numerous scientific studies, these additives can bioaccumulate in the brain and disrupt the neurotransmitters, resulting in temper tantrums, hyperactivity, attention deficit disorder, autism, and a host of other serious neurologic and behavioral problems in children. In one recent study (*Pediatrics* 83: [January 1989]: 7–17), for example, 24 preschool-aged boys diagnosed with attention deficit disorder (ADD) and hyperactivity were placed on a diet free of artificial colors, flavors, preservatives, MSG, chocolate, and caffeine. Over half of the boys exhibited a significant improvement in their behavior while on the additive-free diet. In another study (*Annals of Allergy* 72 [May 1994]: 462–68), doctors took 26 children who had ADD with hyperactivity and placed them on a diet free of artificial additives and common allergens, but this time an astounding 73 percent of the children showed significant improvement. When you think about it, it's no wonder that over 10 percent of schoolchildren nowadays are hyperactive and cannot pay attention. One bowl of an artificially colored and flavored breakfast cereal can turn an otherwise well-behaved little child into a "space cadet," flying high in an uncontrollable frenzy.

So obviously you must always read the complete list of ingredients on all package labels to identify (and avoid) products that contain them. In general you'll find the highest concentration of these synthetic ingredients in processed foods and beverages, such as breakfast cereals, cakes, cookies, pastries, pies, pie fillings, powdered mixes, candies, chips, puddings, powdered drink mixes, fruit punch, sport drinks, soft drinks, frozen dinners/pizzas/desserts/waffles/pancakes, luncheon meats, gravies and sauces, mayonnaise and salad dressings, frostings and toppings, ice cream, canned soups, and soup mixes.

Artificial (Synthetic) Colors and Dyes

Most artificial food colors and dyes are synthetic chemicals derived from coal tar and/or petroleum, substances known to cause many health problems, even in small doses. The most common adverse reactions associated with artificial colors in food products include hyperactivity; attention deficit disorder; and a variety of allergic reactions involving the skin (eczema, contact dermatitis, itching, hives,

> The Feingold Association of the United States (FAUS) publishes an excellent (and inexpensive) handbook and two pamphlets listing hundreds of brand-name foods, beverages, and medications that contain no artificial colors, artificial preservatives, or artificial flavors. For more information, call 800-321-3287 or write to FAUS, PO Box 6550, Alexandria, VA 22306.

bruising), gastrointestinal tract (nausea, abdominal cramps, diarrhea), and respiratory tract (runny nose, ear infections, wheezing, and asthma). There are even rare cases of anaphylactic (allergic) shock. The sad part is that these toxic substances are added only for cosmetic purposes. They provide absolutely no health benefits whatsoever to the consumer.

The government requires manufacturers to list artificial colors on the package labels. Most companies use the official FDA numbers, often with the prefix FD&C, but some use the alternative trade names. Many other artificial colors are registered for use in food and beverages, but these are the ones manufacturers use most frequently:

FD&C Blue No. 1 (Brilliant Blue)
FD&C Blue No. 2 (Indigo Carmine)
FD&C Green No. 3 (Fast Green)
FD&C Red No. 3 (Erythrosine)
FD&C Red No. 40 (Allura Red)
FD&C Yellow No. 5 (Tartrazine)
FD&C Yellow No. 6 (Sunset Yellow)

Of all the artificial colors, FD&C Yellow No. 5 (Tartrazine) causes the most allergic reactions, yet Yellow No. 5 seems to be the "dye of choice" for products consumed by children in large quantities, such as breakfast cereals, puddings, powdered drink mixes, fruit punch, sport drinks, chips, frozen goods (waffles, pancakes, pizzas), pastries, baked goods, frosting, and medicine.

Several of the artificial colors also have been proved to cause cancer, but the FDA refuses to ban them because of the economic impact on food manufacturers. Prime examples are Red No. 3 (cherries, candy), which causes thyroid cancer in animals, and Green No. 3 (candy, cereals, fruit punch), which may cause bladder tumors. Other potential carcinogenic artificial colors include Blue No. 1, Blue No. 2, Red No. 40, and Yellow No. 6.

When you're reading labels, note that several natural colors can be added safely to food, such as annatto (yellow), beet juice (red/pink), blueberry juice (blue), grape juice (red/purple), turmeric (yellow), and beta-carotene (yellow/orange).

Preservatives

Preservatives are antioxidant chemicals that provide many benefits, such as retarding spoilage, prolonging shelf life, and preventing food from changing color or flavor. For most processed foods, preservatives are absolutely essential to prevent the growth of disease-causing bacteria and mold. The trick is to choose products that contain safe preservatives and avoid products that contain the harmful ones.

The following food preservatives help to prevent spoilage and are considered relatively safe for most people:

Vitamin E (tocopherol)
Vitamin C (ascorbic acid/calcium ascorbate/sodium ascorbate)
Calcium propionate
Citric acid/calcium citrate/potassium citrate/sodium citrate
Erythorbic acid/sodium erythorbate
Fumaric acid/calcium fumarate/potassium fumarate/sodium fumarate
Sorbic acid/calcium sorbate/potassium sorbate/sodium sorbate
Benzoic acid/sodium benzoate
Salt (sodium chloride)

In contrast, BHA (butylated hydroxyanisole), BHT (butylated hydroxytoluene), TBHQ (tertiary butyl-hydro-quinone), propyl gallate, sulfiting agents, and nitrates/nitrites are the preservatives most commonly associated with adverse reactions, so avoid products that contain them whenever possible. It's worth noting that BHA, BHT, and TBHQ are synthesized from petrochemicals and therefore can cause many of the same problems as artificial colors (especially the neurologic symptoms, such as hyperactivity and attention deficit disorder).

Sulfiting Agents

Sulfiting agents (sulfur dioxide, sodium or potassium bisulfite, sodium or potassium meta-bisulfite, and sodium sulfite) are used to preserve freshness and to prevent browning. They are frequently added to dried fruits (such as raisins and apricots), cider, frozen vegetables (especially potatoes and french fries), pickles, meats, frozen dinners, salad dressings, salads, sauerkraut and coleslaw, avocado dip, guacamole, relishes, sauces and gravies, lemon concentrates, shrimp, seafood, beer, wine, and many restaurant foods (especially salad bars).

The main drawback associated with sulfite preservatives is the risk of triggering an allergic reaction, such as hives, intense flushing of the skin, nausea, vomiting, abdominal cramps, and difficulty breathing. Some people, especially those with asthma, may suddenly develop anaphylactic shock when they consume food or beverages that contain sulfiting agents, so it's best to avoid sulfites whenever possible.

If you or any member of your family may be sensitive to sulfites, the following precautions are suggested:

- Read the labels of all processed foods and beverages and avoid those that contain any of the sulfiting agents in the list of ingredients.
- Be sure to inform your doctors and dentist so that they don't prescribe a medication that contains sulfites.
- When dining in restaurants, ask the manager if sulfiting agents were used in the preparation of any foods you plan to order.

Nitrites and Nitrates

Nitrites and nitrates are used as preservatives for cured meats (bacon, ham, smoked fish) and most luncheon meats (frankfurters, bologna) to retard spoilage, prevent botulism, and keep the meat from turning gray or brown. The problem is that nitrites can form cancer-causing nitrosamines in the gastrointestinal tract. However, vitamin C can prevent or slow the formation of nitrosamines, so including foods rich in vitamin C along with any meal that contains nitrites will help to minimize your risk. Also, the list of ingredients will tell you if the manufacturer had the good sense to add vitamin C (ascorbic acid/ascorbate) to the cured product.

Artificial (Synthetic) Flavors

Most artificial flavors are synthesized from plant extracts, coal tar, or petroleum and can trigger the same adverse reactions as artificial colors, such as allergies and behavioral disorders. And since nutritious, high-quality food usually tastes good all by itself and does not require flavor enhancement, you'll find that the majority of foods and beverages that contain synthetic flavors are of lower quality. Therefore, I strongly suggest that you avoid products that contain artificial flavors.

Artificial chemicals are used to imitate many flavors, such as vanilla, butter, smoke, honey, apple, apricot, pear, peach, cherry, strawberry, raspberry, grape, plum, pineapple, coconut, melon, orange, lemon, and rose.

Vanillin is the artificial ingredient used most frequently to imitate vanilla flavor in food and beverages. For most people vanillin does not pose a significant health danger, but for sensitive individuals it can cause the adverse reactions mentioned.

What most consumers don't realize is that several different synthetic chemicals must be blended together to imitate a single natural flavor. For example, artificial strawberry flavor is a mixture of geraniol, ethyl methyl phenyl glycidate, methyl-pentenoic acid, vanillin, ethyl pelargonate, isoamyl acetate, propenyl-trimethoxybenzene, and ethyl butyrate. Or, to get an artificial raspberry flavor, food companies combine vanillin, ethylvanillin, alpha-ionone, maltol, hydroxy-phenyl-butanone, dimethyl sulfide, and dimethyl-N-pyrazinyl pyrrole. Except for vanillin, though, the chemicals used to create artificial flavors are not listed individually on package labels (mainly because there isn't enough room to list them all). Instead they are all lumped under the generic category of "flavoring" or "artificial flavoring." (Vanillin is the only artificial flavor clearly labeled by its name.)

Please note that food manufacturers can legally label their products as containing "natural and artificial flavors" even if they add only a drop of natural flavoring to a whole vat of artificial flavor ingredients. Furthermore, the term *natural flavoring* is often used by food companies to disguise the fact that MSG has been added to their products.

MSG

Monosodium glutamate (MSG) is a sodium salt of glutamic acid, one of the vital amino acids found in the human body. However, when MSG is added to food as a flavor enhancer, the concentration of glutamate far exceeds the normal levels found in nature, and that's when health problems start to occur.

Do not feed children products that contain MSG. Glutamate acts as a stimulant to the nervous system, and ingesting too much can cause hyperactivity and difficulty concentrating. Studies have also shown that excess MSG can cause permanent brain damage by stimulating nerve cells to death. In addition, eating foods (especially fermented foods and ingredients) containing MSG can cause a reaction called the "Chinese restaurant syndrome," which consists of headaches, intense flushing of the skin, nausea, vomiting, and heart palpitations.

MSG provides no health benefits whatsoever yet it is still added to many products, such as Chinese and Japanese food, canned soups and soup mixes, gravies, sauces, canned meats and stews, luncheon meats, frozen dinners, fish, nondairy creamers, chips, and condiments. It's simply a cheap way to make poor-quality food and beverages taste better.

Please note that literally hundreds of food products contain MSG hidden in the following three additives: hydrolyzed vegetable protein (HVP), natural flavoring, and autolyzed yeast. Most consumers do not realize that these three additives may actually contain monosodium glutamate.

Artificial Sweeteners

Saccharin (Sweet'n Low, for example) and aspartame (such as Nutrasweet and Equal) are the two artificial sweeteners used most frequently by the food industry.

Saccharin is a noncaloric artificial sweetener that is 300 times sweeter than table sugar. Saccharin is synthesized from petrochemicals and can cause hives, itching, nausea, diarrhea, and wheezing in sensitive individuals. Extremely large doses may cause cancer.

Aspartame is an artificial sweetener made of two amino acids (aspartate and phenylalanine) held together in a chemical bond by methanol (wood alcohol). It is added to many foods and drinks (from diet drinks to desserts) as a substitute for sugar. Whenever possible, avoid giving it to your child for the following reasons:

- Consumption of aspartame is associated with a long list of side effects, including headaches (especially migraines), vertigo

(dizziness), seizures, mood swings, depression, blurred vision, numbness, abdominal cramps, nausea, and vomiting.
- Aspartame contains the amino acid phenylalanine, which can cause permanent brain damage and mental retardation in persons who carry the phenylketonuria (PKU) gene. That's why doctors warn pregnant women to avoid products that contain aspartame.

ALUMINUM, DIOXINS, AND PCBS IN FOOD, WATER, AND CONSUMER PRODUCTS
Aluminum

There is growing evidence of a link between Alzheimer's disease and the accumulation of aluminum in the brain. Major sources of aluminum exposure include baked goods containing aluminum phosphate, most commercial baking powders, many processed cheeses, table salt, cosmetics, antiperspirants and deodorants, toothpastes, most antacids (except Tums), buffered aspirin, municipal tap water, beverages packaged in aluminum cans, and aluminum pots and pans (most pans with a nonstick surface are aluminum-based).

No one knows for sure yet whether the excess aluminum is the cause or the effect of Alzheimer's, but until a final conclusion is reached, I would drastically reduce exposure in the following ways:

- Avoid foods that have aluminum compounds (sodium aluminum phosphate) in the list of ingredients on the package label, such as cake/pancake/biscuit mixes, baked goods, baking powder (except Rumford, which is aluminum-free), nondairy creamers, regular table salt.

   FYI: You can make your own aluminum-free baking powder by combining 1 teaspoon of Arm & Hammer baking soda, 2 teaspoons of cream of tartar, and 2 teaspoons of cornstarch.
- Use wooden or stainless-steel utensils rather than aluminum.
- Avoid aluminum pots and pans, including those with Teflon or Silverstone coating. Stainless steel is a much safer material in general, but avoid all stainless-steel cookware with copper-clad

bottoms, because excess copper can leach into the food. Pyrex and Corning Ware are good choices.

- Have your drinking water analyzed to be sure it does not contain excess aluminum. Aluminum sulfate is used extensively to help purify municipal water supplies, and sometimes significant amounts of the aluminum remain dissolved in the tap water.

- Do not drink beverages packaged in aluminum cans (or paper cartons lined with aluminum material). Medical researchers in Australia found that noncola soft drinks (fruit juice, punch, and juice drinks) in aluminum cans (or aluminum-lined cartons) contained an average of 33.4 micromoles of aluminum per liter, but noncola soft drinks in glass bottles had an average of only 5.6 micromoles of aluminum per liter (that's one-sixth the amount of aluminum). Cola soft drinks in cans averaged 24.4 micromoles of aluminum per liter, versus only 8.9 micromoles of aluminum per liter in glass bottles. So, whenever possible, purchase beverages in glass bottles, not aluminum cans.

- Don't use table salt that contains aluminum anticaking agents.

Dioxins and PCBs

Dioxins and polychlorinated biphenyls (PCBs) are manmade toxic chemicals found in food (especially fish and seafood), drinking water, breast milk, and a wide variety of consumer products. There are approximately 75 different members of the dioxin family of compounds, but when people talk about dioxin, they are usually referring to 2,3,7,8-tetrachlorodibenzo-p-dioxin (TCDD), the most toxic member. Polychlorinated biphenyls (PCBs) are very similar to dioxins in their chemical structure and mode of action.

TCDD and other dioxins are generated in the manufacturing of chlorinated insecticides, herbicides, disinfectants, and wood preservatives. Dioxin is also produced whenever chlorine is used to bleach consumer paper products white. In fact, chlorine bleaching is the reason it's so common to find dioxin contamination in milk cartons, food packaging, paper plates, coffee filters, toilet paper, sanitary napkins, tampons, paper towels, facial tissues, writing paper, and the like. (Please note that peroxide bleaching does not generate dioxins.)

Until their ban in 1978, polychlorinated biphenyls (PCBs) were used extensively in the manufacture of electronic equipment, appliances, electrical capacitors, transformers, fluorescent light ballasts, plasticizers, adhesives, pesticides, inks, lubricants, and carbonless paper.

Dioxins and PCBs do not biodegrade easily. Once introduced into the environment (such as polluted waterways like the Great Lakes and the Mississippi River), they persist and bioaccumulate up the food chain (especially in fish and other aquatic organisms) all the way to humans. Dioxins and PCBs are easily absorbed through the skin, lungs, and digestive system; they are stored for very long periods of time in the fat tissue of the brain, thyroid, adrenals, liver, breasts, ovaries, and testes. Minute amounts of dioxins and PCBs can severely disrupt a person's hormonal (endocrine), reproductive, and immune systems and thereby trigger a wide range of health problems such as headaches, sore joints, insomnia, birth defects, infertility, miscarriages, stillbirths, endometriosis, heart disease, and liver damage. In addition, studies have now linked dioxin exposure to cancers of the liver, bone marrow, blood, and lymph tissue.

An experiment involving a colony of rhesus monkeys illustrates the enormous toxicity of dioxins. The monkeys received food with a dioxin concentration of only 5 parts per trillion over 10 years. At the end of that time 79 percent of the female monkeys developed endometriosis and significant fertility problems. It's worth noting that fish and seafood sold in supermarkets are allowed to contain dioxin contaminants up to 50 parts per trillion, which is 10 times higher than the concentration that caused endometriosis in the monkeys.

You can do several things to substantially reduce your family's exposure to dioxins and PCBs:

• Do not eat fish or drink water from the Great Lakes, the Hudson River, the Mississippi River, or any other bodies of water known to be heavily contaminated with dioxins and PCBs. Lakes and rivers downstream from paper mills, wood-pulp-processing plants, chemical plants, and large factories are usually very polluted. See "Toxins in Fish and Seafood" for additional details.

• If you eat animal products, trim away the fat first, because dioxins and PCBs accumulate in fat.

• Avoid chlorine bleach (sodium hypochlorite) and chlorinated insecticides, herbicides, disinfectants, and wood preservatives.

• Substitute 100 percent cotton cloth products for paper products whenever possible. In situations where you have to use paper products, look for brands that are unbleached. (The only reason paper products are bleached white in the first place is to trick consumers into thinking that they are pure and sterile even though they aren't.) If you must use bleached paper products, call the manufacturers (toll-free consumer numbers are usually printed on the package) and ask what they use to bleach their products. Peroxide-bleached paper products are acceptable, because peroxide does not create dioxins or pollute the environment. Avoid the chlorine-bleached brands unless the manufacturer can guarantee that they contain no detectable dioxins at the parts per trillion level.

• Do not disassemble or tamper with any electrical equipment or appliances manufactured prior to 1979, because they might contain toxic PCB components.

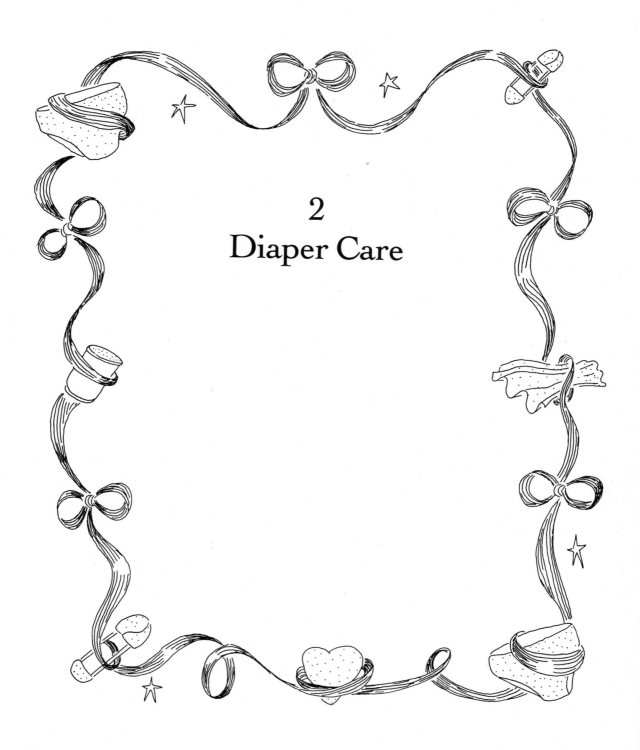

2
Diaper Care

It's estimated that the average child will use approximately 10,000 diapers by the time toilet training is achieved, so deciding whether to use cloth or disposable diapers is important not only for your baby but for the environment as well.

CLOTH VS. DISPOSABLE DIAPERS

Consider the following factors in making your decision.

Absorbency

The absorbency of super- and ultra-absorbent disposables is definitely superior to that of cloth diapers; the absorbent gel securely locks urine inside the diaper, keeping baby's skin dry and preventing accidental leaks on furniture, clothing, and car seats. Tests in hospital newborn nurseries across the country have proved conclusively that a single superabsorbent disposable holds more urine than two cloth diapers.

Diaper Rash Prevention

Diaper rash occurs when stool and urine mix together and remain in direct contact with the skin for longer than 15 minutes. Therefore, the real key to preventing diaper rash is keeping the infant in a clean, dry diaper at all times. In fact a number of scientific studies have found that if diapers are changed as soon as they get wet or dirty, the incidence of diaper rash is about the same for disposables and cloth diapers, although wearing plastic pants over cloth diapers increases the incidence of diaper rash significantly. It's worth noting that the new ultraabsorbent premium disposables significantly decrease the frequency and severity of diaper rash when soiled diapers are not changed right away (during the night, for example).

Comfort

In general, the more leakproof the diapering system, the warmer and less comfortable it is. Compared to disposables, 100 percent cotton cloth diapers are cooler and feel better against the skin, but wearing plastic diaper covers over cloth diapers (to prevent leaks) cancels out their comfort advantage.

Cleanup and Hygiene

Significant cleanup and hygiene problems are associated with cloth diapers, such as leakage of potentially infectious urine and feces, contamination of the hands with germs from rinsing feces off the diaper in the toilet bowl, and pollution of the indoor air with the pungent odor of dirty diapers soaking in a diaper pail.

Disposable diapers leak less than cloth diapers, which helps reduce the presence of germs on clothing, toys, furniture, and caregivers' hands. Two recent scientific studies performed at daycare centers looked at the connection between diapering methods and contamination of hands and toys with feces. Both studies concluded that there was significantly more fecal contamination in rooms where the children wore cloth diapers compared to rooms in which the children wore disposable diapers. The studies suggested that the use of cloth diapers in daycare centers promotes the spread of gastrointestinal viruses, bacteria, and parasites, especially during outbreaks of infectious diarrhea illness.

Convenience

Convenience is the number-one selling point for disposable diapers. However, recent innovations (such as cotton diaper covers with Velcro fasteners and biodegradable disposable paper diaper liners) have made cloth diapering much easier than it used to be.

Ecological Impact

After years of bitter debate and several environmental impact studies, unbiased experts have finally concluded that no one really knows for sure which diaper is best for the planet. The fact is, all diapering systems—disposables, commercially laundered cloth, and home-laundered cloth—pollute the environment.

One of the most widely quoted studies was carried out by Franklin Associates and published in the December 1, 1990, issue of *Science News* (p. 347). Using energy and water consumption, air and water pollution, and solid-waste disposal as the primary areas of ecological concern, the study found the following:

• Home-laundered cloth diapers consume more energy and produce more air pollution than disposables or commercially laundered cloth diapers. (Don't forget that diaper service delivery trucks waste gasoline and pollute the air with exhaust fumes.)
• Home-laundered and commercially laundered cloth diapers consume more water and produce more waterborne waste (strong detergents) than disposables.
• Disposable diapers produce more solid waste than home-laundered or commercially laundered cloth diapers, and they contribute four times as much garbage to landfills. However, according to landfill excavation studies, disposable diapers take up less than 2 percent of the total landfill volume. And the use of ultraabsorbent disposables reduces diaper bulk by an additional 40 percent, which means even less solid waste is produced.

One other important ecological issue concerns the safety of burying soiled disposable diapers (containing disease-causing germs) in landfills. It is against the law to dump human waste in landfills, but for dirty diapers the law is not enforced. To investigate this potential public health hazard, researchers randomly retrieved more than 200 disposable diapers from landfills in New York, Arizona, and Florida. They tested fecal samples from each diaper for a variety of common childhood intestinal germs (such as rotavirus, salmonella bacteria, hepatitis virus, worms, and parasites), but none of the tests showed any evidence of viable disease-causing agents. Furthermore, several additional university studies have concluded that soiled disposable diapers in landfills do not pose a health risk to water supplies, the general public, sanitation workers, or landfill operators.

Allergy/Toxicity

Cloth diapers of 100 percent cotton are hypoallergenic and relatively free of chemicals, but detergents, chlorine bleach, and fabric softeners used to wash them can be a problem if you're not careful. Also, with cloth diapers the standard diaper pail deodorizers pollute the air inside the home and may cause respiratory allergies in susceptible persons.

As for disposable diapers, the chemicals, dyes, and fragrances they contain can cause allergic skin rashes. In fact parents often tell me that their baby will get a diaper rash from one or two particular brands (especially the heavily perfumed economy-priced generics) but not from others.

A toxicity issue gaining notoriety is the allegation that disposable diapers are contaminated with dioxin. Dioxin is an extremely toxic chemical by-product created whenever molecular or elemental chlorine is used to bleach consumer paper products white. To give you an idea of just how toxic dioxin really is, experiments have shown that eating food containing dioxin in concentrations of only five parts per trillion can cause immune system damage. With this in mind, a well-known environmentalist organization has created an uproar by claiming that disposable diapers contain trace amounts of dioxin residues left over from the bleaching process. Naturally, parents are concerned about the possibility that dioxins could migrate out of the diapers and then be absorbed through the baby's skin, and I suppose this could theoretically happen with some of the cheap generics. Spokespersons at Procter and Gamble (Pampers/Luvs), Kimberly-Clark (Huggies), and RMED International (Tushies) state categorically that their diapers have no detectable dioxins, even when tested down to the parts-per-trillion level. Of course, unbleached paper products are always preferable when you can get them, but for many items (disposable diapers, for example), they are not yet commercially available. Please note that peroxide-bleached paper products are acceptable, because peroxide does not generate dioxins or pollute the environment.

Daycare Acceptance

Very few daycare centers will accept a baby in cloth diapers; almost all of them demand that children wear disposables while at the daycare site. As mentioned previously, research at a major medical university proved conclusively that disposable diapers do a much better job of preventing the spread of infectious diarrhea (especially rotavirus diarrhea) at daycare centers by minimizing caregiver contact with contagious germs in the stools and by reducing contamination of surfaces from accidental leaks.

Cost

The average newborn uses 8–14 diapers per day, so the cost per diaper is an important factor to consider. Here's a rough comparison of the average cost of using 12 diapers per day using the three basic diapering methods:

1. Premium brand-name disposables average about $.22 per diaper for the medium size ($2.64 per day or $80.00 per month). However, the benefits of disposables (such as superior absorbency and convenience) are well worth the added expense to many parents.
2. Laundering your own cloth diapers costs only about $.05 per diaper ($.60 per day or $18.00 per month), but it's a time-consuming chore, and the cost advantage may be lost when you consider the value of your time. There can be hidden costs as well, like cleaning bills from accidental soiling of clothing and upholstery or doctor bills for the contagious illnesses spread to

other family members through fecal contamination more often than with disposable diaper use.

3. A commercial diaper service charges an average of about $.15 per diaper ($1.80 per day or $50.00 per month). But there are several major problems with this method. First, diaper services use harsh, water-fouling detergents in the cleaning process. Second, most commercial services have a minimum charge, which means you often pay for diapers that you don't use. Third, and possibly most important, diaper services do not let you label diapers for use by your baby only, so you'd better hope the company follows strict sterilization procedures, because your child will be wearing diapers that were dirtied by the infectious urine and feces of countless numbers of other babies. Think about it for a minute—would you personally wear undergarments that 20 or 30 strangers had previously worn and "soiled," even if the cleaners said they sterilized them? I doubt it. And fourth, many cities don't even have a commercial diaper service.

The Bottom Line

No one can say for sure whether cloth diapers or disposables are better for the environment. If you live in an area of the country where water is abundant, but landfill space is depleted, home-laundered cloth diapers might be the "ecologically correct" choice. On the other hand, disposable diapers might be better in areas of the country that have a water shortage but plenty of landfill space. The point is, each family has its own unique diapering needs, and no single method will work in every situation for every baby. Therefore, your choice of diapers should be based on which of the factors just discussed are most important to you and your community. In the final analysis, you should feel free to choose either kind of diaper or, as some parents do, flexibly combine both diapering methods during the course of the day, using the one most appropriate for a given situation.

BUYING DISPOSABLE DIAPERS

Most of the super- and ultra-absorbent premium disposable diapers work quite well, but many childcare professionals (daycare centers and hospital newborn nurseries, for example) consider Pampers the best conventional brand. Huggies Supremes have handy Velcro fastener tabs and a moisture-proof cover that feels like cloth. The "green" disposables mentioned in the following section are also good choices.

Avoid the cheap generics, because the absorbency is usually poor, the tape fasteners inferior, and they contain higher concentrations of allergy-causing chemicals, perfumes, and powders than the premium brands.

"Green" Disposable Diapers

The word *green* here implies ecological awareness, not the actual color of the diaper; in fact they are actually off-white or beige. The manufacturing of green disposable diapers is less harmful to the environment than conventional disposables, and greens are at least partially biodegradable under typical landfill conditions. Compared to ordinary disposables, these earth-friendly diapers contain fewer chemicals, dyes, and perfumes.

There are several good brands to choose from, but Tushies is my favorite for several reasons: Tushies are dye-free, fragrance-free, and biodegradable. They absorb wetness with a patented natural blend of 30 percent cotton and 70 percent wood pulp cellulose without synthetic chemicals like the acrylic acid polymer gels found in the leading brands. The average retail price for a box of 36 medium-size Tushies is around $11.99 (about $.33 each), and 1 percent of the price of each box sold is donated to American Forests Global Relief, a campaign dedicated to the renewal of forests. Tushies are sold through health food stores, quality drugstores, catalogs, and home delivery. Call 800-34IM DRY (800-344-6379) to order Tushies directly from the manufacturer or to find the name of a store near you that carries them.

Secrets for Success Using Cloth Diapers

Using cloth diapers does not have to be as difficult or time-consuming as it once was. If you decide to try cloth diapers for your baby, consider these practical tips for success:

- One hundred percent cotton is the best material for cloth diapers. Always wash and dry new cloth diapers at least three times before initial use to remove potentially harmful chemicals left over from the manufacturing process.
- Don't use plastic or rubber diaper covers or pants, because they trap heat and wetness, which promote bacterial and fungal (yeast) skin infections. Instead, use modern cotton diaper covers with Velcro fasteners (which hold the diaper in place without dangerous safety pins). One of the best brands on the market is the cotton Biobottom. It's made of 100% cotton terrycloth with a smooth, 100% polyester, water-resistant lining. It can be machine washed and dried. Biobottoms fit snugly to prevent leaks but allow adequate air circulation to the diaper area. Biobottom diaper covers cost about $15 each and can be purchased through the Biobottoms catalog (800-766-1254).
- Standard rectangular cotton cloth diapers will fit inside most Velcro diaper covers if you fold them just right (it takes practice), but there are now cotton diapers also specially shaped like an hourglass to fit perfectly without folding. You can buy these diapers at department stores and through some mail-order catalogs. Another popular option is Bumpkins, a cotton diaper with a built-in waterproof nylon shell and Velcro tabs for a snug fit without safety pins—sort of an all-in-one diapering system. The main drawback to Bumpkins is the price. They can be purchased for about $12 each.

- No matter which cloth diapering system you choose, biodegradable disposable paper diaper *liners* will make removal of feces easier.
- Use hot water and a fragrance-free, dye-free laundry detergent (see Chapter 3 for details) to wash the diapers. Double-rinse to remove soap residue and avoid fabric softeners and antistatic products, because they contain chemicals and perfumes that can cause allergic skin rashes. Drying cotton diapers on high heat in the dryer or simply hanging them outside in the sunlight helps to kill germs.

  20 Mule Team Borax is the safest product you can buy for sanitizing, deodorizing, and whitening laundry. Borax is a naturally-occurring mineral composed solely of sodium, boron, oxygen, and water. Just add ½ cup of borax to the wash along with your regular laundry detergent. It is much safer than toxic chlorine bleach, Lysol, or other chemical additives.

Diaper Pails

Diaper pails can be extremely hazardous for three reasons. First, a toddler may fall headfirst into the pail and drown. Second, a young child may get hold of a deodorizer cake and eat it, with disastrous consequences like chemical burns inside the mouth. Third, the toxic fumes from the deodorizer may cause serious allergy symptoms in susceptible family members. Therefore, if you use a diaper pail, always keep it tightly closed and completely out of the reach of children and never under any circumstances use a deodorizer cake. One of the best brands is the Fisher-Price diaper pail; it's easy for a parent to use but hard for a young child to get into.

Rather than soaking cloth diapers in a pail, many parents prefer to remove most of the feces and then let the diapers air-dry in a separate basket until wash day.

BABY POWDER ALERT

Never use any powders on your baby. Inhaling baby powder can cause severe coughing and sometimes even life-threatening choking. In addition, talcum powder is frequently contaminated with asbestos fibers, and breathing even small amounts of airborne talc particles regularly can be hazardous to the lungs and result in pneumonia (sometimes fatal) or chronic lung disease. Cornstarch is also unacceptable, because it may actually promote the growth of germs that can cause a diaper rash.

HELPFUL HINTS FOR PREVENTING DIAPER RASH

Here are some helpful hints for preventing diaper rash:

- The real secret to preventing diaper rash is to keep your baby's bottom clean and dry, so change the diaper as soon as it gets wet or soiled. Prolonged contact with urine and stool damages the skin and sets the stage for chafing, dermatitis, and yeast infections.
- Unfasten or remove the diaper for periods of 30 minutes several times a day to air-dry the buttocks. And when fastening the diaper, keep the top waistband slightly loose so plenty of air can circulate in the diaper area.
- Don't use plastic, acrylic, or rubber diaper covers or pants (especially overnight), because they trap heat and wetness and promote bacterial and yeast infections.
- Never use alcohol, hydrogen peroxide, iodine, povidone iodine (betadine), or any antiseptic to clean the diaper area; they irritate the skin.
- Soap and/or commercial diaper wipes are too harsh for cleaning your baby's delicate bottom. Besides, there's a better, nontoxic way. First, take a clean, brand-new pump spray bottle and fill it with plain water. (Be sure to label the bottle with your baby's name so you won't accidentally mix it up with another spray bottle that may contain a harmful substance.) When it's time to change diapers, spray the baby's bottom with water and then

gently wipe away the urine and bowel movement with either a moistened washcloth, a soft white paper towel (such as Microwave Bounty), a dye-free, fragrance-free toilet tissue (like Kleenex Unscented or Charmin Free), or facial tissue (Puff's Free, for example). For convenience when you're away from home, carry along some cotton washcloths or soft white paper towels (moistened with plain water) in a zip-lock plastic bag or a snap-lock plastic container (like Rubbermaid or Tupperware).

- To prevent fecal contamination of the genitals, always wipe from front to back and after each wipe either turn to an unused part of the washcloth or get a fresh tissue. Don't rub the skin hard. Blot dry (don't forget the grooves inside the fat folds) and then air-dry for a minute. Do not use an electric hair dryer to dry the baby's skin, because the high-velocity flow of hot air may cause chapping. Furthermore, daily exposure to the high-intensity electromagnetic radiation emitted by the dryer may cause cancer.

- To clean up a big mess quickly, rinse baby's bottom under a running faucet of lukewarm water in the bathtub. Or, if the baby has a rash that hurts when you touch it, you can fill a wash basin with tepid water and dip your baby's bottom in and out of it to remove stool and urine without actually having to rub the skin.

- For those babies who show an increased susceptibility to chapping and diaper rash, a very thin application of plain Vaseline or a dye-free, fragrance-free lotion (see Chapter 4 for brand names) to the diaper area several times a day is often helpful. Don't use lotions, creams, or ointments that contain perfumes, fragrances, or artificial colors (such as FD&C red, yellow, green, blue), because these ingredients tend to cause allergic skin rashes.

- At the first sign of a diaper rash, apply zinc oxide ointment. Zinc oxide is nontoxic, promotes skin healing, and kills germs. The Eckerd and Walgreens store brands are highly recommended; they contain 20 percent zinc oxide in a base of soothing white petrolatum, mineral oil, and beeswax (white wax), without any allergenic fragrances or lanolin, and that makes them a much better choice than the major brand-name diaper rash ointments (such as A and D, Desitin, Dyprotex, and the like). Apply a thick layer of the zinc oxide ointment (like frosting a cake) to the rash several times a day until the skin looks normal again (usually one or two days). It is not necessary to remove all of the ointment at every diaper change. Just wipe away the contaminated outermost layer, then reapply a fresh top coat to the original thickness.

The Four Common Diaper Rashes

Contrary to popular belief, diaper rashes are not all the same; in fact there are more than 25 different types of diaper rash. The common ones you'll see most often, however, are monilia (yeast infection), contact dermatitis, chafing, and impetigo. The location of the rash (genitals, buttocks, or within fat folds and skin creases) is a major diagnostic clue that helps distinguish one from the other.

Monilia (Yeast Infection)

Monilia is a candida yeast infection in the diaper area. The monilia rash is bright red, and it is usually located on and around the genitals or deep within fat folds and skin creases. The sign that helps to distinguish monilia from other diaper rashes is its irregular border with tiny red dots, spots, bumps, or pimples along the edge.

Several different factors can result in an overgrowth of yeast in the diaper area: (1) anything that weakens the immune system (respiratory or intestinal infections, for example), (2) antibiotics that kill the "good" bacteria in the intestines, (3) anything that traps heat and wetness in the diaper area (plastic diaper covers, for instance), (4) diarrhea, or (5) a yeast infection inside the mouth (thrush).

Treatment for monilia diaper rash. Follow all of the suggestions outlined in "Helpful Hints for Preventing Diaper Rash," especially the recommendation to air-dry the buttocks by removing the diaper for 30-minute periods several times a day.

Dermatologists generally recommend applying a thin layer of antiyeast cream to the monilia diaper rash three times a day until the infection is gone (usually about one week). Never put the cream on more often than three times a day, because excessive use will make the rash worse.

Three safe and effective antiyeast creams are sold over the counter: Mycelex OTC Antifungal Cream, Lotrimin AF Antifungal Cream, and Micatin Antifungal Cream.

Toxic Warning

Many prescription diaper rash creams (such as Mycolog, Mytrex, and Lotrisone) contain potent steroids that are readily absorbed into the body through the thin skin in the diaper area. Avoid these creams, because they can produce the following side effects: loss of skin pigmentation, itching and burning of the skin, atrophy or thinning of the skin, permanent stretch marks, suppression of the adrenal glands, increased pressure in the brain, and/or headaches.

Also, please note that Mycelex, Micatin, Mycolog, and Mytrex all sound alike, as do Lotrimin and Lotrisone, but the big difference is that Mycelex, Lotrimin, and Micatin antifungal creams do not contain potentially harmful steroids, so always check the spelling on the label very carefully to be sure you get the right cream from the pharmacy— accidental mix-ups do occur.

Frequent yeast infections could be due to a yeast overgrowth problem inside the mouth or digestive system, and a 10-day course of an oral prescription antiyeast medication called Nystatin Oral Suspension might help. Eliminating fruit juices or other sugary treats from the diet is also worth considering, since sugar promotes yeast growth.

Contact Dermatitis

Contact dermatitis causes a bright red rash with smooth borders, usually on the buttocks. This contrasts with monilia, which occurs primarily on and around the genitals and produces red dots, spots, and bumps along the edge of an irregular border. And, unlike chafing, contact dermatitis normally does not affect the groove inside fat folds.

As the name implies, contact dermatitis diaper rash occurs when a baby's bottom comes into contact with an irritant or an allergenic substance. Common examples include stool and urine mixed together and remaining in contact with the skin for more than 15 minutes, irritant substances in the diet (especially acidic foods), and allergenic chemicals, perfumes, fragrances, or dyes found in lotions, creams, soaps, diapers, and diaper wipes.

Treatment for contact dermatitis diaper rash. First and foremost, avoid (or minimize to the greatest extent possible) contact with the primary irritant or allergenic substance that you suspect is causing the rash. Change diapers as soon as they get wet or soiled, and apply a thick layer of either zinc oxide ointment (Eckerd or Walgreens store brands) or plain Vaseline to the diaper rash to form a protective barrier against prolonged contact with urine and stool. Put on an extrathick coating before the baby goes to sleep at night. Also, follow all of the suggestions outlined in "Helpful Hints for Preventing Diaper Rash," especially the recommendation to air-dry the buttocks by removing the diaper for 30-minute periods several times a day.

For severe cases of contact dermatitis, many dermatologists recommend the application of a thin layer of nonprescription 1 percent hydrocortisone ointment (not the cream) three times a day for two or three days. (Cortizone-10 Ointment is one of the best over-the-counter brands because it does not contain allergenic additives.) Don't put the ointment on more often than three times a day, because excessive use will irritate the skin and make the rash worse. One percent hydrocortisone is a low-potency steroid that usually does not cause the side effects of the high- and medium-potency steroids found in some prescription diaper rash antifungal creams, such as Lotrisone and Mycolog. Of course, you should never use any steroid product without consulting your baby's doctor first.

Chafing

Chafing causes red patches of diaper rash either on the buttocks or deep within the grooves of fat folds and skin creases. The border of the rash is smooth. The lack of spots or bumps along the edge of the rash makes chafing easy to distinguish from monilia. Chafing is caused by the friction of moist skin rubbing against itself or the diaper.

Treatment for chafing. Follow all of the suggestions outlined in "Helpful Hints for Preventing Diaper Rash," especially the recommendation to air-dry the buttocks by removing the diaper for 30-minute periods several times a day. Apply a thin layer of nonprescription zinc oxide ointment (such as the Eckerd or Walgreens store brands) to the diaper rash several times a day until the skin is healed.

Impetigo

Intact skin is a very effective barrier against bacterial invasion. However, when the skin surface is broken by a scratch or a rash, bacteria such as staphylococcus and streptococcus can readily cause a superficial skin infection called *impetigo*. An impetigo diaper rash consists of fluid-filled blisters that are very fragile and break open easily. When the top of a blister peels off, it exposes a shallow, red, round, coin-size sore underneath that looks very much like a burn that might result from touching the tip of a cigarette. A yellowish golden or honey-colored matter may ooze from the open sores and form crusts or scabs. Impetigo sores are full of very contagious bacteria.

Treatment for impetigo. Follow all of the suggestions outlined in "Helpful Hints for Preventing Diaper Rash." To cure impetigo completely and quickly and keep it from spreading, however, you'll need to see your doctor and request an oral antibiotic and topical Bactroban ointment.

I try to avoid using oral antibiotics whenever possible, but here it's worth the small risk of side effects to be sure you kill the bacteria below the surface of the skin, where the ointment may not be able to reach. Duricef (a popular brand of generic cefadroxil) is probably one of the best choices to treat impetigo, because it is reasonably priced, has a pleasant orange-pineapple flavor, is gentle on the stomach, and can be given either with or without food. On the other hand, for children who are allergic to penicillin and/or cephalosporin types of antibiotics, erythromycin is a safe and acceptable alternative. Unfortunately, erythromycin doesn't taste good, and it tends to cause an upset stomach unless it's taken with food.

Bactroban is a prescription antibiotic ointment designed specifically to treat impetigo. Using a cotton swab, apply Bactroban ointment to the top of the impetigo sores three times a day until healing is complete. Use a fresh swab each time so that you don't contaminate the Bactroban tube with germs.

Please note that for treating impetigo none of the over-the-counter antibacterial ointments (Neosporin, Polysporin, bacitracin) even come close to the effectiveness of prescription Bactroban ointment.

One other hint: Bactroban and bacitracin sound alike, so always check the spelling on the tube to be sure you get Bactroban from the pharmacy, because Bactroban is the only one that works fast.

Diaper Rash Danger Signals

The four common diaper rashes can usually be cured by following the preceding suggestions, but always have a doctor examine your baby if a diaper rash is accompanied by one or more of the following danger signals:

- The rash spreads to parts of the body beyond the diaper area.
- The rash does not clear up completely within a few days.
- The baby has a fever or acts sick.

3
Clothing,
Bedding,
and Laundry

Because of their immature liver-detoxification and immune-defense systems, children are much more vulnerable than adults to the health hazards of chemicals in clothing and bedding, such as permanent-press formaldehyde resins, chlorine bleach, dyes, and other toxic compounds. When choosing clothing and bedding for your family, it's important to take several factors into account: cost, comfort (should be soft and breathable), durability (should be rugged), cleaning requirements (should be machine-washable in warm water), potential health problems from the fabric itself and from chemical finishes added to the fabric, animal rights (should be cruelty-free), and the environmental impact of obtaining and processing the raw materials needed to manufacture the fiber into the finished product (should be earth-friendly).

SYNTHETIC FABRICS

Synthetic fabrics are derived from two primary sources: petroleum and cellulose (cotton linters and wood pulp).

The petroleum-based synthetic fabrics include polyester (Dacron, Fortrel, Mylar), polyacrylic (Orlon, Acrilan), polypropylene (Herculon), polyurethane (spandex, Lycra), and polyamide (nylon, Antron). They're designed to look like natural fabrics, but in essence they're soft thermoplastics.

The cellulose-based synthetic fabrics include acetate (Celanese), triacetate (Arnel), and rayon (Coloray, Colorspun, Corval, Fortisan, Topel, and more than 80 other trade names).

Synthetic fabrics are not breathable or absorbent. They're hot and clammy in the summer and cold in the winter. In addition, synthetic fabrics carry an electric charge that produces static cling, often requiring antistatic chemical sprays and fabric softeners that increase the amount of unwanted, unnecessary, and potentially harmful chemicals in the home and environment.

Conventional textile manufacturing of synthetic fabrics wastes water and natural resources, produces large amounts of nonbiodegradable solid waste for landfills, and discharges untold quantities of incinerated toxic sludge and carbon dioxide into the atmosphere (which contributes to the greenhouse effect) as well as adding toxic chemicals (such as dioxins, dyes, and formaldehyde) to waterways.

Generally speaking, the fewer the number of chemical dyes and finishes added to a fabric, the less odor it emits and the less likely it is to cause an adverse reaction. In fact allergic reactions to pure, untreated synthetic fabrics, such as 100 percent nylon and 100 percent polyester, are rare. On the other hand, polyester blends and cellulose-based synthetic fabrics (acetate, triacetate, and rayon) require heavy chemical finishes to resist shrinkage and increase durability, and some of these toxic compounds (especially formaldehyde-based permanent-press resins) can cause serious health problems, such as allergies and chemical sensitivities. And the polyacrylics are even suspected of being carcinogenic and should be avoided.

NATURAL FABRICS

The natural fabrics include cotton, linen (flax), wool, cashmere, and silk. Only cotton, cashmere, and wool will be discussed in detail since linen and silk are too expensive and impractical for children's everyday clothing (not to mention the fact that these fabrics invariably end up at the dry cleaner, getting loaded up with chemicals).

Cotton

The best fabric for clothing is 100 percent cotton, without permanent press. Cotton is king because it is a natural plant fiber that is hypoallergenic, rugged, durable, soft, comfortable, washable, breathable, and reasonably priced. It is produced without killing animals and carries no electric charge (no static cling). Of course 100 percent cotton products without permanent press do need ironing, and they do tend to wrinkle pretty easily, but neatness is not as important as being healthy.

There are three ecological grades of cotton: conventional, green, and organic.

Conventional Cotton

This is the grade most of us are familiar with, the one sold at most retail stores. It's an excellent fabric and highly recommended even though there are a few ecological drawbacks. For example, conventionally grown cotton plants are sprayed heavily with pesticides, which ultimately enter the food chain at several levels (such as runoff into lakes and rivers and in cottonseed oil used in processed foods). During the manufacturing and finishing process most of the pesticide residues on cotton fibers are bleached out or washed away, but then the cotton fibers may receive additional chemical treatments, such as dyes, chlorine bleach, (which generates dioxins), and formaldehyde (particularly in permanent-press items). Fortunately the synthetic dyes are usually so tightly bound to the fabric (colorfast) that they don't bother most people. And there's some more good news: cotton farmers are now learning to minimize their use of pesticides, and half the U.S. textile companies have now switched to hydrogen peroxide for bleaching their cotton.

Clothing and bedding labeled "permanent press," "wrinkle free," or "no-iron" have been treated with formaldehyde resin finishes and should be avoided whenever possible, since contact with immunotoxic formaldehyde can put a permanent crease in a child's immune system.

Conventional cotton fabrics are often blended with synthetic polyester, and almost all polyester/cotton blends are then treated with formaldehyde resins. That's why 100 percent cotton is usually a healthier choice.

"Green" Cotton

This fabric is undyed, unbleached, and formaldehyde-free. Green cotton is actually beige; the term *green* is used to indicate ecological awareness. Compared to conventional cotton, green cotton is more expensive, tends to shrink with each washing, doesn't feel as soft, and has a strong and irritating natural cotton odor that requires several washings to remove.

Organically Grown Cotton

This is basically green cotton raised without pesticides—great for the environment, but it drives up the average price of the fabric about twofold, and for families on a tight budget that's a lot. Furthermore, it has all of the drawbacks of green cotton (shrinkage, scratchiness, and irritating odor).

The Bottom Line

All things considered, clothing and bedding made of conventional 100 percent cotton without permanent press is the best choice for most families. Organically grown or green cotton clothing adds an extra margin of safety for the environment, but you have to put up with shrinkage, reduced softness, and extra expense.

Toxic Warning

Avoid organic or green cotton items such as pillows and mattresses that cannot be washed thoroughly prior to use, because brand-new organic cotton stuffing and ticking usually have a strong natural odor that is extremely irritating to the eyes, nose, throat, and lungs.

Several mail-order companies specialize in selling 100 percent cotton products:

Seventh Generation (800-456-1177)
Janice Corporation (800-JANICES)
Hanna Andersson (800-346-6040 or 800-222-0544)
The Vermont Country Store (802-362-2400)

Cashmere

Cashmere is an excellent natural fabric made from goat hair. It is breathable, resilient, soft, warm, and durable. Cashmere is expensive, but if you live in a cold region, where extrawarm clothing is a must, I highly recommend cashmere for winter coats, sweaters, and socks.

Wool

Wool is a natural fabric that is breathable, resilient, and durable. Unfortunately, it has several drawbacks that make it much less desirable than cotton or cashmere for clothing. The big problem is that many people are allergic to the harsh chemical finishes (dyes, oils, bleaches, formal-

---

Toxic Warning

Never under any circumstances use mothballs in your home. Mothballs usually contain paradichlorobenzene or naphthalene, and breathing these toxic vapors can cause a variety of serious health problems, such as depression, disorientation, chronic fatigue, cancer, sore throat, chronic cough, runny nose, and kidney or liver damage. Even with the closet door tightly closed, the volatile and hazardous vapors from mothballs will eventually permeate the entire house. In addition, a child's accidentally eating a mothball containing neurotoxic paradichlorobenzene could result in seizures.

Moths are interested primarily in wool and fur products that are contaminated with organic matter (food, dander, hair, sweat, and urine), so the best nontoxic strategy for preventing moth damage is to vacuum regularly, keep fabrics clean, and store them in sealed containers or plastic bags. Wearing and brushing clothes frequently and exposing them to sunlight also prevents infestation. I generally advise against cedar chests, cedar blocks, cedar cubes, and the like, because constant exposure to cedar's strong, aromatic scent is irritating to the membrane lining of the eyes, nose, throat, and bronchial tubes.

dehyde, shrinkproofing, and mothproofing) used in the manufacturing of wool. And the wool fiber itself has minute scales, which rub against the skin and cause itching and rashes. Furthermore, wool may be an inhalant allergen, especially for children with allergic or asthmatic tendencies. Another important issue involves the inhumane treatment of sheep. Finally, wool products generally cost more than cotton.

My personal recommendation is to avoid contact with woolen fabrics for the reasons mentioned, but if you're interested in purchasing organic (pesticide-free and chemical-free) wool products obtained from sheep raised humanely and simply sheared (not killed), call Heart of Vermont (800-639-4123) for a free catalog.

FABRIC FINISHES

Some fabrics receive a variety of chemical treatments or finishes designed to make them durable, wrinkle-resistant (permanent-press), shrinkage-resistant, antistatic, stain-repellent, moth-resistant, water-repellent, and mildew-resistant. That's why new clothes and bedding often smell so bad and feel so scratchy at first. Here are a few tips to help you minimize your child's exposure to these potentially toxic chemicals:

• Always wash and dry new clothing and bedding at least three times before initial use. After drying the third time, sprinkle a few drops of plain water on the clothing and see if the water beads up or soaks in; if it beads up, there's still too much formaldehyde-based resin or other chemical finish in the fabric, and the clothing will need several more washings and dryings before it can be worn. If the drops of water soak right into the fabric immediately, a good portion of the harmful chemicals has likely been removed.

• The formaldehyde-based resins in fabric finishes can cause allergic skin reactions, such as itching, eczema, or hives. Therefore, avoid fabrics likely to have received chemical finishes such as rayon, acetate (Celanese), triacetate (Arnel), synthetic fibers blended with natural fibers (polyester/cotton blends, for exam-

ple), corduroy, and any fabric labeled "wash and wear," "permanent-press," "wrinkle-resistent," "no-iron," or "shrink-proof."
FYI: The fabrics least likely to have heavy finishes include 100 percent cotton, 100 percent silk, 100 percent linen, 100 percent wool, 100 percent cashmere, 100 percent nylon, and 100 percent polyester.

- Avoid clothing and fabrics treated with antistatic, stain-repellent, water-repellent, moth-resistant, or mildew-resistant chemical finishes.
- Sanforizing is a nonchemical, controlled-shrinkage process used on many cotton products and some linens. It presents no harm to the consumer.
- Loose-fitting clothing is less apt to cause an adverse skin reaction than tight-fitting clothing, because there is less friction and contact with the skin.

Flame-Retardant and Fire-Resistant Chemicals

Children's clothing that is officially labeled as "sleepwear" or pajamas has to meet federal flammability standards established by law. Unfortunately, the flame-retardant chemicals used on clothing and bedding have not been tested adequately for their possible adverse health effects. For example, TRIS and octa-bromo-biphenyl were withdrawn from the market once it became apparent that they caused cancer in animals, but not before millions of children had been needlessly exposed to these carcinogens over a period of many years.

Deca-bromo-diphenyl oxide (DBDPO or Caliban) is the flame retardant used most frequently for polyester and cotton/polyester blends. The fire-resistant chemicals used most frequently on cotton, flannel, and rayon are the Tetrakis compounds.

Breathing formaldehyde gas levels above 0.1 part per million for an extended period of time will cause many health problems, such as headaches, dizziness, scratchy eyes and throat, nasal congestion, coughing, and immune system abnormalities. Unfortunately, most fabrics treated with flame-resistant chemicals, especially the Tetrakis compounds, continuously emit toxic and allergenic formaldehyde gas (sometimes in concentrations as high as 500 parts per million) at the surface of the fabric. That's why many health-care professionals strongly advise their patients to avoid using clothing or bedding treated with fire-resistant chemicals. To avoid using dangerous fire-resistant chemicals on children's sleepwear or pajamas without violating federal flammability standards, many manufacturers have started using fabrics that are so inherently flame-resistant (such as 100 percent nylon) that they do not require any treatment with toxic flame-retardant chemicals. Another technique commonly employed is using untreated cotton for underwear or long underwear but not labeling such clothing as "sleepwear" or pajamas, even though everyone knows (off the record, of course) that that's what it's going to be used for.

BEDDING, PILLOWS, AND MATTRESSES

Bedding

The best material for sheets, pillowcases, blankets, and bedspreads is 100 percent cotton without permanent press. Remember that "no-iron" cotton/polyester blend sheets and pillowcases are treated with formaldehyde-based resins to make them "wrinkle-free," so always wash and dry new items at least three times before initial use to remove potentially harmful chemical residues left over from the manufacturing process. This advice also applies to "green" and organic cotton sheets and blankets, because they have a strong and irritating natural cotton odor when brand-new (even the ones that claim to be prewashed).

Pillows

Most pillows emit a variety of chemicals and allergenic substances, and when children sleep on them they inhale these harmful substances. Therefore, the healthiest choice is to avoid using pillows altogether, but if your child is old enough to sleep in a regular bed (usually around 2 years old) and wants a pillow, you can make a nontoxic one by folding a few soft 100 percent cotton towels to fit inside a standard-size cotton pillowcase. This method allows for easy washing once a week to remove allergy-causing dust mites and other germs.

If you decide to buy a conventional pillow, hold it close to your nose and give it a good sniff to be sure it doesn't emit any odor before you let your child sleep on it. Don't put plastic coverings of any kind on pillows or mattresses, and avoid pillows stuffed with organic cotton, foam rubber, latex, animal hair, feathers, or down. Down and feathers can cause serious allergy problems, but even worse is the fact that to obtain the feathers, live ducks and geese are plucked (without any regard for the pain they must endure) several times during their life-spans and then finally slaughtered for meat when they've outlived their commercial usefulness.

Mattresses

The most important piece of furniture for the nursery is the crib. Your child will spend 8–18 hours a day sleeping in her crib, so it must be made of healthy materials. As with all furniture in the nursery, the crib frame should be solid hardwood with a nontoxic, no-wax finish. An extra-firm crib mattress is also essential. Avoid mattresses stuffed with animal hair, feathers, or down because of potential allergy problems. Look for a crib mattress that does not have a plastic cover (especially not vinyl) and has not received chemical treatments, such as stainproofing, mothproofing, waterproofing, or pesticides. Inherently flame-resistant materials that do not require flame-retardant chemicals are preferred, since many flame-retardants are carcinogenic, and some release toxic formaldehyde gas when the fabric becomes wet.

Please note that many cities have local mattress manufacturers that will custom-build a mattress without using any chemical treatments as long as the customer has a signed statement from a physician stating that the child needs a chemical-free mattress because of allergies or asthma.

As with pillows, give the crib mattress a sniff test for odors before letting your baby sleep on it. An obvious chemical odor or new smell means the mattress is emitting VOCs that may be harmful to breathe.

LAUNDRY

As mentioned earlier, all new clothing, sheets, pillowcases, towels, and washcloths should be washed at least three times before initial use. The object is to completely wash out the "new" smell from the fabric. You should follow the cleaning instructions on the label, but be aware that laundry detergents, chlorine bleach, presoaks, fabric softeners, and antistatic agents can cause allergic reactions and skin rashes because small quantities of chemicals remain in the fabric after washing. That's why it's so important to choose nontoxic products. Avoid laundry powders and liquids that contain perfumes, fragrances, dyes, artificial colors, or strong petroleum solvents. These unnecessary synthetic chemical additives are allergenic. Instead, use a fragrance-free, dye-free laundry detergent. Tide Free, Cheer Free, and Wisk Free are good choices. It may surprise you to learn that both Ivory Snow and Dreft contain perfume (and Dreft even has a colorant), which makes them less than optimal.

FYI: The term *unscented* can be misleading in that it often means a masking fragrance has been added to overcome an unpleasant natural odor in the product. The "fragrance-free" label, on the other hand, means no fragrances or perfumes have been added.

As mentioned in Chapter 2, 20 Mule Team Borax is a great product for whitening, deodorizing, and sanitizing laundry. Just add the recommended amount of borax to the wash along with your regular laundry detergent.

Avoid chlorine bleach products such as Clorox and Purex, because the chlorine is very irritating and harmful to the eyes, nose, and throat.

Minimize (or avoid altogether) the use of most presoak and stain-remover products, which often contain toxic chemicals, such as chlorine, formaldehyde, benzene, toluene, or tetrachloroethylene (perchloroethylene). 20 Mule Team Borax and Wisk Free are generally safe presoaks.

Avoid fabric softeners and antistatic products (especially aerosol sprays and liquids), because they contain perfumes, fragrances, and hydrocarbons that pollute the indoor air and irritate the nose, throat, and skin.

DRY CLEANING

Try not to buy clothing or bedding that requires dry cleaning, because many of the toxic chemical solvents used in the dry-cleaning process (such as tetrachloroethylene, trichloroethylene, benzene, toluene, and naphthalene) are carcinogenic and can seriously damage the immune system and kidneys. These poisonous fumes can pollute the indoor air for up to a week after your clothes are brought home from the dry cleaner. In situations where garments have to be dry cleaned, follow these suggestions:

- Do not accept dry-cleaned goods that have any residual chemical odor.
- After picking up your clothing from the cleaners, remove and safely dispose of the plastic covering as soon as you get home; then hang the items in a well-ventilated area, such as a balcony or porch, to air out for a few days.

4
Baby Bath,
Shampoo, and
Skin-Care Products

There's nothing softer than a baby's skin, but it's thinner, more delicate, and absorbs toxic chemical compounds more readily than an adult's. Furthermore, anything that causes a rash or otherwise breaks the surface of the skin opens the door to infection. That's why choosing the safest skin-care products is so important. First, though, let's review some bathing basics.

BATHING DOS AND DON'TS

- *Don't* give your newborn a tub bath until the umbilical cord falls off; after that, a complete tub bath two or three times a week is generally adequate, since bathing too often can dry out the skin. Of course, you'll have to wipe your baby's face and neck several times a day with a soft washcloth and plain water to remove milk, food, saliva, and other skin irritants.
- *Don't* bathe your baby in a cold or drafty room. Be sure the room temperature is comfortable.
- *Don't* use hot water for bathing; lukewarm or tepid water is less drying to the skin. A floating water thermometer with an easy-to-read temperature display will help you maintain the bathtub water around an ideal 98–100° F. Always check the water temperature with your hand or elbow to make sure it is comfortably warm before you put the baby in the tub, because hot water can cause serious scald burns in a matter of seconds. And don't run the water while your baby is in the tub; the tap water temperature could change suddenly without your being aware of it.

Please note that you can mail-order the floating water thermometer (and several other safety devices mentioned in the book) through the Perfectly Safe Catalogue (800-837-KIDS).

- *Do* equip your bathtub faucet with a scald protection actuator that instantly shuts off water flow to a trickle when the sensing valve detects a water temperature above 110° F. It costs only about $20, and it's simple to install.

- *Do* cover the faucet spout, knobs, handles, and any other protuberances in the tub with soft, fluffy towels (or specially designed padded covers) to prevent accidental bumps and cuts.

- *Do* remove razors, shampoo bottles, soap bars, and other potentially dangerous articles from the tubside.

- *Do* place a towel in the tub, under the baby, to prevent sliding. Baby bath seats that adhere to the tub floor are also helpful once a child is old enough to sit up on his own.

- *Don't* put more than one or two inches of water in the tub, and never leave your baby alone in the water for any reason whatsoever! A small child can accidentally drown in a matter of seconds.

- *Do* keep all of the bathing equipment within reach so you don't have to let go of the baby.

- *Don't* go overboard with soap. It simply isn't necessary. In fact it's safer, easier, and better for the skin to use only a soft washcloth and plain water for most parts of the body. Reserve the use of soap for those few areas of skin that get oily or dirty, in which case a mild, fragrance-free (or unscented), dye-free cleansing bar (brand names are given in the next section) is preferred.

- *Don't* scrub the skin hard; be gentle.

- *Don't* use soap or cotton-tipped swabs (Q-Tips) to clean inside your baby's ears, nose, urethra, vagina, or anus. It's safer to gently wash the outside entrance to these delicate areas with plain water and a soft washcloth or cotton ball. Remember, what you can't reach with the corner of a washcloth doesn't need cleaning in the first place.

- *Don't* let your baby lie flat in the tub, because water will get into his ear canals and may cause an infection. If water accidentally splashes into his ears, lean his head sideways and gently blot the excess water with the corner of a towel.

- *Don't* use soap or shampoo until right before you plan to take your child out of the tub. Allowing a child to soak for more than a few minutes in sudsy water (including shampoo suds) will remove the natural, protective oils from the skin and irritate the anal-genital area.
- *Don't* under any circumstances give your child a bubble bath or use scented bath oils. All brands of bubble bath (even those specifically designed for children) irritate the urethra and can lead to painful urination and an increased risk of bladder or kidney infections. The suds can also cause soreness and redness in the anal or genital area. Soaking in soapy water is asking for trouble.
- *Do* rinse the skin with fresh, nonsoapy water to remove all soap residue when the bath is finished; then blot or pat the skin dry with a soft cotton towel.
- *Do* drain the tub completely as soon as the bath is over; toddlers have been known to fall in accidentally and drown in as little as two inches of water. Do take your child out of the tub before you drain it, however, because young children may actually become frightened that they will disappear down the drain along with the water.
- *Don't* use an electric hair dryer to dry your baby's skin or hair, because the high-velocity flow of hot air may chap the skin, and prolonged exposure to the large electromagnetic field generated by the dryer may be harmful.
- *Don't* use baby oil, because most brands contain allergenic fragrances that can cause skin rashes.
- *Don't* use baby powders, because the airborne particles are hazardous to breathe. In fact a big inhalation of talcum powder can be fatal; and talc is frequently contaminated with cancer-causing asbestos. Forget cornstarch powder, too, since it promotes the growth of bacteria and yeast.

SOAPS AND CLEANSING BARS

Most soaps and cleansing bars or liquids dry and irritate the skin. In fact cleansing agents that make the skin feel "squeaky clean" actually strip away the natural, protective oils and increase the risk of developing eczema and infections. Furthermore, soaps (including those made for babies) generally contain allergenic substances (artificial colors, fragrances, and preservatives). Antibacterial and deodorant soaps (such as Dial, Safeguard, and Lever 2000) even have potentially harmful antibacterial chemicals (triclosan or triclocarban). For all these reasons, it's better to clean your child's skin with just a soft washcloth and plain water and reserve the use of a mild cleansing bar or liquid for areas that are oily or dirty.

As far as different brands of soap are concerned, advertising claims of mildness are usually exaggerated and not based on scientific studies, so before buying a cleansing bar or liquid for your family, always read the label, paying particular attention to the first three chemicals in the list of ingredients since they will be the ones in highest concentration in that product. For example, the alkali soaps (sodium tallowate and sodium cocoate, for example) and the sulfate detergents (especially lauryl sulfate and laureth sulfate) are the ingredients most likely to dry and irritate sensitive skin, and products that utilize them as primary cleansing agents should be avoided. In contrast, sodium isethionate and sodium cocoyl isethionate are two of the least-irritating cleansing agents, which is why isethionate-based Unscented White Dove and Fragrance Free Aveeno Cleansing Bar for Combination Skin have proved to be the mildest cleansing bars. In fact an independent research study at the University of Pennsylvania tested several popular bar soaps and found Unscented White Dove and Aveeno for Combination Skin the mildest by far, followed in increasing order of harshness by Purpose, Dial, Alpha Keri, Neutrogena, Ivory, Oilatum, Lowila, Jergens, Lubriderm, Cuticura, Basis, Irish Spring, Zest, Camay, and Lava.

Unscented White Dove and Fragrance Free Aveeno for Combination Skin are both nonalkaline, with a nearly neutral pH, but they are not "tear-free," so don't let the suds get anywhere near your child's eyes. And even though both brands are considered mild, I would limit their use to only those areas of skin that are really dirty or oily. For most parts of the body (especially the face), a soft washcloth and plain water work just fine and are much safer for the skin. Note that Unscented White Dove does have a tiny amount of masking fragrance, but not enough to be a problem for most children, especially when you compare it to the heavily perfumed competition.

Tear-free baby bath cleansers have the desirable quality of not stinging the eyes, but their strong fragrances are allergenic and irritating to the nose and throat, which makes them less than optimal. And even though they don't sting immediately on contact, tear-free soap suds can definitely injure the eyes when contact time exceeds more than a few seconds, so in the event any suds accidentally get into the eyes, rinse them out immediately with clean water.

SHAMPOO

Most babies need their hair shampooed about twice a week, but if your child has cradle cap or accumulates more than the average amount of oil or scale on his scalp, you may have to shampoo daily or every other day.

The major manufacturers use the mild amphoteric and nonionic surfactant cleansing agents (such as coco-amphocarboxyglycinate, PEG glyceryl cocoate, and polysorbate-20) in their tear-free baby bath and shampoo products. That's the good news. The bad news is that most baby shampoos also contain chemical compounds (such as artificial colors, fragrances, and preservatives) that are notorious for causing contact dermatitis skin rashes.

Of course, the ideal baby shampoo would be tear-free, dye-free, and fragrance-free and contain a nonallergenic preservative and conditioner. Unfortunately, there is currently no single commercial brand that has all of these desirable qualities. Therefore, no matter which shampoo brand you choose, always rinse the hair thoroughly with plenty of fresh water to remove the potentially harmful chemical compounds and never allow your child to soak in shampoo suds. As with soap, tear-free shampoo can in fact be quite harmful to the eyes, so if tear-free shampoo suds accidentally splash into your child's eyes, rinse them out right away with plenty of clean, lukewarm water.

Of the tear-free baby shampoos, Johnson's No More Tears Baby Shampoo is rated by dermatologists as the one least likely to cause allergic reactions in spite of the fact it contains several allergenic ingredients, such as cocamidopropyl betaine, quaternium-15 (a formaldehyde-releasing preservative), and artificial fragrances and colors.

SCALY SCALP/CRADLE CAP

During their first couple of months some babies develop cradle cap, which consists of thick, yellow, greasy scales on the scalp. It may be caused by a common skin condition called *seborrhea* or by a low-grade infection of the scalp with a fungus called *Pityrosporum*. Either way, it usually clears up after a few months. In the meantime, you can control it somewhat by washing your child's scalp once a day. While the hair is lathered, use a washcloth to rub off the superficial scales. Don't be afraid to gently clean the "soft spot" (fontanel) area. Rinse the scalp thoroughly with plenty of clean running water. Pat dry with a soft cotton towel. It often helps to apply a small amount of an emollient ointment (such as plain Vaseline) to the scaly areas of the scalp once or twice a day, especially right after toweling dry.

Stay away from medicated shampoos that contain coal tar extract or salicylic acid, as these chemicals are potentially harmful to children. Some dermatologists recommend over-the-counter Selsun Blue shampoo as an effective treatment for difficult cases of cradle cap, but others believe it is too strong for babies, so always ask your doctor before trying any such treatment. Typically you would continue to shampoo once a day or every other day with the nonmedicated shampoo you normally use and shampoo just once a week (for one month) with the Selsun Blue. The Selsun Blue bottle must be shaken extremely well before each use. Selsun is not tear-free, so do not get the suds anywhere near your baby's eyes, and always rinse thoroughly with clean water to remove the strong fragrance chemicals.

OINTMENTS, CREAMS, AND MOISTURIZING LOTIONS

A baby's skin is thin and can easily absorb the chemical compounds in creams and lotions, with some areas of skin being more permeable than others. For example, the scalp absorbs three times more, the forehead six times more, and the scrotum over 30 times more topically applied hydrocortisone than the forearm or leg. With this in mind, there are two important principles of skin care for children. First, do not routinely apply lotions, creams, or ointments if your child's skin is already smooth and healthy. ("If it ain't broke, don't fix it.") Second, if the use of a skin-care product does become necessary, choose a brand that is fragrance-free and dye-free whenever possible.

All moisturizing lotions are emulsions, that is, a combination of oil (lipids) and water held together in a homogenous suspension by chemical compounds called *emulsifiers*. The lipids used most frequently include petrolatum, mineral oil, natural fatty acids and their derivatives, and/or lanolin and its derivatives. Moisturizing lotions help soften, lubricate, remoisturize, and heal dry, rough skin; lotions feel less greasy than ointments or creams, but ironically, almost all baby lotions are loaded with artificial colors, fragrances, and other allergenic ingredients that make them unacceptable. Two notable exceptions are Curel Fragrance Free and Aveeno Moisturizing Lotion; these two lotions are currently the best on the market.

For dry or rough patches of skin, apply a thin layer of plain Vaseline once or twice a day (especially right after a bath). Plain Vaseline is dye-free, fragrance-free, and preservative-free; it's one of the safest, least expensive, and most effective emollients you can buy. For eczema or dermatitis, many dermatologists recommend twice-daily application of 1 percent hydrocortisone ointment (not cream). Cortizone-10 Ointment is one of the best over-the-counter brands because it does not contain any allergenic additives.

HERBAL SKIN-CARE PRODUCTS

Beware of herbal skin-care products containing trendy ingredients, such as collagen, keratin, propolis (bee glue), balsam of Peru, Tiger Balm, jojoba oil, clove oil, karaya gum, acacia gum (gum arabic), gum tragacanth, herbal extracts (such as chamomile), witch hazel (contains 2–9 percent tannic acid), spices, honey, wheat germ oil, and the like. These ingredients have no proven benefits, and many of them sensitize the skin and provoke allergic rashes. Just because a product is labeled "natural" or "herbal" does not necessarily mean it's safe to use on your baby's skin.

DECIPHERING SOAP, SHAMPOO, AND SKIN-CARE PRODUCT LABELS

Cosmetic advertising can be very misleading. Words like *mild, natural,* and *hypoallergenic* mean absolutely nothing. The sad truth is an informed consumer must learn to read and decipher ingredient labels to avoid harmful products. To that purpose, the following discussion outlines the major sources of cosmetic ingredients and the eight basic cosmetic ingredient categories. The "FYI" at the end of each category gives a synopsis of the best and the worst ingredients along with their potential allergenicity and toxicity.

One of the main things that makes learning to decode labels easy is that all cosmetic companies use the same chemical building blocks to manufacture their products. Once you know the basics of the cosmetic chemical alphabet, the rest is a snap. And although many of the cosmetic ingredient names are tongue-twisters, they do nevertheless follow obvious patterns that are quite logical. Breaking up long words into their prefixes, stems, and suffixes will help. Prefixes, for example, are often nothing more than simple Latin and Greek derivatives denoting numbers of molecules: mono- (one), di- or bi- (two), tri- (three), tetra- (four), penta- (five), and poly- (many). As mentioned, the earlier that a substance appears in the list of ingredients, the higher the concentration of it in the product.

Major Sources of Cosmetic Ingredients

Natural fatty acids and their derivatives, wool fat (lanolin), and petroleum, hydrocarbons, and beeswax are the major sources of ingredients used in soaps, shampoos, lotions, creams, ointments, and other skin-care products.

Natural Fatty Acids

Caprylic acid, capric acid, lauric acid, myristic acid, palmitic acid, stearic acid, and oleic acid are the natural fatty acids used most extensively by the cosmetics industry. They are obtained primarily from animal fat and plant and vegetable oils. Derivatives of the natural fatty acids are easy to recognize by their stems—*laur* as in lauric acid, *myrist* as in myristate, *palmit* as in palmitate, *cet* as in cetyl alcohol, *stear* as in steareth, and *ole* as in oleamide.

Wool Fat

Lanolin (wool wax), lanolin alcohols, lanolate, laneth, and other lanolin derivatives are obtained from wool fat. The lanolin derivatives are usually easy to spot because their names contain the stem *lan.*

Petroleum

Primary examples of petroleum derivatives include petrolatum (Vaseline or white petrolatum), mineral oil, paraffin wax, microcrystalline wax, and most of the artificial colors.

The Eight Basic Cosmetic Ingredient Categories

The eight basic cosmetic ingredient categories are (1) lipids (oils) and emollients; (2) soaps, detergents, and conditioners; (3) emulsifiers; (4) moisturizers; (5) antioxidants and preservatives; (6) antibacterials; (7) perfumes and fragrances; (8) colors and dyes.

1. Lipids (Oils) and Emollients

Lipids (oils) are the main ingredients in lotions, creams, and ointments. They function as emollients that soothe, soften, lubricate, and protect. They heal dry, rough skin and make it feel smooth and velvety. They also serve as the foundation or vehicle to which other ingredients can be added. The most frequently used lipids and emollients include:

- mineral oil
- petrolatum (Vaseline, white petrolatum)
- paraffin wax/microcrystalline wax
- natural fatty acids (lauric acid, myristic acid, palmitic acid, stearic acid, oleic acid, coconut acid, tallow acid)
- fatty alcohols (lauryl alcohol, myristyl alcohol [1-tetradecanol], cetyl alcohol, stearyl alcohol [1-octadecanol], cetearyl alcohol, oleyl alcohol)
- esters (myristyl myristate, isopropyl myristate, isopropyl palmitate, isopropyl stearate, isopropyl isostearate, isostearyl isostearate, isostearyl neopentanoate, isocetyl palmitate, isocetyl stearate, cetyl esters wax)
- isocetyl alcohol (isohexadecyl alcohol)
- monoglycerides (glyceryl laurate, glyceryl myristate, glyceryl palmitate, glyceryl stearate, glyceryl oleate, glyceryl cocoate, glyceryl lanolate)
- diglycerides (glyceryl dilaurate, glyceryl dimyristate, glyceryl dipalmitate, glyceryl distearate, glyceryl dioleate)
- triglycerides (glyceryl trilaurate, glyceryl trimyristate, glyceryl tripalmitate, glyceryl tristearate, glyceryl trioleate, caprylic/capric triglyceride)
- mixtures of natural monoglycerides, diglycerides, and triglycerides: tallow (animal fatty acid glycerides) and plant and vegetable oil glycerides (avocado oil, cocoa butter, coconut oil, castor oil, corn oil, cottonseed oil, olive oil, palm oil, safflower oil, sesame oil, soybean oil, sunflower oil, wheat germ oil, and the like)
- lanolin, lanolin alcohol, and other lanolin derivatives
- cholesterol, cholesteryl isostearate (IS-CE), and related sterols
- dimethicone/cyclomethicone

FYI: Petrolatum and mineral oil are two of the best lipids for use in skin-care products because they rarely cause any adverse reactions. Most of the other lipids listed also perform quite well, although there are a few exceptions worth noting. For example, lanolin and its derivatives are generally safe to use on a simple case of dry skin, but they can be allergenic when applied to injured or inflamed skin (such as eczema, diaper rash, poison ivy, or burns) and should be avoided until the skin has healed.

2. Soaps, Detergents, and Conditioners

The main function of soaps and detergents is to remove oil and dirt, and as such they are the primary ingredients in shampoos, cleansing bars, and liquid hand soaps. Technically the terms *soap* and *detergent* are not synonymous; true soaps (or alkali soaps) are sodium salts of natural fatty acids, while detergents are synthetic surfactant cleansing agents.

Soaps. The alkali soaps are produced by taking natural fatty acids from either animal fat (beef or sheep tallow) or vegetable oil (especially coconut oil) and mixing them with lye (sodium hydroxide) in a process called *saponification*. The most frequently used soaps are tallow soap and coconut soap. Tallow soap (sodium tallowate) is especially rich in sodium palmitate and stearate. Coconut oil soap (sodium cocoate) is rich in sodium laurate and myristate.

FYI: The natural alkali soaps are strong cleansing agents. Bath bar and liquid hand soaps that utilize them as their primary ingredients have a tendency to dry and irritate sensitive skin and therefore should be avoided. Ivory, Basis, Castile, and Pure & Natural are four examples.

Detergents and conditioners. Detergents are surfactant cleansing agents that are synthesized from chemical compounds; they are the primary ingredients in most shampoos and cleansing bars/liquids. Surfactant cleansing agents are classified into three groups based on the electrical charge that they carry:

1. Anionic surfactants are strong cleansing agents that carry a negative charge. Examples include sodium laureth sulfate, so-

dium lauryl sulfate, ammonium laureth sulfate, ammonium lauryl sulfate, TEA-laureth sulfate, TEA-lauryl sulfate, sodium trideceth sulfate, sodium dodecyl-benzene-sulfonate, sodium isethionate, sodium cocoyl isethionate, dioctyl sodium sulfosuccinate, disodium cocamido MEA-sulfosuccinate, disodium oleamido MEA-sulfosuccinate, disodium laureth sulfosuccinate. (Please note that MEA and TEA are acronyms for monoethanolamine and triethanolamine, respectively.)

2. Amphoteric surfactants are mild cleansing and conditioning agents that carry both a positive and a negative charge. Examples include lauro-amphoacetate, lauro-amphoglycinate, lauro-amphocarboxyglycinate, coco-amphoglycinate, coco-amphocarboxyglycinate, coco-betaine, cocamidopropyl betaine, cocamidopropyl hydroxysultaine.

3. Cationic surfactants are antibacterial, antistatic, and conditioning chemical compounds that carry a positive charge. Examples include cationic surfactants such as quaternium-15 and quaternium-18.

FYI: Sodium isethionate and sodium cocoyl isethionate are two of the mildest anionic surfactant cleansing agents. In contrast, the sulfates (especially the laureth sulfates and the lauryl sulfates) are the strongest anionic synthetic detergents and therefore more likely to irritate sensitive skin.

As a group the amphoteric surfactant cleansing agents are generally milder than the anionics, which is why the amphoterics are used extensively in "tear-free" baby bath and shampoo products; however, please note that cocamidopropyl betaine is a potent contact allergen, and for that reason it's best to avoid skin-care products that contain it, especially those intended for use in children.

Quaternium-15 and quaternium-18 are the two most frequently used cationic surfactants in shampoos. Quaternium-18 untangles hair. Quaternium-15 prevents flyaway hair due to its antistatic properties and also functions as an antibacterial preservative; however, it releases formaldehyde and can provoke an allergic skin rash.

3. Emulsifiers

Emulsifiers are used in creams and lotions to blend the water and lipid (oil) ingredients together and keep them from separating. The surfactant emulsifying agents used most frequently in skin-care products include

TEA-stearate, quaternium-5 (distearyl-dimonium chloride), polysorbate, sorbitan, propylene glycol (PG) esters of natural fatty acids (PG-cocoate, PG-laurate, PG-stearate), polyethylene glycol (PEG) esters of natural fatty acids (PEG-cocoate, PEG-laurate, PEG-stearate, PEG-oleate), polyethylene glycol (PEG) ethers of fatty alcohols (laureth, myreth, ceteth, steareth, ceteareth, oleth, laneth), and ethanolamides of natural fatty acids (cocamide DEA, lauramide DEA, tallowamide DEA). Please note that DEA is an acronym for diethanolamine.

FYI: Polysorbates, sorbitans, propylene glycol esters, and polyethylene glycol (PEG) esters are the preferred emulsifiers since they rarely cause skin problems.

4. Moisturizers

Moisturizer ingredients help the top layers of skin attract and hold water and thus reduce dryness. The moisturizer chemicals (humectants) employed most often by pharmaceutical companies include glycerin (glycerol), lactic acid, sodium lactate, ammonium lactate, sorbitol, urea, propylene glycol (PG), polypropylene glycol (PPG), and polyethylene glycol (PEG).

FYI: Glycerin (glycerol) is the best moisturizer ingredient. Products that contain propylene glycol, lactic acid, or lactate may occasionally cause a temporary stinging sensation when applied to sensitive skin and therefore may not be suitable for some people. Urea concentrations above 2 percent may cause an abnormal reduction in skin thickness when used over a prolonged period of time, so avoid the routine use of products that contain more than 2 percent urea.

5. Antioxidants and Preservatives

Preservatives and/or antioxidants must be added to skin-care products that contain water (soaps, shampoos, lotions, creams) to inhibit the growth of dangerous bacteria and fungi. Most ointments do not require preservatives because they don't contain water. Preservatives are a leading cause of contact dermatitis due to skin-care products. Frequently used preservatives include benzyl alcohol (phenylcarbinol), benzoic acid, sodium benzoate, benzalkonium chloride (zephiran chloride), butylated hydroxyanisole (BHA), butylated hydroxytoluene (BHT), citric acid, ethylenediaminetetraacetic acid (EDTA), etidronate, formaldehyde, glutaraldehyde, bronopol (BNPD or 2-bromo-2-nitropropane-1,3-diol), quaternium-15 (Dowicil 200), DMDM hydantoin (dimethylol-dimethyl hydantoin), imidazolidinyl urea (Germall 115), diazolidinyl urea (Germall II), Kathon CG (methylisothiazolinone + methylchloroisothiazolinone), parabens (methylparaben, propylparaben, butylparaben), sorbic acid, potassium sorbate, thimerosal (merthiolate) and other mercury-containing compounds, and tocopherol (vitamin E).

FYI: BHA, BHT, EDTA, benzalkonium chloride, and benzyl alcohol (phenylcarbinol) are the best preservatives for skin-care products because they are least likely to cause an allergy or adverse reaction. The parabens are also generally safe preservatives and unlikely to provoke an allergic reaction when applied to normal or dry skin, but they can be allergenic when used on injured or inflamed skin (such as eczema, diaper rash, poison ivy, or burns) and should be avoided until the skin has healed.

Benzoic acid, sodium benzoate, sorbic acid, and potassium sorbate are acceptable—but less than optimal—preservatives. They have a tendency to cause redness and hives when used in products designed to stay on the skin, such as lotions.

Kathon CG is the preservative most likely to trigger an allergic reaction, and all products that contain Kathon CG should be avoided completely.

Formaldehyde, glutaraldehyde, and the formaldehyde-releasing preservatives (bronopol, quaternium-15, DMDM hydantoin, imidazolidinyl urea, and diazolidinyl urea) are also associated with allergic reactions and should be avoided whenever possible. I would also stay away from products that contain thimerosal, an allergenic mercury compound.

6. Antibacterials

Triclosan and triclocarban are the two antibacterial chemicals used most frequently in soaps. These chemicals inhibit the growth of bacteria on the skin, but they may be harmful to humans and should be avoided.

7. Perfumes and Fragrances

Fragrances are often complex mixtures of up to 200 separate ingredients. Perfumes and fragrances are added strictly for cosmetic reasons; they serve no useful purpose. Ironically, these worthless ingredients are the ones most likely to provoke allergic reactions. In fact fragrances are the leading cause of allergic contact dermatitis due to cosmetics. Although any fragrance can provoke an adverse reaction, the most allergenic ones are balsam Peru (Peruvian balsam is found in many diaper rash ointments), balsam tolu, benzaldehyde, benzyl cinnamate, cinnamic alcohol, cinnamic aldehyde (cinnamal), citronellol, hydroxycitronellol, clove oil, eugenol, isoeugenol, colophony (rosin), farnesol, geraniol, jasmine, musk ambrette, oak moss, and phenylacetaldehyde (hyacinthin).

FYI: Fragrance-free products are preferred, because they have no fragrances or perfumes added. The term *unscented* often means that a masking fragrance has been added to cover up an unpleasant odor given off by one or more ingredients in the product.

8. Colors and Dyes

The artificial colors and dyes (FD&C red, yellow, orange, green, blue, violet, and the like) can cause adverse skin reactions and should be avoided whenever possible. On the other hand, natural coloring agents such as carotene, iron oxide pigments, kaolin, titanium dioxide, and zinc oxide rarely cause any problems and are safe for almost everyone.

CRUELTY-FREE COSMETICS
AND SKIN-CARE PRODUCTS

Before ending this chapter, let me remind you to avoid cosmetics that are tested on animals. Squirting toxic chemicals into the eyes of innocent animals just to measure how much pain and damage can be inflicted is totally uncalled for. The modern in vitro methods of testing cosmetic ingredients in a laboratory testtube are much more accurate. There can be no excuse for the barbaric, inhumane, and senseless torture of animals merely to satisfy the vanity of humans.

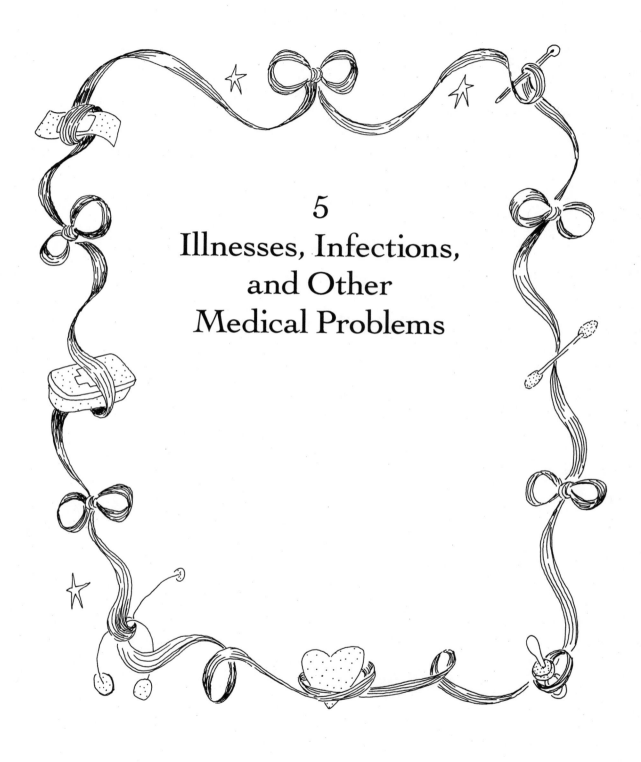

5
Illnesses, Infections,
and Other
Medical Problems

In spite of parents' best efforts to keep their children well, infections and other medical problems are going to occur from time to time. It's an inevitable part of growing up. When your child gets sick, it helps to have some practical guidelines that tell you what symptoms to look for, what to do, and when to call the doctor. To that purpose, this chapter outlines the major causes, danger signs, prevention strategies, and treatment options for childhood illnesses, infections, and other common problems. In addition, several important topics related specifically to newborns are discussed, such as circumcision, colic, jaundice, and SIDS.

CIRCUMCISION

Circumcision is the surgical removal of the foreskin that covers the tip (glans) of the penis. About 75 percent of boys born in the United States are circumcised, but that does not necessarily mean it's the right thing for your son. The following discussion highlights the major points in favor of circumcision and those against it. After examining the evidence, you'll have to judge for yourself whether the benefits outweigh the risks.

The Case for Circumcision

Those in favor of circumcision argue that although the surgery itself has some drawbacks, the following health benefits derived from circumcision will last a lifetime and make it worthwhile:

- Circumcision lowers the risk of developing cancer of the penis to almost zero. Admittedly, cancer of the penis is rare, but it occurs almost exclusively in uncircumcised men.

- Circumcision prevents recurrent infections of the foreskin. Nearly 25 percent of uncircumcised boys have recurrent or chronic inflammation of the foreskin and the tip of the penis. Poor genital hygiene is usually the cause.
- Circumcision prevents phimosis, a medical condition in which the foreskin cannot be drawn back over the head (glans) of the penis. For 90 percent of uncircumcised boys, the foreskin eventually becomes fully retractable by age three. For a substantial number, however, the foreskin never loosens enough to be retracted for proper daily hygiene, and this sets the stage for inflammation and infection. In some cases the opening at the tip of the foreskin eventually becomes so tight it actually blocks the free flow of urine and expands like a balloon every time the child urinates.
- Circumcision protects against bladder and kidney infections. The risk of developing a urinary tract infection in an uncircumcised male is about 1 in 300. Circumcision lowers that risk to less than 1 in 5,000.
- Circumcision may reduce the risk of contracting sexually transmitted diseases (such as syphilis, herpes simplex virus types 1 and 2, HIV, and human papilloma virus) later in life.

The Case Against Circumcision

Opponents of circumcision point out that it's a painful procedure for the baby unless the doctor uses an anesthetic (which very few do), and there's always the risk of complications, the most common one being an unsightly cosmetic result in which the remaining foreskin looks lopsided or ragged or too much skin is removed from the shaft of the penis. Rare complications of circumcision include excessive bleeding, infection of the surgical wound, injury to the urethra, and amputation of the tip of the penis.

Anticircumcision groups also contend that the foreskin enhances sexual sensitivity later in life and that it's unfair to rob the child of something so important without his consent. They believe it's more equitable to wait until a boy is old enough to take an active part in the decision-making process and that by waiting you can determine which boys are going to develop chronic or recurrent problems of the foreskin and which ones aren't. In response to this argument, advocates of newborn circumcision point out that circumcision performed in later childhood or adolescence is much more costly and is associated with a higher risk of complications. Once a baby is more than a few weeks old, most surgeons will perform a circumcision only in a "day surgery" suite using general anesthesia; physician and hospital fees can end up costing thousands of dollars, and many insurance companies won't pick up the tab because they consider it cosmetic surgery. Furthermore, it was reported in *Pediatrics* 92: (December 1993): 791–93 that circumcising an infant during the first few weeks of life has a complication rate of only 0.2 percent, whereas circumcising an older child under general anesthesia has a complication rate of 1.7 percent (an eight-fold increase) and carries with it the potential for serious problems, such as aspiration pneumonia or a reaction called *malignant hyperthermia*, in which the general anesthetic triggers the body temperature to rise uncontrollably to extremely high levels.

Making the Decision

Both sides in the circumcision debate present such valid arguments that it's difficult for most parents to decide what to do. None of the so-called experts can agree on what's best either. Even the American Academy of Pediatrics Task Force on Circumcision was unable to come up with a definite recommendation when it studied the issue extensively in April 1989 and concluded that "newborn circumcision has potential medical benefits and advantages as well as disadvantages and risks." About all you can do is weigh all of the facts mentioned here along with the advice of your doctor and your own religious and family traditions. Just remember, you do have a choice.

If You Decide to Have Your Son Circumcised

If you want to have your baby boy circumcised, but you want to spare him the pain and reduce the risk of a poor cosmetic outcome, you can request (or demand if necessary) that the circumcision be performed by a board-certified pediatric surgeon or pediatric urologist, since they are the doctors specially trained to administer local anesthesia in babies, and their skill at removing the correct amount of foreskin is generally far superior to that of all other physicians. I can tell you without hesitation that it's much smarter to have the real pros do the job right the first time. Believe me, your little boy will thank you someday.

A newborn should not be circumcised until he is at least 24 hours old and healthy enough to be discharged from the nursery. Postpone the circumcision if your baby has a significant medical problem, such as an infection, prematurity, more than just a mild case of jaundice, a birth defect of the genitals (such as hypospadias), a hereditary bleeding disorder (such as hemophilia or von Willebrand's), or some other illness that would increase the risk of complications.

The three standard medical devices currently used to perform circumcisions are the Gomco clamp, the Mogen clamp, and the Plastibell. The metal Gomco clamp is preferred by most pediatric surgeons and urologists because it has the best safety record of the three. However, to avoid a lopsided or otherwise unsightly cosmetic result, be sure the doctor plans to use a surgical marking pen preoperatively to outline on the foreskin exactly where to position the Gomco clamp so as to evenly remove the right amount of skin all the way around.

The Mogen clamp operates somewhat like the blade of a guillotine. The advantage is that it removes the foreskin fast, so there's less suffering, but the surgeon must be extremely careful to position the tip of the penis out of harm's way so as not to accidentally remove it. The Gomco is definitely safer.

The Plastibell has a tendency to leave ragged edges and cause infections, so be sure your doctor does not plan to use it.

With the "sleeve" method of circumcision, the surgeon wields the scalpel freehand without the aid of a clamp or template for guidance. Compared to the Comco or Mogen, the sleeve method takes several minutes longer to complete and thus extends the time of suffering if the foreskin is not anesthetized. It can also result in a poor cosmetic outcome and therefore is less than optimal.

Never let the doctor use an electric cauterizing needle, because it delivers an excruciating shock when applied to unanesthetized skin.

Furthermore, if the needle accidentally contacts the metal Gomco clamp, it can cause a catastrophic electrical injury to the penis.

Local Anesthesia for Circumcision

Some doctors have begun using local anesthetic for pain relief during circumcision. It's called a *dorsal penile nerve block* and is similar to having the dentist numb your tooth before drilling. This is an acceptable way to spare the baby discomfort *as long as the doctor follows very strict guidelines*:

- The local anesthetic must not contain any vasoconstrictors (such as epinephrine), which could cause gangrene due to a spasm of the artery leading to the penis. Lidocaine 1 percent without epinephrine is the best choice for a local anesthetic agent; concentrations above 1 percent are not safe to use in newborns.
- The anesthetic must be injected slowly to avoid excessive stinging.
- The doctor must wait at least five minutes for the numbing to take full effect before clamping or cutting the foreskin.

Complications from a dorsal penile nerve block are uncommon as long as the doctor has been specially trained to administer it to newborns (such as a board-certified pediatric surgeon) and is willing to take the extra time. Ask your doctor if he or she routinely uses a local anesthetic for circumcisions. If the answer is no, or if your doctor acts hesitant in any way, you'd better forget about it, because this technique takes a lot of practice and a spirit of cooperation on the part of the surgeon, and you certainly don't want the job bungled by a "greenhorn" or someone who's doing it just to humor you.

How to Take Care of the Circumcision

The circumcision should heal completely within 7–10 days. In the meantime, follow these suggestions:

- Coat the head of the penis with plain Vaseline after every diaper change for the first three days after the circumcision.

- Don't put bandages or gauze pads on the penis, because they'll stick to the raw skin and cause bleeding.
- When changing diapers, gently clean the penis with cotton balls moistened with plain water. Don't use diaper wipes, soap, alcohol, hydrogen peroxide, iodine, povidone iodine (betadine), or any antiseptics on the raw skin.
- For the first few days after the circumcision, you can expect the wound to ooze a few drops of blood now and then, but persistent or excessive bleeding is abnormal and must be reported to your baby's doctor immediately.
- Watch for signs of an infection, such as the scrotum or the shaft of the penis becoming red and swollen, green pus oozing from the wound, or the baby's crying inconsolably, running fever, or acting sick. Have the doctor check your baby right away if you suspect an infection. Please note, however, that the head of the penis normally develops a thin, yellowish film on its surface for several days following the circumcision; this yellow film is part of the body's natural healing process, so do not try to remove it or rub it off.

If You Decide Against Circumcision

The decision not to circumcise your baby boy must be accompanied by a lifetime commitment to proper genital hygiene to minimize the possibility of infection, inflammation, or cancer of the foreskin. When he's old enough to assume the responsibility, your son must be taught to clean underneath his foreskin daily, and then be monitored to be sure he is dutifully following instructions.

Proper Hygiene for the Uncircumcised Penis

At birth almost all baby boys have a tight, unretractable foreskin. The foreskin becomes fully retractable in about 15 percent of boys by six months, in 50 percent by one year, and in 90 percent by three years. Forcibly pulling back the foreskin over the head of the penis can permanently damage the delicate tissue and cause scarring or bleeding, so until your child's foreskin can be retracted easily, leave it alone!

As soon as the foreskin does show signs of retracting, you should start cleaning underneath it once a day during the bath. Just slide the foreskin back to the point where resistance is met (without using any force whatsoever). Gently cleanse the exposed area with a wet cotton ball (no soap!), and rinse it with clean, lukewarm water. When you're finished, always slide the foreskin back to its normal position over the head of the penis.

Accidental Circumcision

It doesn't happen very often, but occasionally a baby boy is circumcised by mistake, because the parents unknowingly signed the circumcision consent papers during all the confusion in the labor and delivery room. Be sure you read and understand everything you sign in the hospital, and personally communicate your final decision regarding circumcision to the doctor.

Penile Erections

Baby boys normally have brief erections several times a day, especially during certain stages of sleep, when the bladder is full, and at diaper changes. This is perfectly natural.

NEWBORN JAUNDICE

Jaundice is a medical term that means the skin and the whites of the eyes are yellow due to an elevated blood level of a chemical compound called *bilirubin*, a by-product of hemoglobin metabolism in red blood cells. Bilirubin is normally detoxified in the liver and then excreted in the stools, but during the first few days of life the liver detoxification system does not function efficiently, and the bowel movements are irregular, so there's a natural tendency for newborns to accumulate bilirubin.

The level of jaundice is measured by a bilirubin blood test. For newborns over two days old, a bilirubin blood count below 10 mg/dl is considered a low level, 10–15 mg/dl is medium, and above 15 mg/dl is high. Damage to the brain can sometimes occur if the bilirubin blood count exceeds 25 mg/dl; that's why jaundiced newborns need to have their blood bilirubin counts checked regularly until the level peaks and then starts to drop. A tiny pinprick on your baby's heel is all that's needed to obtain a specimen for analysis.

About 50 percent of all full-term, healthy newborns develop a mild case of jaundice, called *physiologic jaundice*, which appears on the third day after birth, reaches its peak on the fourth or fifth day, and disappears by the seventh day. The bilirubin blood count does not exceed 15 mg/dl. This is normal and no treatment is required other than frequent feedings of breast milk or formula. Approximately 3 percent of jaundiced newborns have an underlying illness or medical problem, such as a large internal or external bruise, a blood type incompatibility between mother and infant, a hereditary blood disorder, a bacterial or viral infection, hepatitis, blocked bile ducts, an intestinal obstruction, or hypothyroidism (low thyroid). This type of jaundice is called "pathologic" or abnormal jaundice and it requires close medical supervision. If your baby is jaundiced, ask the doctor whether it is the normal or abnormal kind.

Just because your baby develops jaundice does not necessarily mean he can't be discharged from the hospital. The doctor will take several factors into account before making the final decision for release, such as the baby's age, general health, bilirubin level, prematurity, birth weight, weight loss, feeding and stooling patterns, and the presence of any underlying illness. In the majority of cases mildly jaundiced, healthy, full-term babies can be discharged from the hospital as long as the parents agree to bring the infant to the doctor's office for daily bilirubin blood tests until it's certain the level is stable or dropping.

How to Eliminate Jaundice the Natural and Nontoxic Way

Approximately 99 percent of the bilirubin produced by the body is excreted in the stools. Only 1 percent is eliminated in the urine.

Therefore, the real secret for getting rid of jaundice quickly and naturally is to feed a jaundiced newborn breast milk or formula frequently (every two or three hours around the clock), because a milk feeding normally stimulates a bowel movement, which flushes large amounts of bilirubin out of the body. It is important to note that the baby's first stools, which are dark black bowel movements called *meconium*, promote the reabsorption of bilirubin from the baby's intestines and thereby force the liver to repeat the detoxification cycle all over again; when the stool color finally turns from black to yellow, the meconium has been eliminated, thus breaking the vicious cycle of bilirubin reabsorption, and in most cases the jaundice will start to diminish rather quickly.

If you're breast-feeding and your baby develops jaundice, the nursery staff will almost certainly recommend using sugar water (5 percent glucose water) after each nursing session to help lower the bilirubin. Unfortunately, this well-intentioned advice won't work, because sugar water does not stimulate bowel movements, and as you've just learned, bilirubin is excreted primarily in the stools. Babies need plenty of breast milk and/or formula to get rid of jaundice quickly.

Phototherapy Lights

If your baby's bilirubin count climbs too high, your doctor will probably order phototherapy light treatments. When the blue-spectrum phototherapy light strikes the skin, it transforms the bilirubin molecules (which are located just below the skin surface) into by-products that can be excreted without having to go through the liver detoxification process, thereby reducing the jaundice level more quickly. During phototherapy treatments your baby's eyes must be covered with special patches at all times to prevent permanent damage to the retina from the blue lights; be very careful the patches don't slip down over your child's nostrils and block her breathing.

Feed your baby formula or breast milk at least once every two or three hours around the clock to promote the frequent passage of stools and to prevent dehydration from evaporation of water through the skin. I realize that most parents who choose to breast-feed their baby would prefer not to use formula supplements, but if a baby is jaundiced enough to require phototherapy, it is definitely in her best interest to lower the bilirubin count as quickly as possible, and I can tell you from practical experience that formula supplements help a lot. Of course, if you happen to be one of those lucky few with such an abundant supply of breast milk that your baby is having frequent bowel movements and is not losing any weight at all, then the formula supplements will probably not be necessary. Ask your doctor to be sure.

> *If your infant develops jaundice, someone is almost certainly going to recommend placing your child's crib near a window so that indirect sun can shine on her as a substitute for phototherapy lights. Please do not follow this misguided advice! Why? First, it doesn't work. Second, full-spectrum sunlight (as opposed to blue-spectrum phototherapy lights) contains infrared rays, which can cause serious overheating, and ultraviolet rays, which can damage the skin and eyes.*

INFANT COLIC

Colic is a condition that causes an otherwise healthy infant to cry intensely and inconsolably for hours on end every day. During these nerve-shattering, explosive crying spasms, the baby turns red in the face, arches her back furiously, clenches her fists, thrashes her arms to and fro, draws up her legs, and passes a lot of gas. Colic usually starts at 7–14 days of age. In fact, if your baby doesn't show signs of colic by the 14th day, it is very unlikely that he or she will develop it. Infant colic normally stops by three months of age (although it occasionally lasts until the fourth or fifth month in some babies).

Approximately one in five infants develops colic, and of those about 20 percent have an underlying formula allergy or intolerance, which causes gas and stomach cramps. For the other 80 percent, however, colic is the result of inborn temperament. In other words, the vast majority of colicky babies are colicky because they are born with a high-strung, supersensitive nature that makes them jumpy, uptight, and basically difficult to handle. They have a low tolerance for discomfort and overreact to everything. Simple things that wouldn't normally bother the average infant will drive temperamental colicky babies into an absolute frenzy.

Interestingly, the difficult temperamental traits that can cause colic in the first place may actually work to your child's advantage later on. For example, high levels of energy and intensity can provide your child with the drive to become a go-getter in school and in competitive fields such as law, medicine, athletics, and business. Supersensitive taste, smell, vision, and hearing can also be a real asset in many professions, especially art, music, and cooking. The list goes on and on. The point is, colicky babies are hard to handle at first, but they usually grow up to be very pleasant, intelligent, happy children who are creative, dynamic, and a lot of fun to have around (although they may remain a bit high-strung, headstrong, driven, and finicky). These kids generally make good grades and become successful in a wide range of endeavors, so look to the future and keep thinking about all the good times yet to come.

"Normal" Crying vs. Infant Colic

Almost all babies have certain times during the day (especially in the evening) when they cry for no apparent reason. It's their way of releasing nervous tension. In fact, you can expect a healthy, good-natured, four-week-old infant to spend an average of one hour a day crying. However, you won't have any trouble telling the difference between "normal" crying spells and the hours and hours of ear-piercing screams associated with infant colic. Believe me, there's no comparison!

Is It Colic or Something Serious?

There are many other conditions besides colic that can cause an infant to cry a lot. Never assume that a cranky disposition or constant crying is due to colic until a doctor examines your baby and checks out the possibility of an underlying problem, such as a formula allergy or intolerance, ear infection, bladder or kidney infection, hernia, constipation, or insufficient milk supply.

The following symptoms are important clues that something besides colic might be responsible for the crying spells:

- The baby cries nonstop all day long, rather than for just a few hours at the same time each evening.
- The cranky behavior and inconsolable crying spells do not start until after the first month.
- The crying is accompanied by additional symptoms of illness, such as weight loss, decrease in appetite, fever, vomiting, diarrhea, blood or mucus in the stools, constipation, urine with a strong odor, a lump or mass in the groin area, skin rash (eczema or hives), runny nose, congestion, wheezing, or coughing.

Natural and Nontoxic Soothing Techniques for Colicky Babies

Please do not give in to the temptation of a quick fix with brain-numbing sedatives (phenobarbital, Donnatal), antispasmodics (Levsin, Bentyl), or paregoric (which is actually tincture of opium); such drugs can produce very serious side effects in babies. Instead of zonking out your infant with habit-forming drugs, try some of the natural soothing techniques listed here.

No Smoking

Never allow any smoking inside your house or car. Tobacco smoke makes the baby's eyes, nose, and throat feel sore and scratchy, which automatically increases the crying. Also, don't smoke during pregnancy, because your baby will suffer nicotine withdrawal symptoms after delivery.

Calming Movements and Sounds

Gentle, rhythmic movements and sounds often have a calming effect on colicky babies, so try these suggestions:

- Either cradle the infant snugly in your arms or hold her upright with her tummy cuddled against your chest (in a burping position); then sing a song or softly hum a lullaby while rocking in an old-fashioned rocking chair or strolling through the house.

- When you're exhausted from rocking in the chair or pacing the floor, try a cradle. An automatic swing can also be very useful, but be sure the baby's head has adequate support and never leave your infant alone while she is swinging. Depending on your baby's temperament, she may prefer rocking at a slow, medium, or fast tempo (whether in your arms, a cradle, or a swing), so experiment with different rhythms until you find the one that works best.
- If the weather is nice, go for a walk. The fresh air, change of scenery, and rhythmic vibration of the stroller can often lull a crying infant right to sleep.

Caution: A newborn's eyes are sensitive, so avoid direct exposure to sunlight, and if the baby cries, squints, or her eyes start to water, it usually means the light is too bright and you'd better go back indoors.

Car Rides

If car rides help your infant settle down but you don't like the idea of driving around aimlessly several hours a day, you might be interested in a new electronic device called SleepTight, which fastens to the infant's crib and simulates the rhythmic vibration and sound of a car driving on the highway. Unfortunately, it costs $99.95 plus shipping, so I would recommend it only for babies who respond favorably to a real car ride first. The other drawback is that all electric motors generate electromagnetic fields (see Chapter 6) that may be hazardous, so I would use the SleepTight only when absolutely necessary, and I would position the motor as

Someone will probably suggest placing your baby in an infant seat on top of a running clothes dryer as a substitute for a car ride. Please don't take this advice. The vibrations may cause the seat to walk off the edge of the dryer, and the dryer's electric current generates a strong electromagnetic field that may be hazardous if you get too close to it for prolonged periods of time.

far away from the baby as possible. To order SleepTight, call 800-NO-COLIC. Overnight delivery is available, and since SleepTight is classified as a medical device, it may be covered by your insurance if the doctor writes a prescription. It's worth checking.

Positive Reinforcement

Cuddle and gently stroke your baby a minimum of 50 times a day when she is not crying. The idea is to give lots of positive reinforcement for "good" behavior all day long. Obviously you should continue to cuddle your infant during the colicky episodes, but if you pick up a baby only when she cries, you'll teach her that crying is the only way to get attention, and that's definitely not the message you want reinforced.

Carrying the baby around with you in a kangaroo-pouch infant carrier is a great way to provide plenty of love and contact while giving your arms a much needed rest. Two of the best baby carry pouches on the market are the Snugli from Gerry Baby Products (800-525-2472), and the Kapoochi from Medela (800-435-8316).

Pacifiers

Pacifiers are especially helpful to calm down a baby in between feedings when he or she is not actually hungry.

Avoiding Overstimulation

If your baby is supersensitive and gets overstimulated easily, the following suggestions will help:

- If at all possible, try to establish a regular schedule for feeding, sleeping, bathing, playing, and other daily activities so the baby can count on certain things happening at the same time every day. The more predictable and monotonous, the better.
- Handle the baby gently, avoid jostling or bouncing him, and talk softly and slowly. Colicky babies respond poorly to loud or incessant chattering.

- Keep visitors to an absolute minimum and avoid crowds completely.
- The atmosphere at feeding time must be calm, quiet, and relaxed, without any neighbors, relatives, or children making noise or causing distractions.
- Avoid bright lights and direct sunlight.
- Furnish the infant's room in soft, solid pastel colors rather than wild, flashy prints or plaids. The decorative scheme should be serene and tranquil.
- Use soft, smooth, lightweight 100 percent cotton clothing and bedding instead of scratchy wool or synthetic materials. See Chapter 3 for details and brand names.
- Many colicky babies have a highly developed sense of smell. Strong odors can trigger crying spells, so temporarily stop using perfume and any cosmetic products with a fragrance. And switch to fragrance-free household products whenever possible.

Providing Security

Calm, gentle, and firm handling makes a fussy infant feel secure, whereas holding her like a piece of fragile china may heighten her anxiety. Babies need to sense that the person handling them is in control and not afraid to take charge and set reasonable limits. Please note that *firm* means steady and sure—not rough—so avoid jostling, bouncing, and jerky movements.

Womb Sounds and White Noise

The steady drone of monotonous sounds, such as the ticking of a clock or a metronome or recordings of heartbeats (reminiscent of mother's heartbeat in the womb), may help your baby relax and sleep. Softly played jazz or classical music (or any music you listened to a lot during your pregnancy) may also calm things down. You may want to try recordings of white noise, such as wind, rain, ocean waves, surf, or waterfalls. Do not run the vacuum cleaner as a method of producing white noise, because you'll stir up harmful dust and generate a hazardous electromagnetic field.

Hot-Water Bottles

Some colicky infants enjoy having a hot-water bottle filled with warm (*not hot*) water, wrapped in a cotton towel, and placed next to their tummies. However, be careful not to do anything that might cause the baby to become overheated (do not swaddle your baby, for example), because overheating is a risk factor for sudden infant death syndrome (SIDS). And never use electric heating pads, because in addition to overheating, there's the danger of a short circuit and subsequent fire or electrocution, not to mention the electromagnetic radiation generated by the flow of electricity in the wires.

Avoiding Overfeeding

Don't automatically offer food to a colicky infant every time she cries, or the child will end up feeling stuffed or bloated, much like an adult who's just polished off a huge Thanksgiving dinner. A newborn's stomach is small and fills to capacity very quickly, so feed your baby sensible portions at reasonable time intervals. Although it's not always possible, try to wait at least two hours between feedings; a pacifier or bottle of plain water may help tide her over.

Reducing Intestinal Gas

Try the following suggestions:

- Gently burp your infant every five minutes during feeding sessions.
- Hold your baby in a semiupright position (at approximately a 45-degree angle) during feedings so that swallowed air will stay at the top of the stomach, where it can be burped up easily. When an infant is fed lying flat on her back, air bubbles get trapped in the intestine (bowel) and cause painful gas cramps.
- If you're using a bottle for feedings, keep it tilted at an angle so

the nipple is always filled with milk, not air bubbles. Try the Johnson's Baby Healthflow angled bottle; the angle allows a more upright feeding position and reduces swallowing of air. And use a nipple with a hole that drips slowly enough to prevent the baby from swallowing too fast.

- Try to limit each feeding session to 40 minutes, because most infants start swallowing more air than milk after that amount of time. If your baby wants to keep sucking after a feeding, use a pacifier.

Over-the-counter simethicone drops (such as Mylicon Drops or Phazyme Drops) are supposed to reduce intestinal gas by their anti-foaming action. However, simethicone is actually an alternative name for silicone (technically known as *poly-dimethyl-siloxane*). The FDA recently banned the use of silicone in breast implants because of reports that silicone exposure can trigger memory loss and autoimmune diseases (such as lupus, rheumatoid arthritis, and scleroderma) in susceptible people, so until the FDA comes to a final conclusion about the safety of silicone in breast implants, I would avoid using oral simethicone drops.

Baths

A warm, soothing bath almost always helps a colicky baby relax. For optimal results, keep the lighting dim, be sure there are no drafts, move slowly, talk softly, and keep noises to a minimum.

Glycerin Suppositories

If the baby is having difficulty trying to expel trapped intestinal gas, the gentle insertion of an infant-size glycerin suppository (or a rectal thermometer) about ½ inch into the anus almost always stimulates the passage of gas. Infant-size glycerin suppositories are sold over the counter in the laxative section of the pharmacy. Be careful not to make a regular habit of using these anal stimulation techniques, however, because your baby may become dependent on them or you might irritate his anus.

Switching Formulas

If you've been feeding your baby a milk-based formula (Similac, En-famil, SMA, Gerber), and you suspect your baby has gas and stomach cramps due to an underlying cow's milk protein allergy or lactose sugar intolerance, ask your doctor about switching to one of the lactose-free soy formulas (Isomil, Gerber Soy, I-Soyalac) for a few days and see if the colic improves. If the soy-based formula doesn't work, a three-day trial using a hypoallergenic formula (Alimentum or Nutramigen) would certainly be worthwhile. Both products are available at most super-markets and pharmacies. Of course, a hypoallergenic formula is a little more expensive, but if it works, you won't care how much it costs. Follow the mixing instructions on the package label and always shake the formula well before pouring it into the bottle.

If all else fails, some doctors report that fresh, pasteurized goat's milk has worked wonders for babies with sensitive digestive systems. Be careful, however, because most brands of fresh goat's milk are not vitamin-fortified, and your baby will need a daily multivitamin supple-ment; ask your doctor to be sure. To locate a grocery store near you that carries fresh, pasteurized Meyenberg goat's milk, call 800-343-1185. Please note that the canned, evaporated liquid and powder versions of goat's milk taste horrible and therefore should not be used.

Reviewing Your Diet if You're Breast-Feeding

A portion of almost everything you eat or drink eventually winds up in the breast milk, so review your diet very carefully, cutting out the offending foods as described in "Nutrition for Breast-Feeding Mothers" in Chapter 1. Besides the problem foods listed there, those that might be making the colic worse include tomatoes, asparagus, cabbage, broc-coli, peppermint, and artificial sweeteners. In addition, try to buy products with no artificial colors (FD&C red, blue, green, yellow, tartrazine, etc.), no artificial flavors (vanillin, butter flavor, smoke flavor, etc.), no flavor enhancers (MSG), and no artificial sweeteners (aspartame, saccharin).

Stopping Vitamins

Infant multivitamin drops may occasionally cause gastroesophageal reflux (heartburn), stomach cramps, and gas in some babies. Furthermore, the B-complex vitamins may also trigger neurologic overstimulation and hyperexcitability by upsetting the proper balance of neurotransmitters in the brain. Ask your doctor if it's OK to stop giving vitamins for a few days and see if the colic improves.

Treating Heartburn

If the crying spells occur mainly when your baby is lying flat and faceup or leaning backward in a semireclining position (in an infant carrier or car seat), painful heartburn due to gastroesophageal reflux could be the problem. Treatment suggestions can be found in the section on gastroesophageal reflux and heartburn.

Six Coping Strategies for Mom and Dad

Taking care of a colicky baby is physically and mentally stressful, so parents must develop effective coping strategies for themselves as well as their infant.

1. I cannot emphasize strongly enough how essential it is for your mental well-being to get out of the house and away from the infant for at least one hour every day. Leave the baby with your spouse, a relative, or a trusted friend and do something that relaxes you. Whether it's shopping, exercising, or something else, you must have some time to yourself.
2. Don't blame yourself because your baby has colic! It's not your fault, and feeling guilty will aggravate the situation. Remember, your baby is not angry at you or trying to aggravate you on purpose, so don't take it personally. And above all, don't let a colicky infant make you feel incompetent. Even the most experienced parents and health-care professionals have a hard time trying to cope with these temperamental children.
3. Force yourself to sleep or nap whenever the baby does. When you're well rested, you're better able to keep the situation in perspective.
4. When you feel tense and nervous, perform the muscle relaxation techniques you learned during Lamaze or childbirth

classes. It takes only a few minutes, and it will really help you unwind.

5. You must continue to eat well-balanced, nutritionally complete meals, and don't forget to take the vitamin supplements prescribed by your doctor. Without a proper diet, you won't have the energy needed to handle a colicky baby.

6. Normally it's not a good idea to let your baby cry if you can help it, because crying increases air swallowing, which makes the gas pain worse. But if all else fails and you're at your wit's end, you may have to take short breaks away from the baby and go into another room where it's quiet. Use your time-out to read, listen to music, exercise, nap, pray, or meditate. You need and deserve frequent breaks to revitalize yourself, so don't feel guilty if you have to intermittently ignore the nerve-racking cries. Sometimes it's the only thing that will relieve the tension.

NEWBORN EYE PROBLEMS

Standard policy in most hospitals calls for the routine application of an antibiotic into babies' eyes within the first few hours after birth to prevent infection from germs acquired during passage through the birth canal. Unfortunately, many hospitals use toxic silver nitrate eyedrops, which typically cause the eyes to swell and fill with pus and in some cases can even cause blockage of the tear ducts for several months. To prevent this problem, ask ahead of time about the standard policy for eye prophylaxis in the hospital where you intend to deliver your baby; if silver nitrate is used, request erythromycin ophthalmic ointment instead. Better yet, a study published in *Pediatrics* 92 (December 1993): 755–60, concluded that it is perfectly reasonable for parents to request that no drops or antibiotics be placed in their newborn's eyes as long as the mother has received regular prenatal care and has been screened for sexually transmitted diseases.

Eyelid Mattering

Newborns usually start producing tears within the first two weeks, but their tear drainage system is quite small and tends to get blocked or clogged very easily. When this happens, the tears overflow down the cheek, and yellow mucus may collect along the edge of the eyelids and in the corner of the eye. Sometimes all you have to do is gently wipe away the mattering with a cotton ball and lukewarm water, but if it keeps coming back and causes the eyelids to stick together, you'll have to ask your doctor for a prescription antibiotic ophthalmic ointment, such as Polysporin ophthalmic ointment or erythromycin ophthalmic ointment. (The hospital nursery often sends home a tube of eye ointment along with the other baby items.) The best time to apply the medication is while your baby is sleeping, because his eyelids are closed and he's wiggling less. Squeeze a small amount of the prescription eye ointment onto the tip of a cotton swab and then gently sweep it along the eyelid margin where the eyelashes grow—not inside the eye. The eye ointment is usually applied three times a day until the infection clears up. If the ointment seems to make the eye red or itchy, it could mean your child is allergic to one of the ingredients, in which case you should stop the applications and call your doctor for further instructions.

When to Call the Doctor About Eyelid Mattering

Have the doctor examine your child right away if any of the following danger signs accompany the eyelid mattering:

- The white part of the eye is red or pink.
- The iris looks hazy or cloudy.
- The eye has a constant drainage of mucus that requires frequent wiping.
- The eyelid is red and swollen.
- The child has a fever or acts sick.
- The child is squinting or blinking a lot because of extreme sensitivity to light.

- The child is fussy or cranky for no apparent reason.
- The eyelid mattering continues for more than two days.

Eyelash or Fuzz in the Eye

If an eyelash or a piece of fuzz or lint gets into your baby's eyes, gently flush it away with a sterile eyewash, such as Eye-Stream Sterile Eye Irrigating Solution.

Toxic Warning

Avoid eyedrops that contain the preservative thimerosal (also known by the trademark Merthiolate), because thimerosal is a mercury compound that can cause severe allergic reactions.

TEETHING AND TOOTH CARE

Most babies start teething between 6 and 10 months of age, although some may wait as long as 14 months. (If a child's parents were late to get their teeth, the child is likely to be late as well, since tooth eruption patterns are very hereditary.) The sequence of tooth eruption is quite variable, but the first teeth to come in are usually the 2 lower front teeth at 6–10 months, followed by the 2 upper front teeth. The next ones to sprout are typically the 2 upper and 2 lower lateral incisors at 10–14 months. Between 12 and 18 months the first 4 molars usually erupt, followed by the 4 cuspids (canine or eyeteeth) at 18–26 months. By the time your child is 3 years old, he should have his last 4 molars for a final total of 20 baby teeth. The permanent teeth generally start coming in at around 6 or 7 years.

Symptoms of Teething

Our culture has a bad habit of blaming just about every symptom of illness on teething, so it's important to know exactly what problems teething can and cannot cause. For example, teething may cause crankiness, drooling, gum gnashing, loss of appetite, mild diarrhea, difficulty sleeping, and a slight elevation of body temperature up to 101° F. Teething does not, however, cause vomiting or fever above 101° F. Fever above 101° F almost always means a child has an infection (such as an ear infection, tonsillitis, sinusitis, and the like), which may require a visit to the doctor. Incidentally, babies between three and six months of age tend to produce saliva faster than they can swallow it, so drooling in this age group is not necessarily a sign of teething.

Dangerous Teething Remedies

Please resist the temptation to use over-the-counter teething medicine, because the active ingredients in these products can numb your baby's throat so much she chokes. In addition, the "caine" anesthetics (such as benzocaine, lidocaine, and xylocaine) can cause allergic reactions when applied topically to inflamed tissue. They can also reach toxic levels in the bloodstream after repeated applications. Teething medicine often contains artificial colors as well.

Nor should you rub whiskey or any alcoholic beverage on your baby's gums, since this may cause choking, and as little as 2 teaspoons can cause intoxication and an upset stomach.

Stay away from paregoric too. Very few people realize that paregoric is actually tincture of opium and can lead to narcotic addiction and withdrawal symptoms. Needless to say, you do not want to give your baby anything that powerful and dangerous.

Never place clove oil on your baby's gums. Clove oil is volatile, and inhaling the fumes can cause a chemical pneumonia. Furthermore, clove oil is about 85 percent eugenol, a highly allergenic chemical, which you certainly do not want inside your baby's body. This is just one more example of a so-called herbal remedy that sounds harmless but is actually quite hazardous.

Natural and Nontoxic Alternatives for Relief of Teething Pain

For quick pain relief, the best medicine is a dose of acetaminophen (Tylenol, Feverall, Panadol, or Tempra), but don't overdo it, because giving any pain reliever too often makes your baby's liver and kidneys work overtime. Reserve acetaminophen for those times of the day when relief is needed most, such as bedtime. See the section on fever for dosages.

You can also let the baby chew on a safety-approved solid teething ring, pacifier, or toy. Avoid teething rings and toys filled with fluid, because the fluid might be hazardous and may leak out accidentally while the baby is chewing. Some babies prefer a cold teething ring or toy that has been in the refrigerator.

Another possibility is to wash your hands thoroughly and then gently massage the baby's gums with your fingers.

Nursing Caries and Baby Bottle Tooth Decay

The bacteria that cause tooth decay flourish when they have prolonged contact with the sugar in breast milk, formula, and fruit juices. That's why allowing babies to constantly graze on breast milk, formula, or juice between regular feedings, or at naptime or bedtime, promotes cavities (caries) and strips away the protective enamel from the teeth, especially the front four upper teeth. This devastating dental condition is called *nursing caries* or *baby bottle tooth decay* (*BBTD*), since the risk exists for breast-fed as well as bottle-fed children. Unless brought under control quickly, the decay can totally destroy the teeth in a matter of months.

Once your baby's teeth start to erupt, the following preventive steps will help to reduce cavities:

- Clean your baby's teeth at least once a day using the methods described in the following section.
- Do not put your baby to bed with a bottle containing milk, formula, or fruit juice.
- Whether you breast-feed or bottle-feed, don't let your baby graze at will throughout the day or night. After six months of age, feeding times should generally be spaced at least three or four

hours apart. If your baby wants oral stimulation in between feedings, try a pacifier.

- Don't let a bottle or a breast become your baby's constant companion. Offer a soft toy or security blanket instead.
- As your child approaches his first birthday, encourage the use of a cup for drinking liquids. Wean him completely from bottle feeding by 12–14 months of age.
- Take your child to the dentist for regular checkups starting at 12–18 months of age.

Cleaning Your Child's Teeth

As soon as the first few baby teeth come in, it's wise to start cleaning them once a day with a soft-bristled child's toothbrush and plain water. Daily flossing with Butler unwaxed dental floss is also a good habit to establish early in life. Do not use dental floss that is waxed or that contains artificial colors or flavors.

To remove stubborn stains from the teeth, *Arm & Hammer* baking soda on a wet toothbrush is nontoxic and works pretty well. Do not use toothpaste until your child is old enough to rinse his mouth thoroughly and spit, because swallowing the fluoride and other ingredients in toothpaste (artificial colors and flavors, for example) can be harmful and should be avoided. Most toothpaste brands contain high concentrations of fluoride, some as high as 1,200 parts per million. (Compare that to fluoridated municipal tap water, which usually contains only about 1 part per million.) By swallowing toothpaste each day, a child can quickly exceed the recommended daily intake of fluoride and end up with a condition called *fluorosis*, in which excess fluoride prevents the proper development of tooth enamel, resulting in permanent teeth that have ugly gray or white spots.

Fillings

Although cavities and fillings are uncommon for kids under six, it's important to look ahead and be prepared for the day when a dental restoration may become necessary. In addition, the following information is extremely important for women who are pregnant, because toxic dental materials can cause birth defects and immune system damage in the fetus.

So-called silver fillings, also known as *amalgam*, actually contain about 50 percent mercury, 30 percent silver, and various amounts of copper, tin, zinc, and other metals. (As mercury is the major component, they should be called mercury fillings.) The World Health Organization Expert Committee on Inorganic Mercury has concluded that the daily intake of mercury from amalgam dental fillings is the largest single source of mercury exposure in the general population, exceeding all other nonoccupational sources combined, including air, water, and food (including fish).

Mercury is more poisonous than lead, cadmium, or arsenic. Unfortunately, mercury constantly leaches out of amalgam fillings (especially when you drink warm liquids or chew food or gum) and steadily bioaccumulates throughout the body, where it wreaks havoc with the immune system and other vital organs like the brain, pituitary gland, thyroid gland, heart, lungs, liver, adrenal glands, and kidneys. Mercury can even cross the placenta and cause birth defects in the developing fetus. That's why women who have mercury amalgam fillings should not have them worked on or replaced during pregnancy. In fact, starting in 1994, many California dentists will be posting the following signs in their offices: "WARNING: This office uses amalgam filling materials, which contain and expose you to mercury, a chemical known to the State of California to cause birth defects and other reproductive harm. Please consult your dentist for more information."

Since mercury is carcinogenic (causes cancer), teratogenic (causes birth defects), neurotoxic (damages nerves), and immunotoxic, a large number of health problems are associated with mercury accumulation in the body, such as birth defects, miscarriages, infertility, endometriosis, autoimmune diseases (lupus or rheumatoid arthritis, for example), multiple sclerosis, Alzheimerlike disorientation and confusion, memory loss, depression, anxiety, headaches, seizures, vision problems, vertigo, ringing or buzzing in the ears (tinnitus), abnormally fast or slow heartbeat, irregular heartbeat (palpitations), sore throat, metallic taste in the mouth, gingivitis and other gum problems, precancerous lesions in the mouth, skin rashes, hives, allergies, asthma, joint pain, chronic fatigue, frequent infections, chronic yeast infections, kidney disease, high blood pressure, and antibiotic-resistant bacteria in the intestines.

In spite of all the potential health problems associated with mercury amalgam fillings, many dentists continue to use them because they're fast and cheap. Admittedly, no dental material is 100 percent safe, but products that contain mercury are the absolute worst and should never be placed inside the mouth.

Since mercury amalgam fillings are toxic, what can be used in their place? Two good choices are high-noble gold and light-cured composite fillings. Gold is generally the safest and strongest material for dental restorations, but even here you must be careful, because the actual concentration of gold in dental gold fillings and crowns varies from as low as 20 percent to as high as 90 percent, depending on the brand the dental laboratory uses. Dental labs routinely add other metals (silver, copper, palladium, nickel, and beryllium) to gold to make it harder and cheaper. Unfortunately, the lower the percentage of gold and the higher the amount of these other metals, the greater the health risk. Therefore, in cases where a gold filling or crown is necessary, high-noble gold alloy is a lot safer for your child's health in the long run even though it costs more initially. However, you must ask your dentist to order a specific brand name that contains at least 80 percent gold (and without any silver, copper, palladium, nickel, or beryllium), or you may end up with a cheap substitute. One of the best brands is APM-Sterngold 2713, which is 90 percent gold and 10 percent platinum. Another good choice is Jeneric/Pentron RxG, which is 86 percent gold and 10 percent platinum. Be sure to get a written guarantee that your order was filled exactly as requested; this will put the lab on notice that you won't tolerate any shenanigans.

If your child already has a mouthful of mercury amalgam, be careful when getting new fillings or replacing old ones. Whenever gold or stainless steel comes into contact with mercury amalgam inside the mouth, electro-galvanic forces generate a small electric current (like a minibattery) that corrodes the amalgam and greatly accelerates the absorption of toxic mercury into the body. Ironically, college chemistry textbooks describe this phenomenon in detail, and yet many dentists continue to place these metals together in the mouths of their patients every day without realizing the damage they're causing. To avoid becoming a "live wire," do not use gold restorations until all of the mercury fillings have been properly and completely removed.

When a person is having serious health problems that might be related to mercury poisoning, some doctors recommend removing all of the amalgam fillings to see if the symptoms improve. Unfortunately, when the mercury fillings are not removed carefully and properly, the person will inhale mercury vapor and swallow metal particles, which could wind up damaging his health even more. To reduce the risk of such a disaster, during the entire drilling procedure the dentist should isolate the tooth with a "rubber dam," keep a steady spray of cold water coming from the drill, and have the dental assistant continuously irrigate the tooth with plenty of cold water while simultaneously using a high-volume suction device to remove toxic metal vapors and particles. To further minimize inhalation of mercury vapors, the dentist should section the metal filling into chunks, which easily pop out, rather than grinding the filling into airborne dust.

Much of the restorative material dentists put in the human mouth can upset the immune system terribly, but that doesn't mean you should avoid the dentist. On the contrary, regular dental checkups are absolutely essential to prevent cavities from ever developing in the first place. By knowing to request the safest dental products you can easily avoid the immunologic and toxic pitfalls associated with dentistry.

IMMUNIZATION

It's very important for your baby to receive all of the required immunizations, but it's equally important for her to be completely well on the day she gets the vaccines. It's dangerous to administer any immunization when there are signs of an illness—fever, runny nose, hoarseness, coughing, vomiting, diarrhea, and the like—because a vaccine will add stress to your child's immune system at the same time she is trying to fight off an infection.

The required immunizations include DTP, polio, HIB, and MMR. The following chart outlines the routine checkup and immunization schedule for healthy children. Be advised, however, that this schedule is likely to change somewhat over the next few years as new vaccines are granted FDA approval.

AT-A-GLANCE CHART FOR
ROUTINE CHECKUPS AND IMMUNIZATIONS

2 weeks old	Checkup plus PKU and thyroid blood test
1 month old	Checkup plus optional hepatitis B #1
2 months old	Checkup plus DTP #1, polio #1, HIB #1
3 months old	Checkup plus optional hepatitis B #2
4 months old	Checkup plus DTP #2, polio #2, HIB #2
6 months old	Checkup plus DTP #3, polio #3, HIB #3
9 months old	Checkup plus optional hepatitis B #3
12 months old	Checkup plus optional tuberculosis skin test
15 months old	Checkup plus MMR vaccine and HIB booster
18 months old	Checkup plus DTP booster and polio booster

DTP Vaccine

The DTP vaccine provides good protection against diphtheria, tetanus, and pertussis (also know as *whooping cough*). The injection is associated with a few minor reactions, which usually disappear within 24–48 hours:

- The temperature may fluctuate from 101° F to 103° F for a day or two after the vaccine is given.
- The area where the shot is given may become red, swollen, or tender. If this occurs, you can apply a cold compress or an ice

bag to the site for about 15 minutes of each waking hour until the pain and swelling subside. An ice cube wrapped in a paper towel or washcloth will work if you don't have an ice bag handy. Do not apply ice directly against the skin, because this might cause frostbite.

• Some children have a drop in appetite or may be a little cranky or drowsy for a day or two.

Acetaminophen (Tylenol, Tempra, Panadol, or Feverall) helps reduce the fever, soreness, and fretfulness associated with the DTP vaccine. See the dosage chart in the fever section for details.

The DTP Vaccine and Brain Damage

Whether or not the DTP vaccine can cause brain damage is a very controversial issue. Most medical experts have finally concluded that the DTP vaccine does not cause any permanent brain damage, but a few still believe that the pertussis component does, although rarely, with risk estimates varying from about 1 in 300,000 to one in a million. Unfortunately, the media have sensationalized this issue and denied parents the unbiased information they need to make an informed decision about whether to give their child the vaccine. Many parents have the mistaken impression that the pertussis germ has gone away. Don't be lulled into a false sense of security just because you hear about only occasional outbreaks of whooping cough. As many as 4,200 cases of pertussis are documented every year in the United States. The fact is, among babies under a year of age who catch whooping cough and have not received any DTP vaccines over 50 percent will become sick enough to require hospitalization, 16 percent develop pneumonia and need intravenous antibiotics, 2 percent have seizures (convulsions), 20 percent stop breathing and have to be placed temporarily on a breathing machine for several days (assuming they're lucky enough to be in the hospital and not at home sleeping in the crib when such a catastrophic event happens), about 1 baby out of 200 will develop encephalitis or other brain problems that may be permanent, and approximately 1 out of 200 will die from the infection.

Without the DTP vaccine, a baby's actual risk of catching whooping cough and having a serious complication is higher than the theoretical one-in-a-million chance of suffering brain damage from the vaccine itself. Unfortunately, nothing is totally risk-free in this world.

Although the risk of your baby being seriously injured by the DTP vaccine is extremely low to begin with, there are several ways to reduce the risk even more:

1. Don't let your child receive the vaccine if he shows any signs of illness. In the long run, it's much smarter to postpone an immunization for a week or two until your child is well.
2. Don't let your child receive the DTP vaccine if she has ever had any of the following reactions when it was given previously:
   - A severe allergic reaction—hives; swelling of the lips, face, or throat; difficulty breathing
   - Fever of 105° F or above, high-pitched inconsolable crying for more than three hours, collapse, or shock
   - A seizure
   - Encephalitis or other serious brain disorder within 14 days
3. If your child has epilepsy or a serious underlying neurologic disorder that is getting progressively worse, ask your doctor about using the DT vaccine (which does not contain pertussis) instead of the DTP.

Acellular DTP (DTaP)

The acellular DTP (DTaP) is approved for use as a booster in children between the ages of 17 months and 7 years. The new acellular DTaP vaccine does not contain the toxic parts of the pertussis bacteria cells found in the old-fashioned whole-cell DTP. As a result, children receiving the DTaP have substantially less fever and less redness and pain at the injection site. The acellular vaccine costs a few dollars more than the whole-cell DTP, but it's really worth it, so tell your doctor you prefer the acellular DTaP for your child. Incidentally, the FDA is expected to approve the DTaP for use with infants soon.

FYI: The Acel-Imune DTaP manufactured by Lederle is the brand that produces the best immunity and the least side effects.

HIB Vaccine

The HIB vaccine protects against hemophilus influenza type B bacterial infections of the brain (meningitis), windpipe (epiglottitis), lungs (pneumonia), blood (sepsis), bone (osteomyelitis), and joints (septic arthritis). Hemophilus type B is not related to the influenza virus, and the HIB vaccine is not the same thing as a flu shot. The HIB vaccine is very safe, extremely effective, and highly recommended.

MMR and Oral Polio Vaccines

The MMR—measles, mumps, rubella (German measles)—and oral polio vaccines contain live but substantially weakened versions of the original viruses against which they are supposed to protect. Live virus vaccines are just strong enough to make a person immune to the virus without causing a serious infection in most cases. However, if your child (or anyone who comes into contact with your child) has a weak or dysfunctional immune system, tell your doctor ahead of time, because live virus vaccines can occasionally provoke an autoimmune disease such as lupus or rheumatoid arthritis, chronic fatigue syndrome, or a chronic viral infection.

VISITS TO THE DOCTOR'S OFFICE

You will be making frequent trips to the doctor's office during the first two years of your child's life, so here are seven helpful hints that can make those visits more enjoyable and productive:

1. Schedule your routine well-baby visits about a month in advance so you can arrange a time most convenient for you. It's best to have the very first appointment in the morning or the afternoon, because that's when the waiting room is empty (fewer germs) and the doctor is usually on time. After the first few appointments most doctors start to fall behind schedule and you have to wait longer to be seen. The worst time is right before lunch or the last appointment of the day.

2. Don't schedule a routine checkup on a Monday or a Friday if you can help it, because they're the busiest days of the week for most doctors. You want to see your doctor on a day when he or she has plenty of time to talk and answer all your questions. Always bring along a written list of your specific questions beforehand so you won't forget anything.
3. Try not to take other children with you to the doctor's office. You and your doctor will be much more able to focus your attention on the baby if little brothers and sisters aren't running around the exam room distracting everyone.
4. Try to feed your baby about an hour before the appointment so that she won't be crying for food during the exam.
5. While waiting to be called to an exam room, don't let your baby mingle with other children, play with the toys, or crawl around on the floor. Remember, a doctor's office is full of sick kids and contagious germs, and you certainly don't want your child to catch something worse than what she came in with.
6. Bring along a favorite stuffed animal or "security" blanket for the child to hold during the exam.
7. Let the doctor know your basic philosophy and expectations regarding medical care. Most parents prefer a partnership in which they're given the opportunity to discuss the pros and cons before making decisions on certain issues. Many times a compromise between the advice of the doctor and the wishes of an informed parent turns out to be the best approach for the child.

FEVER

Unfortunately, in our supposedly modern culture there's still a lot of deeply ingrained misinformation about fever. These erroneous beliefs are based on old wives' tales and fever folklore handed down from the preantibiotic era. With all these inaccurate superstitions floating around, it's no wonder parents become frightened when their child has a fever. This section is designed to reduce fever phobia by arming you with the facts and a sensible plan of action.

Fever Facts

Fact 1

The body temperature for a baby or child normally ranges from 97° F to 100° F, depending on whether the temperature is taken in the armpit, mouth, or rectum. Your child has a fever if the rectal temperature is higher than 100.6° F or if the oral or armpit temperature is above 99.6° F. (A rectal temperature is normally about 1° F higher than an oral or armpit temperature. It's also worth noting that the body temperature in the evening typically runs about 1° F higher than in the morning.)

Fever can be graded as low (101–102° F), medium (103–104° F), or high (105–106° F), but the degree of fever is not a reliable indicator of how sick a child really is. In other words, the height of the fever is not necessarily indicative of the seriousness of the infection. It's much more important to look at a child's behavior, appetite, and sleeping pattern when trying to decide if a serious infection is present. If your child is over three months old and alert, active, happy, playing and sleeping as usual, and eating or drinking normally, a serious infection is not likely. On the other hand, if your child is crying and refusing to play, eat, or drink, a visit to the doctor would be wise even if the fever is only low-grade.

Fact 2

Fever is a symptom of illness, not a disease itself. When a child has a fever, 99 percent of the time the underlying cause is an infection (usually viral or bacterial). Since most infections are contagious, a feverish child should be isolated from others until the temperature remains normal for at least 24 hours.

Fact 3

Fever by itself does not cause brain damage unless the temperature goes higher than 107° F. Fortunately, it is rare for common childhood infections to cause a fever above 106° F.

Fact 4

Teething does not cause fever higher than 101° F rectally. Do not assume teething is the cause of your child's fever.

Fact 5

Fever in the range of 101–102° F actually boosts the immune system's ability to fight off viral and bacterial infections. In other words, low-grade fever can serve a very useful purpose and should not automatically be considered harmful unless the child is under three months old, the child has a history of seizures during febrile illnesses, or the child's general health is impaired or weakened by a disease of the immune system, blood, lungs, heart, brain, kidneys, or other vital organ.

Fact 6

The body temperature usually bounces up and down erratically during the first two or three days of an infection. Shivering is the mechanism the body uses to raise the fever; sweating brings it back down.

FYI: Cortisol is the primary anti-inflammatory steroid hormone produced by the adrenal glands. The blood cortisol is normally at its peak in the morning (6:00–9:00 A.M.) and at its low point around midnight. The lower the blood cortisol, the higher the fever can go. That's why the fever often rises an additional degree or two in the evening and at night but then comes back down again in the morning. It also explains why sick children feel so much worse at night.

Choosing a Thermometer

The three thermometers that give the most accurate readings are the digital electronic thermometer, the infrared heat-sensing ear thermometer, and the mercury-glass thermometer.

Please note that temperature-sensing pacifiers, liquid crystal temperature strips placed across the forehead, and feeling the forehead with your hand are notoriously inaccurate and cannot be recommended.

Digital Electronic Thermometer

A digital electronic thermometer is your best buy. It makes the job of taking your child's temperature as easy as pie, and it costs only about $9. The digital electronic thermometer measures the peak temperature accurately and very quickly, and you don't even have to keep track of time, since a buzzer automatically beeps when the peak temperature is reached. Furthermore, the bold digital numbers are easy to read, and there's no glass to break. Becton-Dickinson (B-D) and Sunbeam are good brand names. Disposable plastic thermometer probe covers make cleanup easy and minimize the chance of spreading the infection to other family members. (Do not use the same thermometer for taking oral and rectal temperatures.)

Infrared Heat-Sensing Ear Thermometer

The ultimate high-tech thermometer is the ear thermometer by Thermoscan (800-EAR-TEMP). It measures the infrared heat generated by the eardrum and surrounding tissue and then automatically converts that reading into an oral or rectal equivalent. Just place the tip of the probe in the ear canal, press a button, and in one second you have a digital readout of the body temperature. Of course, something this comfortable and convenient was bound to have a price tag of $99, although many parents feel it's worth saving the time and avoiding the mess, crying, and struggling with the rectal thermometer. Please note, however, that ear thermometers are prone to give false high readings (sometimes as much as two degrees), so for Thermoscan recordings above 103° F you should double-check the accuracy with a rectal thermometer (preferably the digital type mentioned above).

Mercury-Glass Thermometer

The old-fashioned mercury-glass thermometer is definitely low-tech. It costs only about $3, but it measures the peak temperature very slowly, the numbers are hard to read, and the glass may break, resulting in a cut or release of mercury. Personally, I would buy a digital electronic thermometer instead, but if you decide to use a mercury thermometer, follow these suggestions:

- The glass thermometer with the short silver tip is for rectal temperatures; the one with the long silver tip is for oral or armpit temperatures.
- Shake the mercury level below 97° F before taking the temperature.
- Hold the thermometer in place long enough to obtain a peak temperature reading (three minutes for the rectal method, four minutes for the oral method, or seven minutes under the armpit).
- Never leave your child unattended with a thermometer in the rectum, mouth, or armpit.

Taking Your Child's Temperature

It's not necessary to take your baby's temperature every day. In fact, about the only time you need to check the temperature is when your child feels hot, refuses regular feedings, or acts sick or fussy. If your baby does have a fever, taking the temperature two or three times a day (early morning and late afternoon or evening) is usually adequate until the infection has run its course and the temperature remains in the normal range for 24 hours. Overdressing, swaddling, or overbundling a baby can cause a false high temperature reading, so be sure to remove any unnecessary clothing or blankets at least 15 minutes before you take the temperature.

Rectal Temperature Method

The rectal temperature method is the most accurate. Lubricate the silver bulb or the plastic probe cover of the thermometer with plain Vaseline petroleum jelly. Place the infant facedown across your lap and restrain his legs firmly with your hand. Spread the buttocks and gently insert the silver bulb of the thermometer about half an inch into the anus (rectum). Keep the thermometer in that position by holding the buttocks together firmly with your hand until the peak temperature is reached (about one minute for the digital electronic thermometer or three minutes for the mercury-glass one). *Never leave the child unattended.*

Armpit Temperature Method

The armpit (axillary) temperature method can provide only a rough approximation of the rectal temperature, but it's certainly more accurate than just feeling the forehead with your hand.

Place the silver bulb of the thermometer in your child's bare, dry armpit. Maintain the thermometer in that position by holding your child's upper arm firmly against the side of his chest with your hand until the peak temperature is reached (about two minutes for the digital electronic thermometer or seven minutes for the mercury-glass one). *Never leave the child unattended.*

Oral Temperature Method

The oral temperature method is recommended only for cooperative children over six years old. Don't let your child drink any hot or cold beverages for at least 15 minutes prior to taking an oral temperature.

Place the silver bulb of the thermometer underneath one side of the tongue—not on the top or front. Keep the thermometer in that position until the peak temperature is reached (about one minute for the digital electronic thermometer or four minutes for the mercury-glass one). Instruct your child to breathe through her nose and keep her lips closed tightly around the thermometer without biting it.

When to Call the Doctor about Fever

If your child has a fever as defined under "Fever Facts," the following procedure will help you figure out when to call the doctor.

Step 1: Is your child younger than three months old? If the answer is no, go to step 2. If the answer is yes, have the doctor examine your child immediately.

Step 2: How healthy is your child in general? If your child is normally healthy, go to step 3. If your child's general health is impaired or weakened by a disease of the immune system, blood, lungs, heart, brain, kidneys, or other vital organ, call the doctor.

Step 3: Has your child ever had a seizure (convulsion) caused by fever? If the answer is no, go to step 4. If your child has a history of seizures during febrile illnesses, call the doctor.

Step 4: Does your child have fever higher than 102° F? If the answer is no, go to step 5. If the answer is yes, have the doctor examine your child.

Step 5: Is the fever accompanied by any of the danger signs listed below? If the answer is no, follow the advice in the next section, "Treatment for Fever," and continue to watch closely for the onset of any danger signs. If the answer is yes, have the doctor examine your child. Danger signs include the following:

- The child's fever does not go away completely after two days.
- The child has symptoms of shock (fast heartbeat, collapse).
- The child is whimpering or crying inconsolably.
- The child refuses to eat or drink.
- The child's "soft spot" on top of the heat is puffy or bulging.
- The child's neck is stiff, or the child cries in pain when bending the neck or moving the head up and down or sideways.
- The child is disoriented, delirious, combative.
- The child is extremely sleepy and difficult to arouse.
- The child suddenly faints or has a seizure.
- The child is dizzy, becomes unsteady or uncoordinated, or cannot maintain her balance.
- The child shows signs of dehydration, such as a 5 percent drop in body weight, dry mouth (little or no saliva), sunken eyes, hardly any tears when crying, failure to pass any urine for 10 hours, extreme thirst, weakness that makes her unable to stand or sit, fast heartbeat, rapid breathing.
- The child passes more than four large diarrhea stools within a 24-hour period.
- The child is passing red, maroon, or black stools.
- The child is vomiting blood or green bile. (Please note that bile is green, and stomach acid is yellow. It's also helpful to review what your child has eaten or drunk within the last 24 hours, because red, purple, or green food coloring [Jell-O or Popsicles, for example] is often mistaken for blood or bile in vomitus or stools. And if you're breast-feeding, examine your nipples for signs of cracking or bleeding, because your child may have just swallowed some blood-tinged breast milk.)

- The child vomits more than just a few times.
- The child has severe abdominal (stomach) pain or cramps.
- The child's abdomen (stomach) is bloated or tender to the touch.
- The child is passing white or beige stools.
- The child's skin and the whites of the eyes are yellow (jaundice).
- The child cries when passing stools or urine.
- The child's urine has a strong odor or looks cloudy, red, or dark brown.
- The child's groin, testicle, or scrotum is swollen and/or tender.
- The child is breathing very fast (over 50 breaths per minute while sleeping).
- The child has cough spasms every few minutes.
- The child's breathing is labored or wheezy.
- The child is short of breath (trouble catching his breath or sucking in air).
- The child's chest or lower neck (right below the Adam's apple) sinks or draws inward with each breath.
- The child has bad breath.
- The child has constant drainage of yellow, green, or bloody mucus from the nose.
- The child complains of a sore throat or is drooling a lot more than usual.
- The child has red spots or blisters on the tongue, the gums, the back of the throat, and/or the roof of the mouth.
- The child's tonsils are red and swollen with white pus pockets on them.
- The child's neck is sore, or the lymph glands in the neck (or elsewhere) are swollen and tender.
- The child is rubbing her ears or complaining of an earache.
- The child's ear canal is draining orange wax or yellowish green pus.
- The child is shaking her head back and forth as if something is hurting.
- The child's eye is red or has a constant drainage of yellow or green mucus that requires frequent wiping.

• The child's eyelid is red and swollen.
• The child complains of eye pain, blurred vision, or double vision.
• The child has a red, tender, or swollen area of the body.
• The child suddenly develops a large lump for no apparent reason.
• The child is limping or refuses to move an arm or a leg.
• The child breaks out in purple spots or bruises or starts to bleed for no apparent reason.
• The child breaks out in red spots or a skin rash that looks like measles, a sunburn, or hives.
• The child has a progressively expanding red patch of skin or a red streak spreading up her arm or leg.
• The child swallowed a poisonous substance.
• The child has any symptom that is causing significant distress or concerns you, and you don't know what to do.

Treatment for Fever

The following suggestions will help control a fever safely and make your child feel more comfortable.

• Avoid overdressing, swaddling, or overbundling. Dress your child comfortably in soft, lightweight 100 percent cotton clothing, such as pajamas and socks. You can add a cotton blanket if your child is shivering or feels chilled.
• Keep the room temperature in a comfortable range—not too hot and not too cold. Avoid drafts from air vents and fans.
• A few babies enjoy light sponging with plain tepid water and a washcloth when they have a fever, but in most cases bathing makes feverish children shiver, cry, and feel very uncomfortable. In fact, shivering itself drives the temperature higher and totally defeats the purpose of sponging. That's why the fever usually shoots right back up again as soon as the bath is over and why I normally do not recommend wasting time and effort with sponge bathing.

```
┌─────────────────────────────────────────────────┐
│                  Toxic Warning                   │
│  Never give alcohol baths to reduce fever,       │
│  because breathing the toxic fumes can cause     │
│  alcohol poisoning and result in hypoglycemia    │
│  (low blood sugar), coma, or seizures.           │
└─────────────────────────────────────────────────┘
```

- Encourage—but don't force—your child to drink plenty of cool liquids and keep the diet light and bland. For babies who are breast-feeding, it's usually a good idea to continue nursing.
- At the present time the safest medication for fever reduction in children is acetaminophen. There are several popular brand names including Tylenol, Tempra, Feverall, and Panadol. You can give the recommended dose of acetaminophen every four hours up to five times in a 24-hour period. Acetaminophen will usually reduce the fever a few degrees and make your child feel better, but it will not shorten the natural course of the infection that is causing the fever, nor will it eliminate the fever entirely or stop the erratic body temperature fluctuations caused by the underlying infection.

  Acetaminophen comes in many different milligram strengths (80, 120, 160, 320, 325, 500) and forms (infant drops, children's syrup or suspension, children's chewable tablets, junior tablets, caplets, capsules, and suppositories), so always read the label very carefully to find out the number of milligrams (mg) per unit dose for the brand you've purchased. The following chart outlines the standard acetaminophen dosage schedule for infants and children based on body weight from 9 to 36 pounds.

Weight	Recommended Dose of Acetaminophen
9–13 pounds	40 milligrams every 4 hours
14–19 pounds	80 milligrams every 4 hours
20–25 pounds	120 milligrams every 4 hours
26–36 pounds	160 milligrams every 4 hours

Note that the major brands of acetaminophen list two recommended dosages on their package, one based on the body weight of a child and the other based on age. The dosage based on body weight is more accurate, since some children weigh quite a bit more or less than average for their age.

For parents who are concerned about artificial colors and flavors, there's an acetaminophen brand called Feverall Sprinkle Caps. Feverall is a taste-free, dye-free acetaminophen powder you mix into the child's favorite beverage; it's sold over the counter and comes in 80-milligram and 160-milligram capsules, so be sure to buy the right size for your child. Feverall also comes in rectal suppositories of 80 milligrams, 120 milligrams, and 320 milligrams. Your local pharmacist can order Feverall for you, or you can call Upsher-Smith Laboratories at 800-654-2299 for the name of a retail store in your neighborhood that carries Feverall products.

For children over 14 pounds who cannot tolerate or don't like the taste of the liquid form of acetaminophen, try this. Place an 80-milligram acetaminophen children's chewable tablet in a teaspoon, then crush the tablet by pressing another teaspoon down on top of it. The powder can then be sprinkled onto a teaspoon of cereal, applesauce, pudding, or strained bananas.

Parents who give their child acetaminophen infant drops should not let the dropper touch their baby's mouth or lips when administering the medicine, because if the baby's lips touch the dropper, the entire bottle will become contaminated with germs after putting the top back on. To avoid this problem, squirt the prescribed amount of acetaminophen drops into a baby spoon or medicine dispenser spoon and then give it to your child. Better yet, put the correct amount of acetaminophen drops in one or two ounces of water, juice, or formula and then let the baby drink it in a diluted form; this method generally causes less gagging.

Acetaminophen Warnings

Acetaminophen is effective for reducing fever, aches, and pains when used as directed, but please observe these warnings:

Warning 1. Never under any circumstances exceed the recom-

....

mended dose of acetaminophen (or any other fever-reducing medicine), because larger or more frequent doses will poison your child and will not reduce the fever any better than the suggested dosage.

Warning 2. Tylenol, Tempra, Feverall, and Panadol are different brand names, but all four contain acetaminophen, so do not give them at the same time. And be careful not to inadvertently give cold and flu medicines that also contain acetaminophen.

Warning 3. Do not refill an acetaminophen infant drops bottle with acetaminophen children's syrup or suspension liquid, because they are not equivalent. The infant drops usually contain 80 milligrams of acetaminophen per 0.8 milliliter, whereas children's syrup or suspension liquid typically has only about 25 milligrams per 0.8 milliliter. In other words, for most major brands of acetaminophen, the infant drops are approximately three times more concentrated than the children's syrup or suspension liquid.

Warning 4. Acetaminophen must be detoxified by the liver to be eliminated safely from the body; therefore, children who have diseases of the liver should not receive acetaminophen.

Aspirin and Ibuprofen Alert

The American Academy of Pediatrics strongly warns against giving aspirin (also known as *salicylate* or *salicylic acid*) to children or teenagers who have chickenpox, the flu, or other viral infections. This warning is based on the observation of a link between taking aspirin for viral illnesses and the subsequent development of Reye's syndrome, a rare but serious illness.

Although most doctors rely on acetaminophen as their first choice to reduce fever in children, liquid ibuprofen (Children's Motrin or Children's Advil) products are now available, by prescription only, for use as fever reducers. Unfortunately, ibuprofen can produce many of the same side effects as aspirin, such as nausea, stomachache, heartburn, vomiting, stomach ulcers, impaired blood clotting, asthma, and allergic reactions. Furthermore, ibuprofen is relatively new, and unforseen side effects might become apparent as its use becomes more widespread. Aspirin was used for decades before its association with Reye's syndrome was discovered; whether a similar link will eventually be found between ibuprofen and Reye's syndrome remains to be seen. The point is, since fever is not harmful in most cases anyway, you shouldn't risk using ibuprofen for routine reduction of a fever below 103° F. On the other hand, I would recommend ibuprofen in these situations: if the fever exceeds 103° F and acetaminophen by itself is not providing adequate fever reduction, if your child has a history of seizures during febrile illnesses, or if your child has a medical condition that requires strict control of fever.

PREVENTING INFECTIONS

There are four basic kinds of germs: viruses, bacteria, parasites, and fungi. Viruses and bacteria are responsible for over 95 percent of common childhood infections, and the following list will give you some idea of the mind-boggling number your child can catch. The symptoms usually associated with a particular infection are in parentheses, and the asterisks identify the infections that can be prevented by vaccination.

Viruses

- Rhinoviruses (common cold symptoms: runny nose, congestion, sniffles, sneezing, watery eyes, mild fever)
- Influenza virus types A* and B* (flu symptoms: fever, sore throat, runny nose, congestion, sneezing, watery eyes, hoarseness, deep cough, fatigue)
- Parainfluenza virus types 1, 2, 3, 4A, and 4B (fever, sore throat, hoarseness, croupy cough)
- Respiratory syncytial virus or RSV (fever, ear infection, runny nose, congestion, hoarseness, wheezing, deep cough)
- Herpes simplex virus types 1 and 2 (fever blisters or cold sores)
- Herpesvirus-6 (roseola: three-day fever followed by measleslike skin rash)
- Epstein-Barr virus or EBV (mononucleosis symptoms, fever, sore throat, tonsillitis, swollen lymph glands in the neck, severe fatigue)

- Cytomegalovirus or CMV (mononucleosislike illness)
- Varicella-zoster virus (Chickenpox blisters and scabs all over the body)
- Hepatitis virus types A and B* (fever, vomiting, jaundice, dark brown urine, white or beige stools)
- Coxsackie virus and echovirus (fever, sore throat, vomiting, diarrhea, measleslike rash, blisters on the hands, feet, and inside the mouth)
- Polio virus types 1*, 2*, and 3* (paralysis)
- Rotavirus (vomiting, diarrhea, dehydration, runny nose, congestion, cough)
- Adenoviruses (sore throat, runny nose, cough, congestion, pinkeye, fever, vomiting, diarrhea)
- Measles* (seven-day measles skin rash, high fever, sore throat, red eyes, runny nose, congestion, severe croupy cough)
- Mumps* (swollen salivary glands in the cheeks and underneath the jaw)
- Rubella* (three-day measles or German measles skin rash)
- Human parvovirus B-19 (measleslike skin rash called *fifth disease*)

Bacteria

- Diphtheria* (sore throat, tonsillitis, labored breathing)
- Pertussis* (runny nose, congestion, severe whooping cough)
- Tetanus* (severe muscle spasms and lockjaw)
- Streptococcus (strep throat, tonsillitis, scarlet fever, impetigo blisters)
- Staphylococcus (impetigo blisters, boils)
- Meningococcus (meningitis, blood infection)
- Pneumococcus (meningitis, blood infection, pneumonia, ear infection)
- Hemophilus type B* (meningitis, epiglottitis, pneumonia, blood infection)
- Tuberculosis (meningitis, pneumonia)
- Salmonella (fever, vomiting, diarrhea, abdominal pain)

- Shigella (fever, vomiting, diarrhea, abdominal pain)
- E. coli (fever, vomiting, diarrhea, abdominal pain)
- Campylobacter (fever, vomiting, diarrhea, abdominal pain)

How Germs Spread

To reduce your baby's risk of getting sick, it helps to know how germs spread. Unfortunately, contagious germs are everywhere. They are in the air you breathe, in the food you eat, in secretions from the nose and eyes, saliva, tears, vomitus, stool, urine, blood, and sores, and on everything you touch, including doorknobs, toilet handles and seats, diaper pails, sinks, drinking fountains, money, keys, telephones, cups, glasses, utensils, table or desk surfaces, combs, towels, toothbrushes, teething rings, pacifiers, toys, water-play tables, and other playthings. And since children are always rubbing their noses and eyes, putting their hands and dirty objects in their mouths, eating or preparing meals without washing their hands first, sharing each others' food and utensils, using the toilet without washing their hands afterward, sneezing and coughing on each other, and touching each others' hands in all sorts of everyday activities, it's easy to see how infections can spread from person to person so fast.

Most parents don't realize that the aftereffects of many so-called routine childhood infections can last for months, years, or throughout a person's life. For example, the body's immune system can normally get rid of a respiratory virus in about 7–10 days, but the virus often causes significant damage to the nasal and bronchial membranes, which keeps the eardrums full of mucus and makes the bronchial tubes prone to asthmatic wheezing for months. Or, when an infant or toddler catches an intestinal virus infection, damage to her digestive system can be so extensive that she may suffer with diarrhea for months. Of course, we wouldn't want to forget about the herpes family of viruses—herpes simplex virus types 1 and 2, herpesvirus 6 (roseola), chickenpox, CMV, and Epstein-Barr virus (mononucleosis)—which stay inside the body forever once you're infected with them and have the ability to reactivate from time to time, especially during periods of physical or emotional stress.

Exposing your child to the general public too early in life is asking for frequent infections, some of them quite serious and long-lasting. It's a fact that the greater the number of children your baby is around, the greater the number of infections she will catch. Young children who attend a nursery, daycare center, or similar kind of facility get sick a lot more often than those who stay at home. Remember, a two-year-old has a stronger immune system than a one-year-old, and a one-year-old stronger than a six-month-old, so the older a child is before she is exposed to large groups of contagious children, the better.

11 Ways to Keep Your Baby Well

You can drastically reduce—by at least 75 percent—the number of contagious infections you and your baby will catch by following these tips:

1. Be sure your baby receives all of the recommended vaccinations.
2. Don't expose your child to cigarette, cigar, or pipe smoke. Tobacco smoke exposure increases your child's susceptibility to contagious germs by damaging the protective membrane lining of his nose, throat, and bronchial tubes.
3. For the first six months, don't take your baby to public places (such as shopping malls, supermarkets, church, or movie theaters) where large groups of people (and their germs) are gathered. If at all possible, try not to send your child to a daycare center, church nursery, or similar kind of facility until she is at least two years old.
4. Wash your hands thoroughly with plenty of soap and water after every diaper change or use of the toilet, before preparing or eating meals or snacks, and after every contact with nasal or eye secretions, mucus, blood, saliva, urine, vomitus, bowel movements, or sores. Use sanitary liquid soap dispensers and disposable paper towels. Frequent hand washing gets rid of most but not all of the contagious germs picked up on your

fingers. However, you don't want to make your child germ phobic, so don't go overboard on hand washing. Prudent moderation is the key.

Toxic Warning

Do not under any circumstances use disinfectant aerosol sprays; they spew toxic chemicals into the air that can seriously harm the lungs, and besides, they won't reduce the number of respiratory infections your child will catch.

---

5. Avoid rubbing your eyes or nose unless your hands have just been washed.
6. Use disposable tissues to wipe or blow your nose, discard the tissues in a receptacle with a lid, and wash your hands immediately afterward.
7. Stay away from anyone who is sneezing or coughing with a cold or the flu.
8. Never let children (not even siblings) share food, drinks, glasses, cups, plates, utensils, combs, brushes, towels, toothbrushes, teething rings, pacifiers, medicine bottles, nose drops, nasal aspirators, and the like.
9. A fever blister or cold sore on the lip is caused by a contagious virus called *herpes simplex*. The infection rarely causes any permanent harm to children over two months old who have normal immune systems, but it *can* cause meningitis or encephalitis in newborn babies, so anyone who has a fever blister must follow certain precautions (especially when around newborns):
   - Don't touch or pick at the blister or scab, because you'll contaminate your hands with contagious herpesviruses, which could then spread to the baby.
   - Wash your hands thoroughly with plenty of soap and water before touching or feeding the baby.

- If you have a cold sore on your lip, don't kiss the baby or breathe directly into her face until the blister or scab is completely gone.

10. Try to avoid situations that provoke physical or emotional stress, since stress weakens the immune system and thus increases susceptibility to infections of all kinds.

11. Respiratory infections are caused by viruses and bacteria—not by a chill per se—but when a child gets chilled, the physical stress can weaken his immune system just enough to make him susceptible to germs that would ordinarily not have been able to infect him had his immune system been working at peak efficiency. So be sure your child is dressed adequately for going outside on cold and blustery days.

NOSE, THROAT, AND CHEST INFECTIONS

A child who develops a problem in the nose, throat, or chest will generally display one or more of the following respiratory symptoms: sneezing, nasal congestion, sniffles, runny nose, sore throat, excessive drooling, hoarseness, coughing, wheezing, noisy breathing, rapid breathing, shortness of breath, or labored breathing. The major causes of nose, throat, and chest problems in children are respiratory infections, tobacco smoke exposure, and allergies to foods or air pollutants. Chapter 1 explores the issue of food allergies, Chapter 6 discusses tobacco smoke and air pollutants in detail, and respiratory infections (colds, flu, and the like) are covered in this section.

Infection vs. Allergy

How can you tell whether respiratory symptoms are due to an allergy or to a contagious infection? Actually, it's pretty easy. Statistically, there's a 90 percent probability that a child with respiratory symptoms has a contagious infection, not an allergy. Definite signs of an infection include fever or yellowish green mucus drainage from the nose. However, even if the body temperature is normal and the nasal discharge is clear or white, the odds are nine to one that the child has an infection and is probably contagious.

The hallmark symptom of an allergy is intense itching of the eyes and nose. The throat, roof of the mouth, or skin (hives or eczema) may also be very itchy. If itching and respiratory symptoms are provoked by exposure to certain foods or air pollutants, consult your doctor or an allergist for advice on possible allergy testing. A little detective work on your part (in collaboration with your child's doctor or allergist) can often uncover the offending allergenic item so it can be avoided.

"Sick-All-the-Time" Syndrome

When a child has a constant runny nose, a persistent cough, or frequent respiratory infections and never seems to get well—what some call the "sick-all-the-time" syndrome—over 90 percent of the time the problem turns out to be tobacco smoke exposure and/or attendance at a daycare center or nursery where contagious respiratory infections are rampant. Allergies are responsible about 10 percent of the time.

Healthy young preschool-age children who are not exposed to tobacco smoke and don't go to daycare centers or nurseries catch about 6 to 9 respiratory infections per year. Breathing tobacco smoke or going to crowded places where people and their germs gather in groups more than doubles the number of infections to 15 to 20 per year (that averages out to about one every 2 or 3 weeks). When you consider that a typical infection takes 7–10 days to run its course, that leaves only a few "well" days before the next infection sets in, especially during the fall and winter months. A study in the June 1994 issue of *Pediatrics* (vol. 93, pp. 977–85) found that youngsters who attend daycare centers are almost 12 times more likely to catch pneumonia than children who stay at home.

Uncommon causes of the "sick-all-the-time" syndrome include cystic fibrosis (about 1 out of evey 2,000 Caucasian children) and genetically inherited diseases of the immune system (approximately 1 out of every 1,000 children in the general population). A few simple and inexpensive laboratory tests can usually diagnose these problems quickly.

The warning signs of a possible immune system disease in a child include one or more of the following:

- More than eight ear infections within one year
- Intravenous antibiotics required to cure an ear or sinus infection
- Two or more straight months on oral antibiotics with little improvement
- Two or more cases of pneumonia within one year
- More than one episode of a deep-seated bacterial or fungal infection of the brain (meningitis), bone (osteomyelitis or mastoiditis), blood (sepsis), skin (cellulitis or abscess), or internal organ (abscess)
- Failure of a baby to gain weight or grow properly
- Persistent thrush in the mouth after one year of age
- Member of the immediate family with an immune deficiency
- Family history of a genetically inherited disease of the immune system

The Jeffrey Modell Foundation provides a toll-free hot line (800-JEFF-844) to answer parents' questions about disorders of the immune system in infants and children.

Common Colds

The symptoms of a "common cold" include a runny nose, sniffles, nasal congestion, sneezing, watery eyes, a mild sore throat, poor appetite, and sometimes a low-grade fever or mild cough. More than 100 different rhinoviruses and a mind-boggling number of other viruses and bacteria can cause cold symptoms. Nasal secretions contain the highest concentration of rhinoviruses, but they can also be found in saliva and in eye secretions. Common cold viruses spread from person to person when people sneeze and cough contagious viruses into the air (airborne transmission) and rub their nose and eyes after contaminating their hands with contagious mucus.

The incubation period for rhinoviruses is usually two to five days from the time of exposure to the onset of symptoms. An uncomplicated cold usually runs its course within seven days. If the symptoms last longer than a week, chances are the original virus infection has turned into a secondary bacterial infection that requires an antibiotic.

Each time a child has a cold, he develops immunity to the specific virus responsible for that infection, but since there are more than 200 different viruses that can cause common cold symptoms, there will always be a new virus floating around the community ready to attack.

Flu

Flu symptoms consist of severe nasal congestion and drainage, sneezing, watery eyes, a very sore throat, hoarseness, a deep cough with a lot of mucus production, muscle aches and pains, nausea, headache, chills, and fever above 102° F.

Influenza virus type A and influenza virus type B are the two major virus strains that cause flu symptoms. However, parainfluenza, adenovirus, and respiratory syncytial virus (RSV) infections can also mimic the flu.

Flu viruses spread from person to person through sneezing, coughing, and contact with contagious mucus.

The incubation period for influenza virus types A and B is usually 1 to 3 days from the time of exposure to the onset of symptoms. An uncomplicated case of the flu typically runs its course within 10 days. Flu symptoms that last longer than 10 days usually mean the original virus infection has spawned a secondary bacterial infection that requires an antibiotic.

Viral Croup Cough

Viral croup is a term used to describe a hoarse, dry, hacking cough that sounds like a dog or a seal barking. The illness typically starts with a runny nose, sore throat, and low-grade fever of 101° F; then, after a day or two, the infection spreads to the vocal cords and windpipe, where it causes laryngitis, hoarseness, noisy breathing, and a distinctive "seal bark" croupy cough.

Parainfluenza viruses (types 1, 2, 3, 4A, and 4B) and influenza viruses (types A and B) are the leading causes of croup. Both viruses are quite contagious and spread through sneezing, coughing, and contact with contagious mucus.

The incubation period for parainfluenza viruses is usually two to six days from the time of exposure to the onset of symptoms.

Pneumonia

Pneumonia is an infection (usually viral or bacterial) of the lungs. Most of the time, a child with pneumonia will have nonstop cough spasms, rapid breathing, fever, and often vomiting. There may also be wheezing, shortness of breath, or heavy sighing. The chest or lower neck (right below the Adam's apple) may sink or draw inward with each breath. Sometimes the only symptom is a cough that persists for more than a week.

One of the hallmarks of pneumonia is rapid breathing. You can test for this at home. Just take a watch with a second hand, and while your child is sound asleep, count each breath he takes for 60 seconds. You don't even need a stethoscope to do this. If your child is congested (which he probably is, or you wouldn't be doing this test in the first place), the breathing will be loud enough to hear each breath easily. You can also observe the movement of the child's chest with each breath. There's a strong possibility of pneumonia if the respiratory rate exceeds 50 breaths per minute in a sleeping baby under one year of age or 45 breaths per minute in a child over one year old. (When babies are awake and active, their breathing rate often exceeds 50 breaths per minute. That's why, for greater accuracy, a baby should be sound asleep when you count his or her breathing rate looking for signs of pneumonia.) Please note, however, that some youngsters will maintain a relatively normal respiratory rate even though they have pneumonia. Always call the doctor right away if you suspect your child has pneumonia.

Secondary Bacterial Infections

Most respiratory infections are caused by viruses, which cannot be cured by antibiotics. However, as a viral infection runs its course, the immune system often becomes so weakened that a secondary bacterial infection takes hold—in the ears, sinuses, or lungs—especially in children under three years of age. Be on the lookout for one of the three cardinal signs of a secondary bacterial infection: (1) the symptoms of the respiratory infection last longer than 7–10 days without any noticeable improvement, (2) a fever suddenly develops toward the middle or end of the infection, or (3) the symptoms start to clear up after the first few days but then suddenly get worse again. Secondary bacterial infections usually respond quickly to antibiotic therapy.

When to Call the Doctor About a Cold or the Flu

If your child has symptoms of a respiratory infection, such as a common cold or the flu, the following stepwise plan will help you figure out when to call the doctor:

Step 1: Is your child younger than three months old? If the answer is no, go to step 2. If the answer is yes, have the doctor examine your child.

Step 2: How healthy is your child in general? If your child is normally healthy, go to step 3. If your child's general health is impaired or weakened by a disease of the immune system, blood, lungs, heart, brain, kidneys, or other vital organ, call the doctor.

Step 3: Does your child have a fever higher than 102° F? If the answer is no, go to step 4. If the answer is yes, have the doctor examine your child.

Step 4: Is the respiratory infection accompanied by any danger signs? If the answer is no, go to step 5. If the answer is yes, have the doctor examine your child. The major danger signs to look for with regard to respiratory infections are outlined here, but for a more detailed list, refer to the section on fever.

- The child is breathing very fast (over 50 breaths per minute while sleeping).
- The child has cough spasms every few minutes.
- The child's breathing is labored or wheezy.

- The child is short of breath (trouble catching his breath or sucking in air).
- The child's chest or lower neck (right below the Adam's apple) sinks or draws inward with each breath.
- The child has bad breath.
- The child has constant drainage of yellow, green, or bloody mucus from the nose.
- The child complains of a sore throat or is drooling a lot more than usual.
- The child has red spots or blisters on the tongue, the gums, the back of the throat, and/or the roof of the mouth.
- The child's tonsils are red and swollen with white pus pockets on them.
- The child's neck is sore, or the lymph glands in the neck (or elsewhere) are swollen and tender.
- The child is rubbing her ears or complaining of an earache.
- The child's ear canal is draining orange wax or yellowish green pus.
- The child is shaking her head back and forth as if something is hurting.
- The child's eye is red or has a constant drainage of yellow or green mucus that requires frequent wiping.
- The child has any symptom that is causing significant distress or concerns you, and you don't know what to do.

Step 5: Have the respiratory symptoms lasted longer than one week, or were the symptoms of the infection starting to clear up after the first few days but then suddenly got worse again? If the answer to either question is yes, have the doctor examine your child. If the answer to both questions is no, continue to watch closely for the onset of any danger signs and consider the following treatment suggestions.

Home Treatment Suggestions for Respiratory Infections

If your child's nasal mucus drainage changes color from clear or white to yellow or green, and along with the change in color his appetite drops, or he starts crying, acting unusually fussy, or running a fever, it means the infection is getting worse, and you should see the doctor right way. You should also see the doctor if the infection has not run its course in a week. On the other hand, if your child is playful and has a normal temperature and a reasonably good appetite, the infection is probably progressing normally, and the drainage is likely to dry up completely within a few days.

General Treatment Suggestions for Respiratory Infections

When your child has a respiratory infection, you can help things along by following these general suggestions as well as the specific recommendations for runny noses and coughs that follow.

- First and foremost, you must totally avoid tobacco smoke exposure! Never allow any smoking inside your house or car. Tobacco smoke damages the nasal and bronchial membranes so badly they cannot fight off respiratory germs. Even a brief exposure to smoke once a day is very harmful. Antibiotics, antihistamines, and cough syrups cannot even begin to counteract the damaging effects of tobacco smoke.

- Keep your child indoors at home for the first few days of the illness, because going back and forth from indoors to outdoors makes the infection worse. Most colds will resolve on their own if the child can just stay home and rest. There's no substitute for a parent's tender loving care around the clock during an illness. In our on-the-go society, we have a tendency to underestimate the value of good, old-fashioned rest at home. A study conducted at the University of Pittsburgh found that, on average, children with colds actually get well two days sooner if cared for at home rather than at a daycare facility. Resting and playing quietly indoors, staying in pajamas, reading, and relaxing makes the pain and fever more bearable for sick children, just as it does for sick adults. The last thing a sick child needs is to be subjected to the three-ring circus of day care.

- Strong fumes or odors irritate the nose and throat, so avoid exposure to perfumes, colognes, household cleaning agents, ammonia, fresh paint or varnish, turpentine, gasoline, automobile exhaust, insect sprays or foggers, wood-burning stoves or fireplaces, candle smoke, kerosene heaters, and the like.

- Don't use baby powders or aerosol sprays (such as hair spray, insect spray, Lysol spray, and air fresheners/deodorizers) anywhere near your child; the airborne particles irritate the nose and lungs.
- Avoid drafts from fans and air vents.
- To stop the spread of germs, all household members must wash their hands thoroughly with plenty of soap and water before every meal and after every contact with the sick person's hands, nasal or eye secretions, saliva, urine, and bowel movements. Strict personal hygiene is essential.
- To reduce fever and relieve aches and pains, acetaminophen is a good choice. Acetaminophen is the active ingredient in Tylenol, Feverall, Tempra, and Panadol. See the section on fever for details on dosage.
- Offer a light, bland, soft, nonspicy diet and plenty of cool, soothing liquids appropriate for the age of the child. Warm liquids may help to thin mucus and unclog nasal passages.

For Nasal Congestion and Runny Noses

If your baby's nose is full of mucus or sounds dry and stuffy, use plain saline (saltwater) nose drops, two or three drops in each nostril, as often as necessary to make the breathing easier. (It's particularly helpful right before a feeding so the baby can eat and breathe at the same time.) You'll be able to aim the nose drops better if you lay the child faceup in your lap and tilt his head back slightly so his nostrils point up toward the ceiling. After you apply the nose drops, the baby will often sneeze and clear the nasal passages, but if not, you can suction the mucus out with a nasal aspirator. Squeeze the air out of the rubber bulb, snug the tip up to one nostril, and then suction while gently pressing the other nostril shut with your finger. Be careful not to share nose drop bottles or nasal aspirators among family members; label such items to avoid a mix-up.

Decongestant nose drops (Neosynephrine, Afrin, Dristan, and others) contain stimulants that can cause insomnia, hyperactivity, or a rapid heartbeat, so do not use any drops with the word *decongestant* on the package label. And avoid nose drops that contain the allergenic preservative thimerosal, because thimerosal is a mercury compound, and you obviously would not want to squirt a toxic heavy metal like mercury up your child's nose, especially when there are safer alternatives.

A soft, dye-free, fragrance-free tissue is preferred for wiping runny noses. A dab of plain Vaseline around the nostrils and lips several times a day also helps prevent chapping. It's worth noting that although white petrolatum is derived from petroleum (and as you know from reading this book, I usually shy away from petroleum products), plain Vaseline is safe and effective for almost everyone and remarkably free of any side effects.

Toxic Warning
Do not use Vicks Vaporub, mentholatum, or any ointments containing camphor, menthol, or eucalyptus. The fumes from these products irritate the nose and throat, and accidental ingestion can poison young children.

Don't give your child antihistamines or decongestants unless your doctor specifically instructs you to do so. There are at least six good reasons why many pediatricians don't routinely recommend these medications for children:

1. Antihistamines and decongestants do not prevent or cure respiratory infections (common cold or flu). Furthermore, several recent scientific studies have shown that cold medicines—PediaCare, Dimetapp, Novahistine, Actifed, Triaminic, and the like—do not relieve the symptoms of a cold or the flu or shorten the course of the illness any better than a sugar pill. Ironically, in some of these experiments the kids who took the placebo got well more quickly.

2. Antihistamines and decongestants can cause a lot of bothersome side effects, such as insomnia, nervousness, nightmares, hallucinations, delirium, drowsiness, impaired thinking, slow reaction time, loss of balance, blurred vision, muscle spasms, tremors, loss of appetite, constipation, dry mouth, nausea, vomiting, difficult urination, high blood pressure, and rapid or irregular heartbeats (palpitations).

3. Taking antihistamines lowers the seizure threshold in the brain and thus increases the risk that a child may have a convulsion during the illness.

4. Antihistamines can sometimes make mucus so thick and sticky it gets clogged up inside the sinuses and eardrums instead of draining out as it's supposed to; this blockage sets the stage for a secondary bacterial infection.

5. The American Academy of Pediatrics Committee on Drugs concluded more than 10 years ago that combination cold and cough medications should not be used in treating respiratory infections in infants and children.

6. The American Association of Poison Control Centers reports that cold medicines are a leading cause of accidental poisoning in children under six years of age.

In spite of scientific evidence to the contrary, many parents are convinced that antihistamines and decongestants do relieve cold and flu symptoms. If you are absolutely determined to give your child one of the standard cold medications, over-the-counter Benadryl Dye-Free Elixir (diphenhydramine) is one of the safest, because it does not contain alcohol or stimulant decongestants. If Benadryl causes too much drowsiness, consider Chlor-Trimeton (chlorpheniramine) as an alternative. Atarax syrup is a dye-free antihistamine, but it contains alcohol and menthol (both undesirable), it's expensive, it's available by prescription only, it causes drowsiness, and many kids don't like the taste.

For Coughs

Cough syrups are about as ineffective as the antihistamine/decongestant medications just mentioned. Research studies have shown that prescription and over-the-counter cough syrups containing various combinations and strengths of the three basic active ingredients (guaifenesin, codeine, and dextromethorphan) do not work any better at suppressing nighttime coughs than nonmedicated placebo cherry syrup. Nevertheless, I realize that it's almost impossible to resist trying a cough syrup when your child has a miserable cough, so here are a few tips:

- Don't give cough syrups to children under one year of age, because of the possible side effects, such as allergic reactions or suppression of the breathing control center in the brain.
- Cough drops and lozenges are choking hazards and should not be given to children younger than eight years old.
- If a cough is "productive" and helping to clear or loosen a lot of phlegm (mucus) from the throat and bronchial tubes, it's probably not a good idea to suppress it. On the other hand, if the cough is a dry, hacking nuisance and not serving any useful purpose, you can try a nonprescription cough syrup that contains dextromethorphan without an expectorant, such as Benylin DM Pediatric Cough Formula, Delsym 12-Hour Cough Relief, or Robitussin Pediatric Cough Suppressant. It's worth noting that most cough syrups contain artificial colors and flavors, both of which can cause some youngsters to become hyperactive for several hours after taking just one dose.
- Guaifenesin is the active ingredient promoted as an "expectorant" in many popular cough syrups. Guaifenesin is supposed to loosen phlegm and make coughs more productive, but I've never seen any evidence that it works. One thing I can tell you for sure, guaifenesin tastes so awful that it makes a lot of kids sick to their stomachs and vomit. Therefore, since guaifenesin serves no useful purpose, I would avoid cough syrups that contain it or any other expectorant.
- To loosen phlegm, my patients seem to get good results by simply drinking warm, soothing liquids. Incidentally, most parents don't realize that when a child sniffs, coughs, or clears his throat and swallows, the phlegm goes right into the stomach and through the digestive system. It does not drain back into the lungs, so there's no need to make your child spit out phlegm as

an adult might. Swallowing thick gobs of mucus can cause nausea or vomiting, however, so encourage your child to blow his nose once he's old enough to do so.

If your child has viral croup and wakes up in the middle of the night with the classic seal bark cough, there's an old-fashioned non-toxic remedy that usually works fast. Take your child into the bathroom, turn the shower on warm, close the door so the moisture will accumulate like fog, and sit with him while he breathes the warm mist. (Do not leave him unattended!) Breathing moist air will usually loosen the thick dry mucus in the windpipe and stop viral croup coughing spasms within 20 minutes. As soon as your child can breathe easily again, let him have a few swallows of water if desired, and then he can go back to sleep, but keep a close watch over him and call the doctor right away if any danger signs develop. Running a steam vaporizer in the room for a few hours usually helps viral croup (see the following notes on its proper use).

Humidifiers

Humidifiers and vaporizers almost always do more harm than good. The excess humidity introduced into the room by such devices promotes the growth of allergenic mold and house dust mites in the wallpaper, carpet, and furniture. That's why a lot of kids (especially those with allergies) seem to get worse when a humidifier is used regularly, so I don't recommend using humidifiers except for the treatment of viral croup coughing spasms.

There are three basic humidifiers: cool mist, ultrasonic, and steam vaporizers. Each has its own advantages and disadvantages.

I do not recommend cool-mist humidifiers because they pump out millions of harmful bacteria and mold spores into the air, even when the tank is meticulously cleaned and dried every day. The germs manage to hide in parts of the machine you can't reach to clean. Some manufacturers recommend sanitizing humidifiers with a dilute solution of chlorine bleach, but chlorine bleach is toxic and should not be used. When using any chemical to clean a humidifier, always rinse the unit thoroughly with plain water to remove all traces of the chemical before refilling the water tank.

Modern ultrasonic humidifiers are whisper-quiet and have excellent volume controls, but they generate ultrafine mist, which (depending on the water source) may contain unacceptably high levels of minerals, aluminum, asbestos, lead, radon, volatile organic compounds (VOCs), and other dangerous substances that should not be inhaled. Using bottled distilled water reduces the mineral problem but not necessarily the volatile organic compounds VOCs.

The old-fashioned steam vaporizers do not spew live germs into the air. The main concern with them is the risk of accidental scald burns.

If you decide to use a humidifying device, the old-fashioned steam vaporizer has the least potential for harm as long as you follow all of the safety precautions recommended by the manufacturer plus the following:

- Empty out the old water and rinse out the inside of the vaporizer tank with plain water and a clean washcloth every morning. Add fresh, bottled distilled water before each night's use.
- To prevent accidental scald burns, keep the vaporizer at least six feet away from the child and up high enough to be completely out of reach at all times. Set it in a stable place where it cannot tip over and run the electric cord behind a piece of furniture so the child cannot possibly get to it. And never leave a young child alone in a room where a steam vaporizer is running. Constant adult supervision is essential.
- Don't run the humidifier or vaporizer for more than a few hours at a time; running it all night long will make the room very cold and damp, one of the worst things for a sick child. Furthermore, keep the bedroom door open when the vaporizer is turned on in order to equalize the room temperature, because if the room gets too hot, the swelling in the throat and windpipe could get worse. If the unit has a volume control dial, set it to deliver a thin mist, not a fog.
- Do not put Vicks Vaporub, Mentholatum, or any ointment or

medication containing camphor, menthol, or eucalyptus in the vaporizer. As mentioned earlier, the fumes from these products irritate the nose and throat, and accidental ingestion can poison young children.

EAR INFECTIONS

The medical term for an infection of the eardrum or middle ear is *otitis media*. Eardrum infections usually start when the eustachian tubes get blocked. The eustachian tube is a short, tiny passageway that connects the middle ear to the back of the nose; it normalizes air pressure inside the middle ear and allows fluid secreted by the membrane lining the middle ear to drain into the nose and throat. When the eustachian tube gets congested, fluid cannot drain properly from the middle ear; the ear feels full and won't pop, and before long a secondary bacterial infection sets in, which leads to a buildup of mucus, pus, pressure, and pain behind the eardrum. Young children are particularly prone to middle-ear infections, because their eustachian tubes are small and do not function efficiently.

Children rarely develop middle-ear infections without first having a runny nose or nasal congestion. Tobacco smoke exposure and respiratory infections (colds, flu, and the like) are responsible for over 90 percent of all middle-ear infections, since they are the two leading causes of swelling and blockage of the nose and eustachian tubes. Allergies, immune system disorders, a genetically inherited susceptibility to ear problems, and drinking formula bottles while lying flat account for about 10 percent of ear infections.

An ear infection itself is not contagious. However, if an earache is due to a cold or the flu, the accompanying respiratory infection is very contagious, especially if the infected child is sneezing or coughing.

Symptoms of an Ear Infection

The main symptom of an ear infection in older children is an earache, but since an infant or toddler can't tell you his ear hurts, you'll have to be on the lookout for nonverbal cues, especially when your baby has a runny nose or a respiratory infection. Any of the following symptoms could mean your child has a middle-ear infection: fever; unusual fussiness or crying; pulling or rubbing on the ears; signs of hearing loss, such as decreased responsiveness to your voice and other sounds; suddenly waking up several times at night for no apparent reason; dizziness, vertigo, or loss of balance; drainage of orange, yellowish green, or bloody fluid from the ear canal; vomiting; or shaking the head back and forth as if something is hurting.

When to Call the Doctor

An earache by itself is rarely an emergency, but have the doctor examine your child within 12–24 hours whenever you suspect that your child has an ear infection so that proper treatment can be started. In the meantime, the best thing for pain relief is an oral dose of acetaminophen (Tylenol, for example). Follow the dosage instructions in the section on fever.

I do not recommend anesthetic eardrops for earaches. Eardrops contain ingredients that can cause an allergic inflammation of the outer-ear canal. And if the eardrum has burst, the eardrops may get trapped inside the inner ear and burn for hours.

The pain from an eardrum infection usually stops by itself within four to eight hours whether you give your child an antibiotic or not, but just because the pain goes away does not mean the infection is gone— in fact it usually isn't—so always have the doctor examine your child's ear so that the proper treatment can be started. An ear infection left untreated can lead to permanent hearing loss or to a serious infection in the mastoid bone next to the middle ear. If your doctor diagnoses a middle-ear infection, he or she will prescribe an oral antibiotic to be taken for 10–14 days and recommend a follow-up visit to be sure the eardrum has healed completely.

Natural and Nontoxic Prevention of Ear Infections

Children who have frequent or chronic ear infections are usually referred to an ear, nose, and throat (ENT) specialist for surgical implantation of tiny plastic tubes into the eardrums to normalize the middle-ear air pressure and thereby prevent the buildup of pus and fluid. The surgery is usually performed under general anesthesia, costs more then $1,000, and may leave a permanent scar on the eardrum, resulting in hearing loss and other problems many years down the line. This unpleasant scenario can be prevented 90 percent of the time by following seven precautions:

1. First and foremost, you must totally avoid all tobacco smoke exposure. Never allow any smoking whatsoever inside your house or car. Even a brief exposure to tobacco smoke once a day is very harmful. By damaging the delicate membrane lining of the nose and eustachian tubes, tobacco smoke lowers the body's ability to fight off respiratory germs. It also blocks the middle ear by triggering the secretion of thick gobs of mucus. All the cold remedies and antibiotics in the world cannot counteract the damaging effects of tobacco smoke. A lot of people suffer from the erroneous idea that if they use an air filter or avoid smoking in the baby's room it won't hurt anything. That's just wishful thinking. Smoking anywhere in the house eventually circulates into all the rooms. Incidentally, air filters don't even come close to screening out the toxic pollutants. If you must smoke, please go outside for your child's sake.

2. Try to keep your child from catching frequent respiratory infections early in life. The younger a child is, the greater the chance his middle ear will become blocked and infected. Even though the body's immune system can normally get rid of a respiratory virus in about 7–10 days, the damage left behind by the virus often keeps the middle ear full of fluid and susceptible to secondary bacterial infections for weeks or sometimes months. And the earlier in life this vicious cycle starts (six weeks old versus one year old, for example), the more likely a child will have persistent problems with his ears. Therefore, don't take your baby to public places where large groups of people (and their germs) are gathered (such as church, shopping malls,

supermarkets, movie theaters) until he is at least six months old and try not to send your child to a daycare center, church nursery, or similar facility until he is at least two years old. (Older children are much less prone to get ear infections when they catch a cold or the flu because their eustachian tubes function more efficiently and their immune systems are stronger.)

3. Don't let your baby lie flat while drinking from a bottle, because the horizontal position lets milk collect near the adenoids and blocks the eustachian tubes. Always hold your child in an upright or semiupright position during feedings. That means no bottles in the crib during naps or at night and no propped bottles.

4. If the weather is very cold or windy, don't take your child outside if you can help it. If it's unavoidable, at least cover his ears with a hat.

5. Avoid drafts from fans or air vents.

6. Don't let infants or toddlers submerse their ears in water, even in the bathtub.

7. Avoid public swimming pools frequented by toddlers and young children, because the water (especially in the "kiddie pool") is loaded with contagious respiratory and fecal germs that the chlorine doesn't kill.

If your child continues to get frequent ear infections despite your following these suggestions, you should ask your doctor about testing for allergies and immune system disorders. In addition, you might consider the possibility of a vitamin or mineral deficiency or a sensitivity to something in the diet, such as refined white sugar or bleached and brominated flour.

STOMACH AND INTESTINAL PROBLEMS

Stomach and intestinal problems are common in children. Typical symptoms include heartburn, spitting up, vomiting, diarrhea, intestinal gas, and constipation.

Gastroesophageal Reflux, Spitting Up, and Heartburn

Gastroesophageal reflux is a medical condition in which the stomach tends to regurgitate its contents up the esophagus. Normally, when a person swallows, the lower esophageal sphincter (a ringlike muscle located at the junction of the lower esophagus and stomach entrance) automatically relaxes and allows food and liquid to enter the stomach; once the meal is finished, the sphincter muscle is supposed to contract and remain tightly closed to prevent regurgitation as the stomach squeezes the food. In about 10 percent of babies, however, the lower esophageal sphincter is immature and relaxes for prolonged periods of time, allowing the stomach contents to reflux back into the esophagus, sometimes rather forcefully and painfully. The sphincter muscle usually matures and begins to function properly in most children by 9–12 months of age, but in the meantime, after verifying the diagnosis with your doctor, there are several measures you can take to ease your baby's discomfort (outlined later in this section).

Common symptoms of gastroesophageal reflux include spitting up, vomiting, and heartburn. Heartburn (acid indigestion) usually manifests itself as intense crying spasms due to the burning pain of stomach acid regurgitating up the esophagus. Sometimes the symptoms are more subtle, such as grunting noises, squirming and fidgeting in apparent discomfort, or making repetitive gagging or swallowing movements due to the unpleasant sensation of stomach acid in the back of the throat. Typically the symptoms improve when you hold the baby in a vertical or forward-leaning position, and they get much worse when you place the baby flat on his back or lean him backward in a semireclining position (as in an infant carrier seat or car seat, for example).

Chronic hoarseness or coughing, wheezing, failure to gain weight, difficulty swallowing, and/or seizurelike muscle spasms are infrequent symptoms of gastroesophageal reflux.

Rarely, in babies under one year of age, gastroesophageal reflux can trigger a life-threatening neurologic reflex that automatically shuts the windpipe, stops the breathing, and drastically slows the heartbeat; if this happens while the baby is awake, he will appear frantic or in shock (like a choking person with a foreign object stuck in his throat) and may collapse; immediately dial 911 for emergency medical services and start appropriate CPR maneuvers. If your baby ever experiences one of these rare, life-threatening choking episodes, ask your doctor about renting an apnea/heart monitor to use during sleep to reduce the risk of sudden infant death syndrome (SIDS).

Leading Causes of Spitting Up and Heartburn

The leading causes of spitting up and heartburn in babies include gastroesophageal reflux, gulping formula or breast milk too fast, over-feeding, improper feeding or burping techniques, fastening the diaper too tightly around the waist after feedings, and an allergic reaction or intolerance to formula, breast milk, fruit juice, solid food, medicine, or vitamins.

Natural and Nontoxic Ways to Reduce Spitting Up, Heartburn, and Gastroesophageal Reflux

As long as your baby is gaining weight properly, feels good, and does not show any of the danger signs listed in the sections on fever and vomiting, the simple measures outlined here may help. But always check with your doctor first and have your child examined if spitting up or heartburn persists.

- Avoid overfeeding. Don't automatically feed an infant every time she cries. A newborn's stomach is small and fills to capacity very quickly, so offer your baby smaller portions every two or three hours rather than large amounts every four to six hours.

• Hold your infant in an upright or semiupright (45-degree angle) position during feedings. Don't feed your baby while she is lying flat and never feed her with a propped bottle.

• Fastening a diaper too tightly at the waist or flexing the legs into a full squat or frog posture increases pressure on your baby's stomach and makes the spitting up worse, so keep her diaper loose, especially after feedings, and try to avoid flexing the legs beyond a half-squat or normal sitting position.

• Avoid overstimulation at feeding time and avoid any unnecessary jostling for about two hours after a feeding, because it takes that long for the milk to move out of the stomach and into the intestines.

• Whenever the baby has a crying spell due to heartburn (acid indigestion), hold her upright against your shoulder in a vertical or forward-leaning position. Also, a few swallows of plain water may help wash down the stomach acid.

• If you suspect that an antibiotic, vitamin drops, or some other medication is causing the problem, contact your child's doctor before giving the next regularly scheduled dose to find out if the medicine or dosage needs to be changed. Vitamin C (ascorbic acid) and the B vitamins found in regular infant multivitamin drops can cause nausea and regurgitation in some babies, even when the drops are given during a feeding and washed down with formula or breast milk. Ask your doctor if it is OK to stop giving the vitamins for a week and see if the stomach problems improve.

• Infants who are prone to gastroesophageal reflux tend to cry and spit up more when they lean backward in a semireclining position (such as an infant carrier seat or car seat) or when they lie flat on their back or on their left side. If your baby fits this pattern, she will probably prefer being carried around in an upright position or in a kangaroo-pouch infant carrier, such as the Snugli from Gerry Baby Products (800-525-2472) or the Kapoochi from Medela (800-435-8316).

As far as sleeping positions are concerned, most babies with gastroesophageal reflux will regurgitate less and therefore sleep more safely and more comfortably lying on their stomach rather than on their back. Elevating the head of the crib about 15–20 degrees (on a secure platform) may further reduce the reflux for some. On the other hand, there are some babies who spit up less while lying on their backs. The point is, you'll have to experiment with different sleeping positions and crib elevations until you find the magic combination that's most comfortable for your baby. Do not make your baby sleep in a position that causes obvious discomfort or other symptoms of gastroesophageal reflux.

When gastroesophageal reflux causes significant heartburn or vomiting, some doctors suggest using Gerber instant rice or oatmeal cereal to help thicken the formula or breast milk so it stays down in the stomach. For example, mixing 1 tablespoon of cereal per ounce of formula yields a blend that is thin enough to pass through a nipple with an enlarged hole (or a so-called cross-cut or juice nipple, which you can buy at the supermarket). Another alternative is to mix 2 tablespoons of cereal in one ounce of formula, expressed breast milk, or water and offer the baby 5 or 6 teaspoons of the mixture during each feeding session.

• Peppermint, chocolate, tomatoes, and all fruit juices (especially orange and other citrus) tend to aggravate gastroesophageal reflux, so avoid these items completely if your child suffers from this problem.

• If you've been feeding your baby a milk-based formula and suspect the problem is an underlying cow's milk protein allergy or lactose sugar intolerance, consider the suggestions for switching formulas in the section on infant colic earlier in this chapter.

• Because a baby's sense of smell and taste are so well-developed, the food you offer should have a pleasant aroma and flavor for proper digestion to occur. Of the three national brand-name baby foods, Gerber has the best taste by far. Always perform your own taste test before you offer the food to your baby. (Don't share the same spoon, because saliva contains germs, which can transmit infections.) If it smells and tastes awful to you, chances are it's going to make your child spit up or have acid indigestion.

- If you're breast-feeding, a portion of almost everything you eat eventually winds up in the breast milk, so review your diet very carefully for any food or beverage that might be causing the spitting up or heartburn. Peppermint, chocolate, caffeine, tomatoes, and citrus juices are particularly likely to cause problems. See the breast-feeding information in Chapter 1 for a more detailed list.

Vomiting

Vomiting means an ounce or more of milk or food gushes with projectile force out of the mouth and sometimes even the nose. It's often preceded by retching or abdominal straining and obvious distress and discomfort. (If you have trouble judging the actual volume of the vomitus, just measure out one ounce of formula or milk and then pour it onto a washcloth or towel for comparison.) Spitting up (in contrast to vomiting) means a small amount of food or milk (less than an ounce) spurts effortlessly out of the baby's mouth without any straining or distress.

When a baby vomits infrequently (no more than twice a day), acts happy and feels good, continues to gain weight properly, and has no other symptoms of illness, the cause usually turns out to be gastroesophageal reflux, gulping formula or breast milk too fast, overfeeding, improper feeding or burping techniques, or fastening the diaper too tightly around the waist.

Leading Causes of Vomiting in a Sick Child

Many different disorders can make a child suddenly become sick and start vomiting, but viral and bacterial infections are the leading causes by far. Additional problems to consider include an allergy or adverse reaction to formula, food, medicine, or vitamins or a blockage in the digestive system, such as pyloric stenosis or an intestinal obstruction.

When to Call the Doctor About Vomiting

Have the doctor examine a child who has suddenly become sick and started vomiting if any of the following occur:

- The vomiting is accompanied by any of the danger signs outlined in the section on fever.
- The vomiting doesn't stop after 12 hours.
- The vomitus has blood or green bile in it. (Bile is green, and stomach acid is yellow.)
- The child has severe abdominal (stomach) pain or cramps.
- The child's abdomen (stomach) is bloated or tender to the touch.
- The child shows signs of dehydration, such as a 5 percent drop in body weight, dry mouth (little or no saliva), sunken eyes, hardly any tears when crying, failure to pass any urine for 10 hours, extreme thirst, too weak to stand or sit, fast heartbeat, rapid breathing.
- The child has fever higher than 101° F.
- The child sustained a head injury that caused a brain concussion, skull fracture, or loss of consciousness.
- The child swallowed an object (coin, button, pin, or whatever) that might be blocking the digestive system.
- The child has any symptom that is causing significant distress.

Home Treatment Suggestions for Vomiting
Due to an Intestinal Virus Infection

If your child is vomiting because of an intestinal virus infection and no other signs of a serious illness appear, the following suggestions should help, but always check with your baby's doctor first.

- Let your child's stomach rest for a few hours (no food or drink except for sips of plain water) and then follow the "Oral Rehydration Therapy for Vomiting and Diarrhea" outlined in detail at the end of the section on diarrhea. Offer small sips (1 or 2 teaspoons) of the suggested oral electrolyte solutions (commercial or homemade) every few minutes and slowly increase the amount as soon as the vomiting shows signs of improvement. Don't force a resistant child to drink if she doesn't want to and don't let a thirsty child drink a large amount of fluid all at once, because either extreme will make the vomiting worse. The best method is to offer small amounts of fluid at frequent intervals.

Discontinue milk-based formula, cow's milk, and dairy products for the first day. If your child normally drinks a soy formula, your doctor will probably have you continue it, but check to be sure.

If you're breast-feeding, it's usually all right to keep nursing your baby since breast milk is easy to digest and contains antibodies to help fight off infections.

- A reliable sign of dehydration is a 5 percent drop in body weight (a 10 percent drop in weight is a sign of severe dehydration), so it's a good idea to weigh your child on an ordinary bathroom scale as soon as the vomiting starts and every eight hours thereafter until it subsides. Record the weight each time. For example, if a child weighs 30 pounds, a 5 percent loss is 1½ pounds $(30 \times .05 = 1.5)$, and a 10 percent weight loss is 3 pounds $(30 \times .10 = 3)$.

If your child is too young to stand on the scale alone, hold her in your arms while you stand on the scale together and then subtract your weight from the total. Remember to reweigh yourself each time, because your body weight fluctuates by a pound or two during the day. And be sure your child wears the same clothing at each weighing because different clothes and shoes can throw the measurement off by as much as a pound or more.

- Don't give your child any fruit juices until he or she is completely well again, because fruit juices have a strong tendency to provoke vomiting and acid indigestion.

- Don't use antivomiting suppositories unless specifically instructed to do so by your doctor, because they often produce unpleasant side effects such as lethargy, disorientation, blurred vision, hyperactivity, and painful muscle spasms. Furthermore, such medications often lull parents and doctors into a false sense of security and delay the recognition of a serious underlying disorder. And although it rarely happens, some antivomiting suppositories can even provoke a seizure.

- Don't use Pepto-Bismol or Alka-Seltzer products that contain aspirin, because salicylates can produce side effects, such as nausea, vomiting, stomach ulcers and bleeding, impaired blood clotting, a severe allergic reaction, or an increased risk of developing the rare but serious illness called *Reye's syndrome*.
- When vomiting is caused by an infection, contagious germs are excreted in the vomitus, bowel movements, and other bodily fluids, so strict personal hygiene is essential.
- Red or purple food coloring may be confused with blood in the vomitus, and green dye looks like bile, so don't give your child food or drinks with these colors until the vomiting has stopped.
- If you suspect that an antibiotic or some other medication is causing the vomiting, contact your child's doctor before giving the next regularly scheduled dose to find out if the medicine or dosage needs to be changed. Vitamin drops contain ingredients that sometimes irritate the stomach, so you may want to stop them temporarily.

Diarrhea

Diarrhea is defined as a noticeable change in a child's normal pattern of stooling such that the bowel movements suddenly become much looser, larger, and/or more frequent. With that definition in mind, diarrhea can be classified as mild, moderate, or severe based on the following criteria:

- Mild: three or four diarrhea stools per day. There is no weight loss, and the child does not act sick.
- Moderate: five or six diarrhea stools per day. The stools almost fill the diaper, and the child will usually act fussy and may lose weight.

• Severe: seven or more watery, explosive diarrhea stools per day. The stools completely fill the diaper and may even run down the legs. The child loses weight quickly and acts very sick. A doctor should examine the child immediately.

Please note that some babies (especially those who are breast-feeding) pass loose stools several times a day, but this is usually not considered diarrhea as long as the child is happy, gaining weight properly, not vomiting, and having no symptoms of illness.

Leading Causes of Diarrhea in Children

There are many reasons why children develop diarrhea, but the leading causes include the following:

Intestinal infection. Viruses (rotavirus, Norwalk viruses, coronaviruses, and adenoviruses), bacteria (E. coli, salmonella, shigella, and campylobacter), and parasites (*Giardia* and *Cryptosporidium*) are the most common causes of acute diarrhea in children. The diarrhea usually lasts about two to seven days, and the infection may be mild, moderate, or severe, depending on how well the child's immune system is functioning at the time of exposure.

Apple juice or prune juice. Drinking more than six ounces of apple juice or prune juice a day can often cause diarrhea in young children.

Food or milk allergy or sensitivity. A child may suddenly become allergic or sensitive to formula, milk, fruit juice, or solid food. The diarrhea stops as soon as the offending item is removed from the diet.

Lactose sugar intolerance. Lactose is the primary sugar in breast milk, cow's milk formulas (Similac, Enfamil, SMA, Gerber), and dairy products (milk, cheese, ice cream). Children with lactose intolerance are deficient in lactase, an intestinal enzyme needed to digest lactose. Shortly after consumption of milk or dairy products, lactose-intolerant persons develop nausea, gas, abdominal cramps, and diarrhea. The symptoms usually subside within 24–48 hours after totally removing lactose sugar from the diet.

Sorbitol sugar intolerance. Sorbitol is a sugar used to sweeten several brands of "sugarless" gum, hard candy, jams, and jellies. Excess consumption of sorbitol sugar can result in gas, abdominal pain, and diarrhea.

Food poisoning or spoiled food. Food poisoning causes nausea, vomiting, gas, painful abdominal cramps, and diarrhea within 1–24 hours after consumption of the contaminated food or drink. Other people who ate or drank the same items have similar symptoms. The diarrhea usually stops after a day or two.

Medication intolerance. Antibiotics are notorious for causing diarrhea. If you suspect a medicine or vitamin is causing your child to have diarrhea, contact the doctor before the next regularly scheduled dose to find out if the medicine or dosage needs to be changed or discontinued completely.

When to Call the Doctor About Diarrhea

Have the doctor examine your child if any of the following danger signs accompany the diarrhea:

- The child has more than four large diarrhea stools within a 24-hour period.
- The diarrhea doesn't clear up after a few days.
- The diarrhea stools have blood and/or mucus in them.
- The child has severe abdominal (stomach) pain or cramps.
- The child's abdomen (stomach) is bloated or tender to the touch.
- The child vomits more than just a few times or the vomitus has blood or green bile in it.
- The child shows signs of dehydration. The first signs include a 5 percent drop in body weight, dry mouth (little or no saliva), sunken eyes, hardly any tears when crying, failure to pass any urine for 10 hours, and extreme thirst; the signs of severe dehydration include a 10 percent drop in body weight, fast heartbeat, rapid breathing, loss of muscle strength (too weak to stand or sit), little or no effort to drink, and failure to pass any urine for 18 hours.
- The child looks sick or is crying inconsolably.
- The child has fever higher than 101° F.

• The child has any symptom that is causing significant distress or concerns you, and you don't know what to do.

Home Treatment Suggestions for Diarrhea
Due to an Intestinal Virus

If your child has only a mild case of diarrhea, there's no need to make any changes at all in the diet. On the other hand, if the diarrhea is due to an intestinal virus infection that's causing a moderate increase in the number of stools without any other signs of a serious illness, the following home treatment suggestions should help, but always check with your child's doctor first:

For a mild case of diarrhea, stick with a routine diet, but keep the menu light, bland, and nonspicy.

For a moderate or severe case of diarrhea, see the doctor right away and follow the "Oral Rehydration Therapy for Vomiting and Diarrhea" outlined at the end of this section. Follow the procedure in the section on vomiting for weighing your child to determine whether she is dehydrated. In addition, the following chart provides a rough guideline (based on body weight) for the minimum number of fluid ounces that an average child with moderate diarrhea (but without any fever or vomiting) needs to drink every 24 hours to prevent dehydration. Of course, these estimates have to be adjusted to meet your child's individual needs depending on additional factors, such as intensity of thirst, urine output, fever, vomiting, severity of diarrhea, and overall response to treatment, so always check with the doctor to be sure you're providing the right amount of fluids for your child.

Let your child drink more than the suggested minimum daily amount if she desires, but to prevent vomiting and bloating it's better to offer small amounts of fluid every 15–30 minutes while she's awake than a large amount all at once.

Keep in mind that *all fruit juices make diarrhea worse, so do not give your child any fruit juices until his or her diarrhea stops completely.* Also don't give the baby red food or drinks, because the red color may be mistaken for blood in the bowel movements.

Children with diarrhea due to a virus infection may temporarily have trouble digesting the lactose in milk-based formulas and dairy products, so you may want to avoid those items for a day or two and switch to a milk-free, lactose-free soy formula, such as Isomil or Isomil DF (*DF* stands for "diarrhea formulation") until the stools firm up.

As with vomiting, it is usually OK to continue breast-feeding your baby during a bout of diarrhea, because even though lactose is the primary sugar in breast milk, the protein and fat portions are very easy to digest, and breast milk contains antibodies to help fight the infection.

Child's Weight	Minimum Fluid Intake per 24 Hours
12 pounds	28 ounces
15 pounds	34 ounces
18 pounds	38 ounces
21 pounds	42 ounces
24 pounds	48 ounces
27 pounds	54 ounces
30 pounds	60 ounces

It's generally a good idea to continue feeding your child bland, starchy foods. Cereals (rice or oatmeal), bread, rolls, plain pasta noodles, and potassium-rich bananas, carrots, and sweet potatoes are good choices. You can also offer applesauce, pears, rice, chicken noodle or chicken with rice soup, plain saltine crackers, mashed potatoes, and boiled or baked chicken or turkey.

Try not to give your child any antidiarrhea medications. The World Health Organization (WHO) and the Centers for Disease Control report that many of the prescription and over-the-counter antidiarrhea medicines—especially the antimotility drugs such as Lomotil and Imodium—prevent the body from flushing out harmful toxins and thereby do more harm than good. And don't use Pepto-Bismol, because it contains salicylate. However, for those parents who feel they have to give their child an antidiarrhea medicine, Diasorb Liquid and Kaopectate (regular flavor) are generally safe choices.

If you suspect that an antibiotic or some other medication is making your child's diarrhea worse, contact your child's doctor before giving the next regularly scheduled dose to find out if the medicine or dosage needs to be changed.

When acute diarrhea is caused by an infection (which it is most of the time), contagious germs are excreted in the stools and in other bodily fluids, so strict personal hygiene is essential to prevent the infection from spreading. Also, diarrhea stools are extremely irritating to the skin, so coat your baby's bottom with a thick layer of Eckerd or Walgreens brand zinc oxide ointment or plain Vaseline at every diaper change to serve as a protective barrier between the skin and the bowel movements. Use superabsorbent disposable diapers to soak up the liquid stool; change the diapers as soon as they get soiled. Gently rinse the diaper area with plain water as explained in Chapter 2.

Oral Rehydration Therapy for Vomiting and Diarrhea

Oral rehydration therapy (ORT) is intended primarily for the short-term (one or two days) treatment of vomiting and/or diarrhea due to an intestinal virus infection. Basically it consists of having your child drink the recommended oral electrolyte solutions (commercial or home-made) to replace the sodium, potassium, chloride, and bicarbonate lost in the vomitus and/or stools. Offer the electrolyte solutions at frequent intervals in small to moderate amounts, because vomiting and bloating will occur if your child drinks a large quantity all at once.

"Commercial" oral electrolyte solutions such as Infalyte and Pedialyte contain the perfect balance of electrolytes—sodium, potassium, chloride, bicarbonate/citrate—but they are expensive, they don't taste very good, and some brands actually cause heartburn and regurgitation. Refrigerating the electrolyte solution, pouring it over ice, or making ice cubes out of it will improve the flavor somewhat, but in spite of all your best efforts your child may refuse to drink it or will actually vomit it right up. (If you decide to try a commercial oral electrolyte solution, I suggest Infalyte, because it has the best taste of all the brands currently available.)

Homemade oral electrolyte solutions are inexpensive and taste much better than the commercial brands, but you must use accurate measuring spoons and cups to measure out each ingredient exactly according to one of the following standard recipes. Too much or too little of an ingredient can result in a dangerous solution that could cause diarrhea, dehydration, and/or serious electrolyte imbalances. I would also suggest trying the cereal-based recipe first, because it provides more calories than the banana-based recipe. Or make both recipes and store them in separate containers, then alternate them to see which one your child likes best. You can either spoon-feed the electrolyte solution or let your child drink it from a cup. Always taste the mixtures before offering them to your child; do not use any solution that has a salty taste. And please note that homemade oral electrolyte solutions are designed for children who are over six months old.

Cereal-Based Oral Electrolyte Solution

Using an accurate measuring spoon, measure out ¼ teaspoon salt, level with a knife, and dissolve the salt in 2 cups of water. Gradually stir in ¾–1 cup dry infant rice or oatmeal cereal (depending on your child's taste preference). Gerber baby cereal is the best brand. The mixture should be easily spoonable and drinkable. Discard any unused portion of the mixture after six hours or if it becomes too thick to drink.

It's worth noting that children with diarrhea lose a considerable amount of potassium in their stools. The cereal-based recipe does not contain much potassium, so if your child is having more than just a mild case of diarrhea, you may want to boost his or her potassium intake by offering supplements of potassium-rich bananas (assuming your child likes bananas and normally has no trouble digesting them). Along with every two cups of cereal-based solution, offer two ounces of strained Gerber bananas or half of a small ripe fresh banana (mashed or in age-appropriate slices). Or you can alternate the banana-based and cereal-based recipes. Incidentally, oatmeal cereal contains twice as much potassium as rice cereal.

Banana-Based Oral Electrolyte Solution

Pour 2 cups of water into a blender or food processor. Using an accurate measuring spoon, measure ¼ teaspoon salt, level with a knife, and add

the salt to the water. Then add 3 teaspoons of regular table (granu-
lated) sugar and a medium-size ripe fresh banana. Blend to a smooth
consistency. Keep the mixture refrigerated and discard any unused
portion after six hours. (Do not use this recipe if your child normally
doesn't like bananas or has trouble digesting them.)

Sport Drinks

For children over one year old who totally reject both the commercial
and the homemade oral electrolyte solutions, some doctors recommend
sport drinks such as Gatorade, or clear carbonated beverages (7UP or
Sprite, for example). The problem with these beverages is that they
have a high sugar content (which often creates an unfavorable osmotic
gradient that makes the diarrhea worse), and they do not have enough
sodium or potassium to maintain the proper electrolyte balance. I
would use them only as a last resort.

Resuming a Routine Diet

By the second day of the illness, your child should try to gradually
resume his or her routine diet. Starchy foods like cereals (rice or
oatmeal), bread, rolls, plain pasta noodles, and potassium-rich bananas
and carrots are especially good choices. You can also offer any of the
following bland solid foods that your child enjoyed prior to the illness:
applesauce, pears, rice, chicken noodle or chicken with rice soup, plain
saltine crackers, mashed potatoes, sweet potatoes, boiled or baked
chicken or turkey. *Do not give your child any fruit juices until he or she
is completely well.*

Continue to supplement the bland solid foods with one of the oral
electrolyte solutions (commercial or homemade) for a day or two if
necessary. You can also start formula feedings again if desired, but
increase the amount offered gradually. Some doctors prefer using a soy
formula (such as Isomil DF) for a few days until the stools firm up,
because soy sugar (sucrose) is easier to digest than cow's milk sugar
(lactose).

Don't worry if the diarrhea gets slightly worse when you resume
bland solid foods and/or formula. It's better to give your child enough
calories to recover from an illness, even though it might cause a little
extra diarrhea. Withholding adequate calories for more than just a few

days leads to malnutrition very quickly. Never starve your baby in a misguided attempt to make the diarrhea go away completely. It's much smarter to get your child back on a nutritious diet as soon as possible even though the stools may remain slightly loose. Always consult your child's doctor for an alternative dietary plan if the resumption of solid foods and/or formula causes any difficulties, such as vomiting, stomach cramps, weight loss, or frothy, foamy diarrhea stools.

Intestinal Gas

There are many reasons why babies have intestinal gas, but the leading causes include

- improper feeding or burping techniques
- infant colic (see the section on colic for complete details)
- allergic reaction or intolerance to formula, breast milk, fruit juice, solid food, medicine, or vitamins
- lactose sugar intolerance

It's normal for babies to have quite a bit of intestinal gas, especially during their first few months, but as long as they're happy and healthy and pass the gas without any problem, no further treatment is necessary. If intestinal gas causes stomach cramps and crying, you'll generally find the treatment suggestions in the section on infant colic quite helpful, but always check with your doctor first.

Constipation

Constipation is defined as a noticeable change in a child's normal pattern of stooling such that the bowel movements suddenly become much firmer (like modeling clay or dry pellets) and less frequent than usual.

There are many reasons why infants and children become constipated, but the leading causes include

- a family history of constipation problems
- formula or solid food allergy or intolerance

- abruptly switching from breast milk to formula or cow's milk
- excess consumption of cow's milk
- inadequate consumption of fiber from fruits, vegetables, and whole grains
- inadequate fluid intake
- irritation or soreness around the anus
- stressful events at home, day care, or school
- antihistamine and/or decongestant usage

The Way Things Should Go

By the fourth or fifth day of your baby's life, her bowel movements should be yellow or mustard-golden and look like tiny birdseed or scrambled eggs mixed with water. (If your baby is not having normal yellow bowel movements by the fifth day, a doctor should examine her right away to check out the possibility of an inadequate milk supply or a digestive system problem.)

During the first six months most babies pass soft yellow to yellowish green stools. Formula-fed babies typically pass 3 to 6 stools a day, while breast-fed infants may have as many as 8 to 10 bowel movements daily. Some babies have a regular biorhythm and stool at almost the same time every day (you could practically set your clock by it), while others are so erratic that they never seem to do anything on schedule. All of these patterns are normal as long as the baby feels good and gains weight properly and the stools remain soft.

Infrequent stooling in an exclusively breast-fed infant under one month old is often due to inadequate breast milk intake. Between the second and fifth months, however, it's not uncommon for breast-fed babies to go through temporary phases of "irregularity" where they have only one very large soft bowel movement once every three or four days for a few weeks and then go right back to being regular again. Most of the time it's normal, but always check with your doctor to be sure there's no underlying problem.

A baby may strain, grunt, and turn red in the face while trying to have a bowel movement, but that doesn't necessarily mean he is constipated. In fact, if your infant is passing at least one soft stool a day, the straining is probably not due to constipation and does not require any special treatment. However, there are some things you can do to help work out the problem. During the straining episodes, let the baby push his feet against your hands while his legs remain flexed in a half-squat or sitting position or simply move his legs back and forth in a bicycle-pedaling motion. These maneuvers help the rectal muscle release a bowel movement with less effort. Just imagine how hard it would be for you to pass a stool if you were lying flat on your back and unable to push your feet against the floor.

Treatment for Simple Constipation

Simple constipation means there aren't any other symptoms of illness. The following suggestions should help, but always consult your doctor first, especially if constipation persists for more than a day or becomes a recurrent or chronic problem.

If your baby usually drinks Similac or Gerber formula, ask your doctor about switching to Enfamil or SMA (or vice versa) or possibly a soy formula and see if the constipation improves. Enfamil and soy-based formulas tend to make the stools change color from yellow to green, but this is no cause for concern. If you are weaning your baby from breast-feeding to formula or cow's milk, make the change gradually, not abruptly.

Make sure your child is drinking enough fluids. Offer four extra ounces of plain water once or twice a day.

For children over one year old, limit their intake of cow's milk to no more than 20 ounces of milk per day and encourage them to eat plenty of nutritious high-fiber foods, such as bran muffins, oatmeal, whole-grain cereals and breads, fresh fruits, and fresh vegetables. Apple, grape, and prune juice are also quite effective.

Many babies respond favorably to 4–5 teaspoons of Gerber pears, applesauce, or prunes twice a day. Another effective regimen is three or four ounces of Gerber fruit juice—prune, apple, apple-prune, or grape—once or twice a day. By trial and error you'll be able to figure out just the right amount to give your child to soften the stools without making them too loose. (Rice cereal and bananas cause constipation in some babies, so it might be wise to eliminate them from the diet until the stools become soft again.)

Do not use corn syrup or honey to relieve constipation in children under one year old, because both products may contain botulism spores, which can be very harmful to babies.

If immediate relief is required, gently insert an infant-size glycerin suppository into the rectum and hold the buttocks together for two minutes so that it has time to dissolve. (Glycerin suppositories are sold over the counter in the laxative section of the pharmacy.) Another trick that works on the same principle is to insert a rectal thermometer about ½ inch into the anus (see the section on fever for detailed instructions). Do not make a habit of using these anal stimulation techniques, however, because your baby may become dependent on them. And never use enemas unless you are specifically instructed to do so by your baby's doctor; improper use of enemas can cause a dangerous imbalance of the blood electrolytes and lead to a seizure.

Stop all antihistamines and decongestants; they significantly disrupt the neurologic impulse to contract the colon and stimulate defecation.

Finally, if your baby's anus looks red or irritated, apply Eckerd or Walgreens brand zinc oxide ointment or plain Vaseline three or four times a day. If the problem doesn't clear up within two days, consult your doctor.

SUDDEN INFANT DEATH SYNDROME (SIDS)

The term *sudden infant death syndrome (SIDS)* is used to describe a condition that causes an infant to die suddenly and unexpectedly during sleep. Statistics indicate that about 1 out of every 500 infants dies of SIDS, but that number is based on general population figures without taking into account factors known to increase the risk of SIDS. In other words, the actual chance of SIDS happening to your baby is going to be a lot lower because, as a modern "ecological parent," you'll be following the precautions outlined in this section.

Over 90 percent of SIDS cases occur when babies are between the ages of three weeks and six months. It very rarely happens to babies older than eight months. Although no one knows the exact cause of

SIDS, most experts believe the underlying problem is that for the first eight months of life a baby's vital organs—heart, windpipe, lungs, and breathing control center in the brain—are immature and thus vulnerable to failing under stress. During this susceptible time period exposure to a SIDS risk factor can sometimes trigger an abnormal heartbeat, choking episode, or abnormal breathing pattern severe enough to be fatal.

12 Risk Factors Linked to SIDS

Twelve risk factors have been linked to SIDS, the four most important being (1) exposure to tobacco smoke, (2) sleeping facedown on the stomach, (3) sleeping on a soft surface, and (4) thermal stress. Please note that the factors 5–12 are not ranked in order of importance.

1. Tobacco Smoke Exposure

It's a proven fact that tobacco smoke contains many toxic poisons—carbon monoxide, formaldehyde, benzene, and the like—that can severely damage a baby's windpipe, lungs, and breathing control center in the brain. According to the latest scientific research, exposing a baby to moderate smoking (1–9 cigarettes per day) doubles the risk of death from SIDS, and exposure to heavy smoking (10 or more cigarettes per day) triples it.

2. Facedown (Prone) Sleeping Position

Allowing a baby to sleep on her stomach facedown (the so-called *prone position*) triples the risk of SIDS. The reason for this association is not completely understood at present. Some doctors speculate that sleeping on the stomach can upset the delicate temperature regulation of the infant. Others say that sleeping facedown places the nose in a position that either obstructs the airway directly or causes the infant to rebreathe too much of her own exhaled carbon dioxide and/or inhale toxic fumes that constantly outgas from certain kinds of mattress and bedding material. Foam rubber mattresses and vinyl plastic mattress coverings, for example, may release several toxic gases, such as phosphine, arsine, and stibine. Breathing high concentrations of these gases promotes the accumulation of acetylcholine within the body and, in susceptible babies, can cause the heart to stop beating properly. These toxic gases are heavier than air and are found in highest concentrations near the surface of the mattress, where a baby sleeping on her stomach would have her nose. Flame-retardants and other chemical treatments can also release these toxic gases.

3. Sleeping on a Soft Surface

An infant 12 months or younger can suffocate during sleep if her face becomes wedged or embedded in a soft surface, such as a pillow, water bed, lambskin or sheepskin rug, quilt, comforter, thick blanket, mattress pad, or beanbag cushion filled with polystyrene beads. When a baby sleeps facedown on soft bedding, she rebreathes her own exhaled air (like a person breathing into a paper bag), and death results when she breathes in too much carbon dioxide and not enough fresh oxygen. Also, when a baby sleeps in the same bed with her parents, either the mother or father may accidentally roll over and smother her without realizing it (so-called overlying).

4. Thermal Stress

Getting too hot (hyperthermia) or too cold (hypothermia) puts excessive stress on the baby's cardiovascular system and breathing control center in the brain. Hyperthermia is usually caused by overheating the infant's room or by heavily overdressing, swaddling, or wrapping the baby in too many blankets, especially during sleep.

5. Infections

Respiratory infections, such as the common cold, flu, croup, pneumonia, or whooping cough, and stomach or intestinal infections can sometimes stress an infant's body enough to trigger a fatal episode of choking, cessation of breathing, gastroesophageal reflux, or an abnormal heartbeat.

6. Gastroesophageal Reflux

This medical term simply means the baby's stomach tends to regurgitate its contents up the esophagus. Actually, the reflux of food and stomach acid is a common occurrence in healthy infants and hardly ever causes much of a problem. On rare occasions, however, gastroesophageal reflux can trigger a life-threatening neurologic reflex that automatically shuts the windpipe, stops the breathing, and/or causes an abnormal heartbeat. See the section on gastroesophageal reflux for details and prevention tips.

7. Abnormal Heartbeat

Many SIDS cases are due to cardiac arrhythmias, disturbances of the normal heart rhythm that cause the baby's heart to beat so slowly (bradycardia), so fast (tachycardia), or so irregularly that it no longer pumps enough blood to keep the baby alive. Abnormal heartbeats can be triggered by an infection, gastroesophageal reflux, a medication, the Long Q-T syndrome, or the W-P-W syndrome. These last two syndromes cause problems in the conduction of electrical signals within the heart, making it susceptible to abnormal and potentially fatal arrhythmias. A routine EKG can usually diagnose the Long Q-T syndrome or the W-P-W syndrome; if either is detected, a cardiologist can prescribe safe and effective preventive treatments.

8. Alcohol

Alcoholic beverages or medicine that contains a high concentration of alcohol can cause a baby to choke or develop an abnormal heartbeat. If you're breast-feeding, don't forget that alcohol gets into your breast milk whenever you drink an alcoholic beverage.

9. Prescription and Over-the-Counter Medicine

When used improperly in babies under 12 months of age, the following prescription and over-the-counter medications can cause serious side effects, such as choking, abnormal breathing patterns, suppression of the breathing control center in the brain, or an abnormal heartbeat:

• Sedatives (phenobarbital, chloral hydrate)
• Narcotics (codeine, paregoric)
• Diarrhea medicine (Lomotil, Parepectolin, Imodium)
• Suppositories to stop vomiting (Phenergan, Tigan)
• Colic or antispasmodic medicine (Levsin, Bentyl, Donnatal)
• Antihistamines and common cold medicines (Dimetapp, Actifed, Triaminic, Novahistine, PediaCare, Benadryl, Atarax, Contac Jr., Chlor-Trimeton, Co-Tylenol, Nyquil, Rondec, Bromfed, Phenergan, and many others)
• Decongestants (Sudafed, pseudoephedrine, phenylpropanolamine)
• Cough syrups (Phenergan, codeine, dextromethorphan, Robitussin, and many others)
• Teething liquids or gels

Please note that this is not a complete list. The brand names mentioned are only common examples for each category of medicine, and the absence of a particular brand from the listing does not in any way imply that it is safe.

10. Infant Botulism

Botulism in a baby under one year of age paralyzes the muscles required for breathing. For details, see "Honey, Corn Syrup, and Botulism" in Chapter 1.

11. Asbestos

Microscopic asbestoslike particles have been found lodged inside the lungs of some babies who've died of SIDS. These particles interfere with the proper flow of oxygen through the lungs. Talcum powder is often contaminated with asbestos or fibers chemically similar to asbestos.

12. MCAD Deficiency

MCAD is an acronym that stands for medium-chain acyl-coA dehydroge-nase, an enzyme essential for the proper metabolism of fatty acids. MCAD deficiency is a genetically inherited abnormality of fatty acid metabolism that can cause symptoms mimicking SIDS or Reye's syn-drome. In fact, approximately 2 percent of infants who die with a diagnosis of SIDS actually have MCAD deficiency. The good news is that now there's a DNA blood test that can easily diagnose MCAD deficiency, and effective preventive treatment is readily available. Any child who dies of SIDS should have his or her blood tested for MCAD deficiency; if the metabolic disorder is detected, all brothers and sisters of the victim should then be tested to identify those who carry the gene but may not have obvious symptoms. Test results are also very helpful for parents of SIDS victims planning future pregnancies.

Preventing
Sudden Infant Death Syndrome

Unfortunately there's no surefire way to tell in advance which infants are susceptible to SIDS and which ones aren't, but you can reduce your baby's risk tremendously by following 15 simple precautions during the first year. The goal is to give your baby's vital organs—heart, windpipe, lungs, brain—enough time to mature before being subjected to stress-ful events. Obviously, the more risk factors you eliminate, the more you lower the chance of SIDS occurring.

1. First and foremost, you must totally avoid all tobacco smoke exposure! Never allow any smoking inside your house or car. Don't smoke during pregnancy and don't let people who are smoking get anywhere near you or your baby.
2. Always ask your doctor about the best sleeping position for your baby, but experts in SIDS research suggest putting most infants (see exceptions) to sleep on their back (faceup) for

naps and at bedtime (at least for the first six months). This one simple precaution can reduce your baby's risk of SIDS by 50 percent.

I generally don't recommend placing infants on their side to sleep, because it tends to bend their neck in an awkward position, makes it easier for them to roll over on their stomach, and in some cases increases regurgitation of stomach contents (especially lying on the left side). In fact, studies have found that sleeping on the side is not as effective in preventing SIDS as sleeping on the back.

Exceptions: The American Academy of Pediatrics believes that babies with the following medical conditions should avoid sleeping on their back or side: (a) infants born with abnormally small or receding lower jaws or other birth defects causing upper airway obstruction and (b) babies who vomit frequently or have significant gastroesophageal reflux (read the section on gastroesophageal reflux for details). In addition, there are some infants who, for unexplained reasons, become very irritable or uncomfortable when placed on their backs. It's generally safer for a baby with one of these problems to sleep on his or her stomach, but ask your doctor first to be sure. Never force an infant to sleep in a position that causes obvious discomfort.

3. The crib and/or bassinet mattress must be firm—not soft or spongy. Cover the mattress with 100 percent cotton sheets. Do not use mattress pads. Avoid crib mattresses with latex or foam rubber interiors or vinyl plastic covers, because they outgas toxic fumes. See Chapter 3 for details on crib mattress selection.
4. Avoid clothing and bedding treated with dangerous chemicals. See Chapter 3 for details on purchasing nontoxic clothing and bedding.
5. Don't let your baby sleep on a pillow, water bed, lambskin or sheepskin rug, quilt, comforter, folded blanket, mattress pad, beanbag cushion filled with polystyrene beads, or any other soft, fluffy, or thick bedding materials, because his face may

become wedged or embedded in the soft surface, making it impossible for him to breathe enough oxygen. Don't place stuffed toys in the crib. To further reduce the risk of accidental suffocation, the baby should sleep in his own crib—not in the parents' bed. Of course, it's OK to place the crib right next to the parents' bed if desired. If you take the baby into your bed to nurse, be sure to put him back in his own crib when he's finished.

6. Don't let your baby get overheated (hyperthermia), especially during sleep. Avoid overheating the house, particularly the baby's room. Keep the indoor temperature in a comfortable range. Never use electric blankets or heating pads. Avoid over-dressing, swaddling, and overbundling and don't cover the baby's head during sleep; all of these things impede heat loss and impair normal body temperature regulation. Avoid heavy sleepwear and blankets that restrict movement. Moderation is the key. One layer of lightweight 100 percent cotton clothing, socks, and a thin, lightweight, 100 percent cotton blanket is usually adequate indoors when the weather is mild, with an additional cotton blanket for colder weather if necessary. And it's worth noting that hypothermia can also be quite stressful to your baby's cardiovascular system, so don't take your infant outdoors for extended periods of time on cold and blustery winter days.

7. Protect your child's immature lungs and respiratory system by avoiding things that have strong fumes or spew chemicals into the air, such as cologne, perfume, baby powder, new furniture, foam insulation, remodeling materials, particleboard/pressed wood and other plywood products, new carpeting or uphol-stery, insect sprays and foggers, aerosol sprays (hair spray, deodorant, Lysol, and the like), air fresheners and room de-odorizers, disinfectants, household cleaning agents, ammo-nia, bleach, fresh paint or varnish, paint thinners or strippers, turpentine, solvents, glue, adhesives, air pollution, smog, smoke from candles or fireplaces, gas or wood-burning stoves, kerosene heaters, gasoline, and automobile exhaust. Chapter 6

provides details on choosing nontoxic/low-toxic materials for
your house. Avoid any home remodeling until the baby is at
least nine months old.

8. Avoid exposure to hazardous airborne particles such as talc,
   asbestos, and heavy metals (lead, mercury, aluminum, etc.).
   Talcum powder is chemically similar to asbestos, so never use
   powder on your baby. And don't use ultrasonic humidifiers,
   because the ultrafine mist often contains unacceptably high
   levels of aluminum, asbestos, lead, and other dangerous im-
   purities.

9. Since infections are very stressful to babies, don't let your
   child get near anyone who has fever, a runny nose or congestion, hoarseness, coughing, vomiting, diarrhea, a skin rash, or
   fever blisters. The safest thing to do is limit the number of
   people who have contact with your baby, and for the first eight
   months, try not to take your child to places where lots of
   people and their germs are gathered, such as shopping malls,
   supermarkets, church, theaters, and daycare centers.

10. When used improperly in babies under one year, the prescrip-
    tion and over-the-counter medications listed under "12 Risk
    Factors Linked to SIDS" can cause serious side effects, so don't
    give them to your child unless it's absolutely necessary and
    only under the supervision of a doctor.

11. If you're breast-feeding, don't forget that everything you take
    enters the breast milk. See Chapter 1 for a list of medications
    and drugs to avoid while breast-feeding.

12. Do not use over-the-counter teething gels and liquids, because
    the ingredients can numb the protective gag reflex in the
    throat and allow the baby to choke. And never use paregoric
    (which is tincture of opium), whiskey, or any alcoholic bever-
    age on the gums for teething.

13. It's dangerous to administer any immunization when there are
    signs of an illness, because an immunization will add extra
    stress to the child's body at the same time she is trying to fight
    off an infection.

14. Do not give your child honey or corn syrup during the first year. And, if you work outside and get dusty and dirty, be sure to bathe and change your clothes as soon as you come home (before handling the baby), because soil is sometimes heavily contaminated with botulism spores.

15. All fruit juices have a tendency to cause spitting up and acid indigestion in babies. Therefore I strongly suggest waiting until your child is at least eight months old before you offer her any fruit juice. And if your child has a tendency toward stomach acid regurgitation, there are several helpful suggestions in the section on gastroesophageal reflux.

6
The Natural and Nontoxic Home

Environmental pollutants can enter the body through the lungs, the digestive system, and the skin. That's why children are often the first ones to show the effects of exposure to pollutants inside the home. They eat, drink, and breathe more pollutants per pound of body weight than adults, and their thinner skin allows greater absorption of pollutants. Youngsters are less able to neutralize dangerous chemicals due to the immaturity of their liver detoxification and immune systems. Also, during the first two years of life the brain is especially susceptible to toxic insult because it is growing so rapidly. Finally, many toxic pollutants are heavier than air, which means the highest concentration is near the floor, where crawling babies and toddlers are playing.

It's not hard or expensive to protect your family from the daily onslaught of environmental poisons in the home. It simply involves knowing how to make the right choices and prudently avoiding obvious sources of danger. Indoor air pollutants, electromagnetic fields, and lead poisoning are the three major areas to consider when trying to make your home as natural and nontoxic as possible.

Please note that the information presented in this chapter is particularly applicable to the nursery, since your baby will be spending more time there than anywhere else in the house.

INDOOR AIR POLLUTANTS

The healthfulness of indoor air depends on how many chemical, biological, and radioactive pollutants it contains. Unfortunately, when you construct airtight homes and schools to lower energy costs, you automatically reduce fresh-air ventilation so that the dirty indoor air recirculates in a "closed loop" fashion, progressively building up higher and higher levels of toxic chemicals and allergens. According to recent government studies, the level of residential indoor air pollution often exceeds the outdoor federal air-quality safety standards by a substantial margin; in fact, the Environmental Protection Agency has found that air-pollutant levels indoors are commonly 10–20 times higher than outdoors.

Air is one of the primary routes of exposure for chemical, biological, and radioactive pollutants. The average baby inhales about 1,100 liters of air every 24 hours, the average five-year-old about 3,500 liters of air per day, and the average adult approximately 10,000 liters of air daily. The point is, no matter how old you are, there's a lot of air passing into and out of your lungs on a daily basis. Couple this with the fact that, on average, children spend approximately 90 percent of their time indoors, and you can see why it's so important to keep the air inside your home as healthy as it can possibly be.

Common Symptoms and Health Effects of Breathing Air Pollutants

When a chemical or biological pollutant comes into contact with the human body, it can trigger a toxic reaction in which the affected organs or systems malfunction or fail completely, or it can provoke an allergic reaction in which the affected organs or systems become itchy, irritated, red, and swollen and begin to secrete copious amounts of mucus in an attempt to wash away the toxic substance. Therefore, the symptoms caused by breathing indoor air pollutants are quite varied and depend on the level and duration of the exposure, the specific bodily organs or systems targeted by the pollutant, the type of reaction triggered (toxic versus allergic), and the ability of the liver and immune system to detoxify and neutralize the pollutant.

Breathing indoor air pollutants can cause any of the following physical symptoms either singly or in combination: headaches, dizziness, blurred vision, red and watery eyes, burning or itchy eyes, sneezing, nasal congestion, runny nose, postnasal drip, sore throat, hoarseness, coughing, wheezing, breathing difficulties, shortness of breath, chest pain, irregular heartbeat, jaundice, nausea, vomiting, diarrhea, abdominal pain, water retention or generalized swelling, eczema, and hives and other skin rashes.

Mental, behavioral, or brain dysfunction symptoms may include insomnia, depression, anxiety, panic attacks, mood swings, Alzheimer-like disorientation and confusion, memory loss, forgetfulness, hallucinations, loss of coordination, irritability, hyperactivity, and attention deficit disorder.

Chronic exposure to air pollutants can also damage and weaken the immune system, resulting in immune-related illnesses such as cancer, frequent infections, sick-all-the-time syndrome, allergies, asthma, multiple chemical sensitivity (MCS) or environmental illness (EI), chronic fatigue, immune system dysfunction, endometriosis, lupus, rheumatoid arthritis, and multiple sclerosis.

If your child or another family member exhibits any of these health problems without a readily apparent explanation, consider the possibility of toxic air pollutants as the underlying cause, especially if the symptoms go away when you leave the home but promptly relapse as soon as you return.

Major Sources of Indoor Air Pollutants

The major indoor air pollutants are volatile organic compounds such as benzene, toluene, xylene, styrene, 4-PC, and formaldehyde; carbon monoxide; nitrogen oxides; sulfur dioxide; radon; asbestos; ozone; chlorine; ammonia; biological inhalant allergens such as plant pollens, molds, fungi, and house dust mites; and cigarette, cigar, or pipe smoke.

Volatile Organic Compounds (VOCs)

By definition, any chemical that contains carbon atoms is an organic compound, and in addition, if it evaporates or gives off gas fumes (outgasses) into the air, it is called a *volatile organic compound*. VOCs are everywhere—in the air, water, food, and soil. Some VOCs occur naturally, and others are synthetic. Everyone is routinely exposed to

VOCs during daily activities—you cannot escape them completely, but you can minimize your family's exposure by limiting your use of products that contain them whenever reasonably possible.

The following list summarizes the building materials, furnishings, appliances, and consumer products that are major sources of VOCs in the home. The more you can avoid using these particular items, the healthier your indoor air will be.

- Tobacco smoke
- Appliances or any devices that burn natural gas, propane, butane, heating oil, kerosene, gasoline, wood, coal, or charcoal (such as ovens, ranges, heaters, stoves, clothes dryers, hot water heaters, furnaces/boilers, fireplaces, space heaters, and grills)
- Sterno canned heat cooking fuel
- Foam padding and foam insulation, especially urea-formaldehyde foam insulation, or UFFI
- Synthetic carpets and carpet pads
- Vinyl floors
- Plastic products, especially soft vinyl
- Carbonless paper, wallpaper, scented paper products
- Synthetic curtains, drapes, upholstery, mattresses, pillows
- Permanent-press/wrinkle-free/no-iron clothing, bedding, and other fabrics
- Dry-cleaning chemicals for clothing, carpets, upholstery
- Mothballs, mothcakes, moth crystals, moth flakes
- Fire retardants, water repellents, wood preservers
- Housepaints, varnishes, urethanes, lacquers, paint thinners and strippers, turpentine
- Glues, cements, adhesives, tapes, sealers, caulks, resins
- Waxes and polishes for floors, furniture, and metals
- Cosmetics, shampoo, toothpaste, deodorants, aftershave lotions, perfumes, colognes, fragrances, hair spray, nail polish and polish remover

- Household cleaning products, oven cleaners, drain openers, toilet bowl cleaners, toilet bowl cake/tab/block deodorizers and sanitizers, stain and spot removers, solvents, degreasers, carpet cleaners, laundry detergents, presoaks, fabric softeners, automatic dishwasher powders and liquids, disinfectants, sanitizers
- Air fresheners, room deodorizers, airwicks, stick-ups, potpourri
- Pesticides (insecticides, fungicides, herbicides, flea collars)
- Glued-wood, resin-bonded wood, and pressed-wood products such as plywood, chipboard, particleboard, pressboard, and medium-density fiberboard used for subfloors, cabinets, shelves, countertops, molding, paneling, wood veneers, and furniture
- Photocopiers, laser printers
- Inks, dyes, pens, art and craft materials
- Cigarette lighter fluid, charcoal lighter fluid, correction fluid
- Aerosol spray cans
- Tap water (municipal or private well)

It's worth noting that water vapor inhalation and skin absorption during bathing or showering may contribute 50 percent or more of your total VOC daily exposure, so have your tap water tested for VOCs as explained under "Drinking Water" in Chapter 1.

Formaldehyde. Formaldehyde is a probable human carcinogen and an especially toxic VOC. Almost all of the sources for the VOCs listed emit formaldehyde, but the major sources in the home are floor covering adhesives, tobacco smoke, foam insulation, wallpapering, upholstery, glued-wood furniture, cabinets, paneling, and plywood construction materials.

If you suspect a formaldehyde problem in your home, if you live in a mobile home (which often will have high levels of formaldehyde because it's constructed with a lot of plywood, particleboard, paneling, and vinyl floors, coupled with a metal exterior that traps all the toxic vapors inside), or if a family member is experiencing health problems for which there is no readily apparent explanation, consider having your indoor air tested for formaldehyde by an environmental professional or call the EPA at 800-554-1404. You might also try the following home test kit:

- Air Quality Research (800-242-7472) sells the PF1 Formaldehyde Monitorkit ($72.50) with which you collect the air sample and then mail the kit back to the company for analysis.

Carbon Monoxide

Carbon monoxide is an invisible, colorless, odorless, tasteless gas that can cause many different physical and/or mental symptoms, depending on the level of exposure. The first signs of poisoning are similar to the flu and include fatigue, mild headache, dizziness, nausea, and vomiting. As the carbon monoxide reaches medium levels, the symptoms become more severe, such as a throbbing headache, depression, irritability, drowsiness, Alzheimerlike disorientation and confusion, shortness of breath, blurred vision, and an irregular or fast heartbeat. Carbon monoxide can eventually reach such high levels that the victims fall into a deep sleep or coma and in some cases die from suffocation as the carbon monoxide robs the vital organs of essential oxygen.

Major sources of carbon monoxide in the home are devices that burn natural gas, propane, butane heating oil, kerosene, wood, coal, or charcoal (such as ovens, ranges, heaters, stoves, clothes dryers, hot water heaters, furnaces/boilers, fireplaces, space heaters, and grills); gasoline-powered generators, especially in motor homes; automobile or lawn mower exhaust seeping into the living space by way of an attached garage or basement garage; and tobacco smoke.

Approximately 1,000 people die each year from accidental carbon monoxide poisoning. It can occur in any home—old or new—so I strongly recommend purchasing a carbon monoxide detector, which continuously monitors indoor air and sounds an alarm if dangerous levels of carbon monoxide are reached. Just be sure the one you buy is approved by the Underwriters Laboratories (UL) and test it weekly. Several good brands of carbon monoxide detectors are available, but two of the best ones are the CO Sensor-200 ($50, made by American

Sensors Electronics, Markham, Ont., Canada; 800-387-4219/905-477-3320) and the First Alert ($40, made by BRK Electronics, Aurora, IL; 800-323-9005). Both brands are available at hardware stores. American Sensors Electronics also sells propane and natural gas detectors.

Nitrogen Oxides

Exposure to nitrogen oxides can cause a variety of health problems, such as scratchy and watery eyes, nasal congestion, runny nose, sore throat, shortness of breath, asthma and wheezing, coughing, and frequent respiratory infections (colds, flu).

The major sources of nitrogen oxides are similar to those for carbon monoxide. Please note that heating a gas oven to 400° F for one hour in an unvented kitchen produces indoor carbon monoxide and nitrogen dioxide gas levels three times higher than that of a typical Los Angeles smog attack.

Sulfur Dioxide

Exposure to sulfur dioxide can cause the same symptoms as those listed for nitrogen oxides. The major sources for sulfur dioxide are combustion of gasoline, kerosene, wood, coal, and charcoal.

Radon

Radon is a naturally occurring, radioactive, odorless, and colorless gas found in rocks and soil containing high concentrations of uranium. Radon gas migrates through the soil and groundwater and can pollute indoor air by seeping into homes through cracks or other openings in the basement or foundation, or contaminated tap water, especially from private wells.

Radon gas exposure is the second leading cause of lung cancer (tobacco smoke is first) in the United States, so my advice is to have your home indoor air and tap water tested for it. Testing is the only way to be sure, and test kits for airborne radon are inexpensive, easy to use, and available at many home improvement centers.

For more information on radon, call your regional EPA office or the EPA radon hot line at 800-SOS-RADON.

Asbestos

Until its recent ban, asbestos was used extensively for fireproofing, electrical insulation, and other applications requiring heat or chemical resistance. Homes built in the 1950s, 1960s, and early 1970s are most likely to have asbestos contamination.

Never disturb or remove asbestos material by yourself, because breathing the fibers can cause irreversible lung damage and scarring or even lung cancer. If you suspect an asbestos problem, call the EPA at 202-554-1404 for professional guidance.

Ozone

Ozone located in the upper atmosphere is essential for life on earth because it blocks harmful ultraviolet rays, but ozone near the surface of the earth is a highly unstable and extremely powerful oxidizing agent that is extremely irritating to the eyes, nose, throat, and bronchial tubes. Major sources include electric motors, electrostatic precipitator air filters, electric portable room air purifiers and ionizers, and electronic equipment such as televisions, VCRs, computers, photocopiers, and printers.

Chlorine

Chlorine gas is extremely irritating to the eyes, nose, throat, and bronchial tubes. Major indoor sources include chlorinated municipal tap water and chlorine-based household cleaning products, such as bleach, disinfectants, detergents, scouring powders, and automatic dishwasher powders and liquids.

Ammonia

Ammonia gas is extremely irritating to the eyes, nose, throat, and bronchial tubes. Ammonia-based household cleaning products are the major sources of ammonia gas indoors.

Biological Inhalant Allergens

The biological inhalant allergens come from bacteria, molds, fungi, plants (tree, grass, weed, and flower pollens), insects, house dust mites, and animals. Exposure can trigger a variety of symptoms such as red watery eyes, sneezing, runny or congested nose, sore throat, coughing, wheezing, asthma, itchy skin rashes, and intense itching of the eyes, nose, and throat.

The major sources are animal dander, fur, hair, or saliva (usually from a dog or cat); bird feathers; plant pollens; mold, mildew, and fungi; roaches and other insects; and house dust mites.

House dust mites are virtually invisible, natural inhabitants of most homes, and their presence does not indicate a lack of cleanliness. They live in the dust particles of carpets, rugs, drapes, sofas, stuffed chairs, mattresses, blankets, quilts, pillows, stuffed toys, and the like. Dust mites feed primarily on sloughed scales and flakes of human and animal skin. They avoid direct contact with humans and do not generally cause any harm except for their ability to trigger allergies in susceptible people.

The indoor relative humidity of a home is one of the most important factors in the control of dust mites. Dust mites thrive and multiply when the indoor relative humidity is in the range of 60–80 percent, but when the indoor relative humidity drops to 50 percent or below, half of the entire adult dust mite population in the home will die within five days, and almost all of the adult mites will die if the humidity can be consistently kept at around 45 percent for two straight weeks.

The following are the six most important steps for reducing your family's exposure to the major biological inhalant allergens.

1. Try to maintain the indoor relative humidity at 40–50 percent to stunt the growth of dust mites, mold, mildew, and fungi. Keep kitchens, bathrooms, laundry rooms, and basements dry and well ventilated. Exhaust fans vented to the outdoors are essential for the bathroom and kitchen, and the clothes dryer must. also have its own exhaust vent to the outside. Repair all water leaks. Avoid the routine use of humidifiers and vaporizers and don't leave standing water in sinks or bathtubs. Running an air-

conditioner is also a very effective way to reduce indoor humidity. A relative humidity gauge, such as the one sold by the Bionaire Corporation (800-253-2764), will help you monitor the effectiveness of your efforts.

2. Avoid wall-to-wall carpets and carpet pads (especially in the bedroom) because they are breeding grounds for mold, fungus, house dust mites, and insects. Limit stuffed furniture, dust-catching knickknacks, and stuffed toys. Do not use carpets or upholstered furniture in the basement or other moisture-prone areas.

3. Vacuum floors and upholstery twice a week with a vacuum cleaner that has a strong suction, a rotating beater brush to loosen ground-in dirt, and a two-ply microfiltration disposable paper bag able to trap dust particles down to the 0.1-micron size. Vacuum cleaners with conventional single-lined bags actually stir up allergenic dust and spread it through the house.

The Sears Kenmore canister model 23651, and the Panasonic upright model MC-6250, are excellent choices for most homes. For those who have asthma or serious inhalant allergy problems and can afford to spend about $700, the Nilfisk GS 90 HEPA Allergy Vacuum (with optional power nozzle and rotating brush) provides four stages of filtration, including a HEPA filter (High-Efficiency Particulate Accumulator). Call 800-NILFISK for further information.

FYI: The February 1993 issue of *Consumer Reports* evaluated several vacuum cleaners and concluded that the water-filter Rainbow vacuum cleaner by Rexair had many drawbacks, including mediocre dust filtration and cleaning, very noisy operation, difficult maintenance requirements, and a price tag in the vicinity of $1,000.

An excellent alternative to portable vacuum cleaners is a central vacuum system that vents the exhaust outdoors. Beam Industries in Webster City, IA (515-832-4620), manufactures high-quality central vacuum systems for existing homes or those under construction at prices starting as low as $450; call for a free brochure.

4. Clean the surfaces of bookshelves, furniture, pictures, blinds, and appliances with a damp cloth so that house dust does not accumulate on them. Avoid feather dusting and dry broom sweeping, which stir up dust and scatter biological inhalant allergens all over the house.

5. Launder sheets, pillowcases, and washable blankets in hot water once a week (cold or lukewarm water will not kill dust mites). Recent studies have proved that using cotton fitted sheets and pillowcases (and washing them once a week in hot water) prevents the growth of house dust mites within mattresses and pillows just as well as plastic encasing materials. Do not encase mattresses and pillows with plastic covers (a measure widely recommended by conventional allergists), because plastic emits toxic VOCs that are quite dangerous to inhale. And give blankets, quilts, pillows, and stuffed toys that cannot be washed in a washing machine a one-hour tumble in the electric clothes dryer once a month, assuming the garment tag or cleaning instruction label says it's OK. (Temperatures in an average clothes dryer range 140°–170° F, which is high enough to kill dust mites.)

6. Dead leaves and other organic debris on the lawn promote mold and fungus growth. Compost piles are also breeding grounds for molds, some of them potentially deadly, such as *Aspergillus fumigatus*, so try to maintain a distance of five miles.

Tobacco Smoke

Tobacco smoke contains a smorgasbord of toxic chemicals: tar, nicotine, carbon monoxide, nitrogen oxides, sulfur dioxide, formaldehyde, hydrogen cyanide, ammonia, benzene, styrene, ethylene oxide, and more than 50 other cancer-causing chemicals. With this one product, you can fill your home and the whole family's lungs with practically every indoor air pollutant listed in this chapter. Therefore, the cheapest and quickest way to dramatically reduce indoor air pollution is to forbid tobacco smoking anywhere in the house or car. In fact, tobacco smoke avoidance is so essential to your child's good health that it warrants several additional comments and warnings.

When a pregnant woman smokes a cigarette or breathes someone else's tobacco smoke, she forces the toxic chemicals just mentioned into her baby's blood. This explains why a recent Swedish study discovered that a mother who smokes during pregnancy doubles her child's risk of developing cancer. In addition, these toxins deprive her unborn infant of oxygen and nutrients needed for body growth and brain development. The end result is often a skinny baby who looks like a refugee from a Third World disaster area. Smoking during pregnancy also causes miscarriages, birth defects, and premature births. And a mother who smokes during pregnancy increases the chance that her child will wind up being shorter and having a lower IQ compared to children whose mothers didn't smoke.

Mothers who smoke during pregnancy "hook" their unborn baby on nicotine. Then, shortly after delivery, the nicotine craving starts, and the baby becomes shaky and irritable. Some infants get so jumpy the slightest noise sets off a startle reflex and crying. For the lucky ones the withdrawal period lasts only a few days, but for some it may take longer. Nicotine withdrawal is not a pretty sight, but it's especially tragic when it occurs in a tiny, defenseless newborn.

As discussed in Chapter 1, when a breast-feeding mother smokes, the toxic and cancer-causing tobacco poisons she inhales travel from her lungs to the breast milk, and at each nursing session the baby drinks the toxic chemicals in the tainted milk. *If you smoke, do not breast-feed your baby.*

The term *passive smoking* means that innocent bystanders are forced to breathe air polluted by tobacco smoke. It's now a proved fact that exposing children to tobacco smoke is equivalent to making them actively puff on a cigarette. In other words, every time you light up around your child, you might just as well stuff a cigarette into her mouth and make her inhale along with you, because "side-stream" smoke from the burning end of a cigarette contains higher levels of cancer-causing chemicals than the smoke inhaled through the filter. It doesn't take a rocket scientist to figure out that smoking around children is tantamount to child abuse.

Several scientific research studies have now proved beyond the shadow of a doubt that exposing a baby to tobacco smoke triples his or her risk of death from sudden infant death syndrome (SIDS). The toxic by-products of tobacco damage the infant's windpipe and stress the breathing control center in the brain, resulting in a parent's worst nightmare.

Infants who are subjected to smoke cry more often and for longer periods of time than those who aren't. And who could blame them? Any sensible person would cry out in anger if someone made them feel miserable by assaulting their eyes, ears, nose, throat, and lungs with tobacco smoke day after day.

Exposing a child to cigarette, cigar, or pipe smoke is the number-one trigger factor for asthma attacks, wheezing, noisy breathing, chronic ear infections, and chronic hacking coughs. Breathing the smoke from just one cigarette a day damages the lining of the nose, throat, ears, and lungs and makes a child prone to frequent respiratory infections, croup, and pneumonia. The infections are more severe and take up to three times longer to clear up compared to infections in children who live in a smoke-free home. It is interesting to note that two out of three children who have chronic ear infections are the victims of tobacco smoke exposure. In most cases the ears will clear up completely within one month if both parents totally eliminate tobacco smoke from their child's environment.

Many parents are sports enthusiasts who look forward to the day when their child can participate in school athletics. Recently, scientific studies uncovered the sobering fact that lung growth is retarded by as much as 10 percent in children who grow up in homes where one or more adults smoke. That means permanent lung damage lowers their exercise stamina and thus saddles them with an automatic 10 percent breathing handicap when competing against children who live in smoke-free homes. Why not give your child the winning edge by not smoking?

A lot of people assume that using an air filter or avoiding smoking in the baby's room will prevent all these problems. That's just wishful thinking and totally wrong! Smoking anywhere in the house eventually contaminates all the rooms, and air filters don't even come close to screening out the toxic pollutants. In addition, smoke residue sticks to glass, metal, wood, clothing, carpets, and upholstery, which means that toxic chemicals will outgas from these surfaces continuously, even when the smoker isn't actively smoking. If you must smoke, always go outside, on the porch, or in the garage and never smoke with your child in the car. Insist that guests in your home or car do the same.

Even if you did smoke during pregnancy, you can undo part of the damage by stopping right now. Ask your doctor about the new and painless ways to quit smoking. It could very well mean the difference between life and death for your child.

Let me end my sermon on the evils of smoking with three interesting items to help put things in even better perspective:

1. Remember the famous Perrier bottled water scandal that occurred a few years ago? Perrier was found to contain 20 parts per billion of cancer-causing benzene, which is four times higher than the EPA maximum allowable limit for benzene in drinking water. When the news hit the airwaves, national hysteria ensued, and a swift recall of the product was instituted. You couldn't give the stuff away. And yet one cigarette contains about 10 times more cancer-causing benzene than that one contaminated eight-ounce bottle of Perrier. Furthermore, EPA studies have shown that benzene air concentrations are 50 percent higher in homes of people who smoke compared to homes of nonsmokers, and since benzene exposure is a significant risk factor for developing leukemia and lymphoma, it should come as no surprise that a child who lives in a house where one person smokes regularly has double the risk of contracting one of these cancers. (If both parents smoke indoors, their child's cancer risk quadruples.)

2. For each cigarette smoked, a person loses approximately seven minutes from his normal life span.

3. The average cigarette contains 0.3 picocuries of radioactive polonium. Smoking one pack of cigarettes a day for one year exposes the lungs to an amount of radiation approximately

equivalent to 250 chest x-rays. Of course, children who breathe this secondhand radioactivity are also placed at increased risk for cancer.

Natural and Nontoxic Ways to Reduce Indoor Air Pollution

The overall indoor air pollution level of a home depends on how well-ventilated the building shell is and how many major sources of pollution are in the home. A home with, say, a fuel-burning furnace, gas appliancies, a wood-burning fireplace, wall-to-wall carpeting, tobacco smoke, and radon is going to have horrible indoor air quality. For such homes the first order of business is always to remove or limit the major sources of pollution as much as possible. Some things can be accomplished easily, inexpensively, and immediately (forbid all smoking indoors and quit using the fireplace), while others (switching from gas to electric appliances, for example) are costly and require long-term planning. Just do the best you can and take it one step at a time.

Ventilation

Good indoor ventilation (exchanging fresh outdoor air for stale or polluted indoor air) is absolutely essential for a healthy house. Most homes rely on leaks in the building's shell for their ventilation. This is often referred to as the *air leakage rate* or breathability of a home. The optimal air leakage rate for the average conventionally built family home is one complete exchange of all the air in the house every one to two hours. This generally allows adequate removal of indoor air pollutants without driving up monthly heating and cooling costs excessively.

So-called *superinsulated* homes take 4–10 hours for one complete air exchange. Do not superinsulate your house completely airtight just to save a few pennies on heating and cooling bills. In the long run you'll trap air pollutants indoors and end up spending a lot more money on trips to the doctor's office for the treatment of pollution-induced illnesses.

One major clue that your home is not "breathing" adequately is the presence of lingering odors after cooking a meal. The aroma of whatever you have for dinner should clear out within four hours. If it doesn't, you may want to have your home ventilation analyzed by a representative from the local power company.

One good way to improve ventilation in your home is to use exhaust fans ducted to the outdoors to remove pollutants immediately, before they have a chance to mix with the air in the rest of the house. For example, a kitchen equipped with a gas range or oven should always have an efficient hood exhaust fan operating whenever the appliance is in use.

Heating and Cooling Systems

An electric heating and cooling system is the best choice for a healthy home. Natural gas, propane, heating oil, kerosene, coal, and wood systems pollute the indoor air with hydrocarbon fumes and combustion by-products to a tremendous degree.

If you must use an oil, gas, coal, or wood system, buy one of the carbon monoxide detectors described earlier and, if possible, locate the furnace/boiler outside, in its own room adjacent to but completely separate from the house. The only opening between the furnace/boiler room and the house should be a well-insulated hole through which the necessary hardware passes. A marginally acceptable location for a fuel-burning furnace/boiler is in the garage. The worst location is inside the house or basement, because oil or gas fumes can easily contaminate the indoor air. To prevent backdrafting of toxic combustion gases directly into the room air, fuel-burning furnaces should be equipped with a separate outside combustion air intake supply and an exhaust flue pipe that exits completely through the roof and actually exceeds the height of the roof by the amount specified in the local fire code. To reduce emissions further, make sure the furnace is adjusted properly to burn efficiently with a blue flame (not a yellow-tipped flame) and equip the furnace with an automatic electric sparking pilot ignition system rather than a continuously burning pilot flame.

Fireplaces, wood-burning stoves, and kerosene or gas space heaters should be banned entirely from the inside of homes because they pollute the indoor air with enormous amounts of toxic combustion gases and particles. If you already have a fireplace, don't use it. In addition, the front of the fireplace should be sealed off from the room with tight-fitting glass doors, which prevent any backdrafting into the living quarters. And the combustion air intake supply for a fireplace or stove should come from a separate outside vent.

Also, avoid radiant heating systems with heat coils in the subfloor or ceiling, because the heat they produce promotes outgassing of chemicals from plywood, sheetrock, cement, insulation, paint, and carpets right into the room air.

If you are interested in purchasing an environmentally safe ceramic space heater specifically designed for people who have severe allergies and chemical sensitivities, contact the Radiant Heater Corporation in Greenport, New York (800-331-6408).

Ductwork

A central air system requires ductwork to distribute conditioned air throughout the house. Follow these guidelines for ductwork:

- The preferred material for ductwork is sheet metal with fiberglass insulation wrapped around the outside of the ducts.
- Never use ductwork with insulation lining the inside of the ducts, because the fibers will eventually start to fray and dislodge into the airstream.
- Be sure the joints between sections of ductwork fit tightly, because loose joints allow radon gas, dust, germs, and insulation particles to contaminate the air. A low-odor aluminum foil tape works great to seal joints, seams, cracks, and holes.
- Do not let the ductwork installers place oil or any petroleum-based protective coating on the metal, because the residue will outgas when heated.
- The return air plenum should be made of sheet metal.
- Avoid plastic dampers and plastic air vent registers and grilles. Metal is better.

• I do not recommend cleaning inside central air ducts because duct cleaning can create horrible air pollution problems unless it is done correctly. However, if you decide to go ahead, make sure the duct cleaning company you hire uses the source removal method and employs a self-contained, truck-mounted powerful vacuum that runs during the entire cleaning procedure, efficiently sucking up all the dirt as it is brushed loose. All commercial biocides, germicides, and fungicides are toxic, so demand in writing that the company not spray any such chemicals inside your ductwork. If necessary, air vent registers and grilles can be removed and thoroughly cleaned and rinsed outdoors.

Humidity Control

As mentioned earlier, the best range for relative humidity indoors is 40–50 percent. Indoor humidity above 60 percent promotes the growth of allergy-causing house dust mites, mold, mildew, and fungi, and indoor humidity less than 35 percent dries out the nose and throat and thereby increases the susceptibility to contagious respiratory infections and nosebleeds. Moderation is the key. That's why I recommend monitoring your indoor air with a relative humidity gauge, such as the one sold by mail order from the Bionaire Corporation (800-253-2764). If your indoor relative humidity is consistently above 60 percent, follow the humidity-controlling suggestions under "Biological Inhalant Allergens" earlier in the chapter. Running an air conditioner in the warm weather months, keeping moisture-prone areas of the house dry and well ventilated, and using exhaust fans vented outdoors are some of the most effective ways to reduce indoor relative humidity.

BUILDING MATERIALS, FURNISHINGS, APPLIANCES, AND CONSUMER PRODUCTS FOR A HEALTHY HOME

Flooring

Since flooring covers such a large surface area, your choice of materials is very important to indoor air quality. The healthiest flooring materials include glazed ceramic tiles; stone tiles, such as marble or granite; and solid hardwood, such as oak, maple, or beech. Try to avoid aromatic softwoods—pine, cedar, fir, spruce—because the strong odor of their natural resins tends to irritate the eyes, nose, and throat.

Wood Floors

Wood flooring can usually be purchased prefinished or unfinished. Since most wood floor stains and sealers are toxic and should be avoided whenever possible, the safest choice is prefinished solid hardwood flooring that has already been sanded, stained, and sealed with water-based acrylic-polyurethane at the factory before installation.

Of the three installation options for hardwood floors—nail-down, glue-down, and floating floor—nail-down is the safest because it avoids glues and adhesives that emit potentially toxic VOCs into the air as well as high-density synthetic foam padding used in the floating system.

Wood flooring can be installed over a concrete or wood subfloor. Solid hardwood planks are preferred for subfloors. Acceptable alternatives for the subfloor include exterior-grade plywood or formaldehyde-free plywood as long as the product is rated for low VOC emissions and doesn't give off much of an odor or natural scent. Do not use interior-grade plywood or particleboard for the subfloor, because they emit enormous amounts of toxic formaldehyde gas and other VOCs.

The optimal method for cleaning wood floors is to use a vacuum cleaner once or twice a week to remove surface dust. Dry broom sweeping will just scatter the dust, and wet-mopping or cleaning with an oil soap will damage or splinter the wood. Avoid conventional floor waxes and polishes because of the ammonia and toxic VOCs they emit.

Tile Floors

Ceramic and stone (marble or granite) are the healthiest tile choices for floors. For ceramic tile flooring, insist on glazed ceramic tile made in the United States, because unglazed tile often requires the application of a toxic sealer, and imported ceramic tiles may contain improperly fired lead glazes that could potentially cause a problem.

Ceramic or stone tile floors offer several advantages over wood
floors:

- Tile isn't hurt by water. Accidental spills and leaks are well
tolerated. This makes tile an especially good choice for wet or
humid areas of your home (such as bathrooms, utility rooms,
entryways, solariums, and the kitchen or basement).
- High-quality glazed ceramic tile (with a high wear rating and
high scratch/hardness rating) is extremely tough and durable
and does not scratch or dent like wood. (Stone tiles are not quite
as resistant to scratches as ceramic.)
- Tile requires very little maintenance to keep it looking like new.
Just run the vacuum cleaner over tile floors once or twice a week
to remove surface dust and use a damp mop for trouble spots.
Avoid broom sweeping (which simply spreads the dust around).

Be very careful about choosing adhesives and grout to bond tiles to
the floor. Avoid tile mastics, grouts, and caulks that contain petroleum-
based solvents, such as toluene and xylene. The healthiest choice for
bonding ceramic or stone tiles to most floor surfaces is thin-set Portland cement mortar (without latex or polymer additives). C-Cure Chemical Company of Houston, Texas (800-292-2874) makes some of the
safest products, such as C-Cure Floor Mix and AR Tile Grout.

Carpets

Wall-to-wall carpeting is the worst choice of floor covering for two
main reasons: (1) Carpets trap dust and serve as a breeding ground for
mold, mildew, fungi, bacteria, dust mites, and fleas. (2) Carpets outgas
more than 100 different VOCs, some of which are emitted in significant
concentrations for months after installation. It's no wonder that breathing this chemical smorgasbord can cause a variety of serious health
problems, such as asthma, shortness of breath, allergies, multiple chemical sensitivity (MCS), headaches, dizziness, nervousness, burning eyes,
nasal congestion, and sore throat.

There's no such thing as a healthy synthetic wall-to-wall carpet, but
some are definitely worse than others. Carpets that utilize styrene-

butadiene rubber (SBR) latex adhesive emit 4-PC (4-phenyl-cyclohex-ene). Breathing 4-PC, the VOC that gives new carpet its distinctive odor, can cause many of the adverse health effects mentioned for VOCs at the beginning of this chapter.

If you do decide to buy wall-to-wall carpeting, the following general suggestions may help:

- Look for a brand without (or with the least amount of) stain-proofing, soil repellents, mothproofing, waterproofing, biocides, fungicides, or other chemical treatments or finishes.
- Choose short-pile rugs, since they hold less dust than deep pile, plush, or shag.
- Never buy carpet tiles, because their polyvinyl chloride (PVC) backing emits formaldehyde and other toxic VOCs.

The following carpet installation tips will help reduce the risk of adverse health effects from new carpeting:

- Ask the carpet company to unwrap, unroll, and air out the new carpet in its warehouse for three days before bringing it into your home; this will allow a large quantity of toxins to outgas first.
- Vacuum the old carpet thoroughly before removing it to reduce the level of dust particles; then vacuum the bare floor after the old carpet and carpet pad have been removed.
- During all phases of the carpet installation and for at least 72 hours thereafter, ventilate the house with plenty of fresh outdoor air. If you can smell the carpet, you're breathing potentially harmful VOCs.
- Wall-to-wall carpeting should be fastened in place using nails and metal clampdown tack strips, not glue.
- Avoid carpet pads made of plastic, foam rubber, latex, or synthetic foam. One of the least-toxic carpet pads is Permaloom Carpet Cushion from Southwest Fibers in Mexia, Texas (800-880-6092). Another acceptable brand is the Hartex Carpet Cushion (800-237-9640).

Note that when a synthetic carpet gets warm, the fabric and backing depolymerize and release significant amounts of toxic chemicals into the air, so never expose the carpet to temperatures above 80° F. For example, avoid heating systems that radiate heat up through the floor, and never let the sun shine directly on a synthetic carpet because the heat from direct sunlight increases chemical emissions to such an extent that you can actually smell the toxic fumes.

An interesting phenomenon worth noting is that toxic synthetic carpets cause certain insects (especially spiders) to curl up and die spontaneously. In fact, the more toxic the carpet is, the more likely you are to find dead spiders, doodlebugs, and roaches without using any insecticides whatsoever. As you might have expected, however, it won't kill fleas.

Although wall-to-wall carpeting is the worst choice for floor covering, area throw rugs or scatter rugs made of 100 percent cotton or wool are usually acceptable as long as they do not have an SBR latex adhesive and have not received heavy chemical treatments. Braided or woven cotton or wool rugs are preferred because they do not require toxic binding adhesives to hold the fibers together, and they can be cleaned regularly without toxic chemicals. Chemically untreated, handwoven Oriental and Navajo Indian rugs are also good choices.

Carpets should be vacuumed at least twice a week with a vacuum cleaner that has a rotating beater brush, a strong suction, and a double-lined (two-ply) microfiltration disposable paper bag that traps dust particles down to the 0.1 micron size. The Sears Kenmore canister model 23651 and the Panasonic upright model MC-6250 are excellent choices. Frequent vacuuming (twice a week) is the nontoxic way to prevent moth damage and flea infestations.

Avoid commercial carpet shampoos and spot removers because of the toxic chemicals they contain. Professional steam cleaning without any chemical additives is relatively safe, but watch out for fragrances and other chemicals many cleaners automatically add.

Furniture

Again, the healthiest material for furniture is solid hardwood (such as oak, maple, cherry, mahogany, poplar) with a nontoxic, no-wax finish.

Avoid furniture made of laminated wood, pressed wood, chipboard, particleboard, and aromatic softwoods.

Furniture without upholstery or cushions is the least allergenic. The worst stuffing materials are feathers, down, foam rubber, latex, and polystyrene (Styrofoam) beads. Plastic (especially vinyl) and leather (genuine and imitation) are the worst materials for furniture upholstery and covers.

If possible, avoid furniture treated with chemicals for stain-, mildew-, and wrinkle-resistance. Avoid the use of furniture wax, polish, and sealers (lacquers and varnishes, for instance), because they emit toxic VOCs that pollute the indoor air. For those who are determined to use a wood furniture or cabinet sealer in spite of my warning, consider the water-based acrylic sealer called Crystal Aire Clear Finish by Pace Chem Industries of Newbury Park, California (805-499-2911).

Warning

To reduce the risk of accidental cuts and bruises, select furniture with smooth edges and rounded corners. Furthermore, any antique or secondhand furniture that has been painted with pre-1980 paint should be tested for lead contamination as explained in the "Lead Poisoning" section of this chapter.

Glues and Adhesives

Elmer's White Glue-All and Elmer's Yellow Carpenter's Wood Glue are generally acceptable products. Avoid "super" glues, epoxy glues, and airplane glues. Especially avoid petroleum-solvent-based carpet glues and adhesives, because they usually cover a large surface area (which means they emit enormous amounts of toxic VOCs for long periods of time).

Wallpaper

Avoid wallpaper because it emits formaldehyde, vinyl chloride, and other toxic VOCs. In addition, wallpaper often contains insecticides and fungicides.

Household Cleaning Agents, Cleansers, Deodorizers, and Disinfectants

Avoid most household cleansers, detergents, stain and spot removers, scouring powders, deodorizers, disinfectants, and sanitizers because they contain toxic substances, such as chlorine bleach (sodium hypochlorite), ammonia, formaldehyde, phenylphenol (Lysol), synthetic dyes, fragrances, pine tree derivatives, petroleum distillates, and other harmful VOCs. Do not buy products that come in aerosol spray cans, because the propellant is often more toxic than the active ingredient and the chemical mist will land on your skin and get in your eyes and lungs, where it can do a lot of harm.

Safer Alternatives for General Household Cleaning. There are four relatively safe household cleaning products that work very well and can be purchased at most supermarkets:

1. Bon Ami (calcium carbonate and feldspar) powder cleans and scours.
2. Arm & Hammer baking soda (sodium bicarbonate) cleans, scours, absorbs odors, and removes soap scum.
3. 20 Mule Team Borax (sodium, boron, oxygen) cleans, brightens laundry, deodorizes, disinfects, and removes stains.
4. Heinz distilled white vinegar cuts grease and removes lime deposits and hard-water scale. It cleans and shines glass, windows, mirrors, chrome, and appliances.

Some people make their own general-purpose household cleanser by mixing one cup of plain water and one cup of Heinz distilled white vinegar in a pump spray bottle.

Faucet aerators. In many parts of the country, hard water and lime deposits accumulate on faucet aerators. To remove such deposits safely, unscrew the aerator and place the metal parts in a glass jar of full-strength distilled white vinegar. After soaking for a few hours, the deposits will wipe right off, and the aerator will look almost like new.

Windows. Avoid ammonia-based glass and window cleaners. Instead, make your own window cleaner by mixing 2 tablespoons of distilled white vinegar and 2 cups of water in a pump spray bottle.

Toilets. Do not use chemical toilet bowl cleaners or toilet bowl cake/tab/block deodorizers or sanitizers, because they give off strong, toxic fumes. The safer way to clean toilet bowls is with Bon Ami powder for the superficial stains. For the deep stains and stubborn hard-water rings, a pumice scouring stick designed for cleaning porcelain and tile surfaces works like a charm. The Pumie Scouring Stick, by United States Pumice Company of Chatsworth, California, is sold at most supermarkets and home improvement centers. You can also order the Ring Eraser (a pumicelike block with an easy-grasp wood handle for cleaning porcelain toilet bowls) from The Vermont Country Store (802-362-2400).

Dishwashers. Avoid most commercial automatic dishwasher powders and liquids, because they contain toxic VOCs, fragrances, and chlorine. One of the less offensive brands is plain Electra-Sol.

Ovens. Avoid chemical oven cleaners whenever possible, because they contain extremely harsh ingredients such as lye, ammonia, and petroleum distillates. The best alternative is an electric self-cleaning oven. (Avoid the so-called continuous-cleaning ovens, because they continuously emit synthetic chemicals into the air.)

When you're cooking something that might spill over, put a sheet of aluminum foil or a metal cookie sheet on the lower rack. Or bake in a covered pan when possible. By being careful, you won't have to clean your oven with anything but plain water and a washcloth. On rare occasions when something does spill, as soon as the oven cools down, use a wet washcloth to wipe up the mess so it won't bake in deeper the next time you use the oven.

Clogged drains. An old-fashioned plunger is the best choice for opening a clogged drain. It's about as cheap, nontoxic, and low-tech as you can get, and yet it works beautifully almost every time. You should have two plungers, one for toilets and the other for bathtubs and sinks.

Another device that can come in handy is called an *air plunger*. Just pump it up, place it over the drain, pull the lever, and whoosh. You should be able to find an air plunger at hardware stores or home improvement centers.

Avoid commercial drain cleaners (such as Drāno and Liquid-Plumr); they contain lye and other toxic substances.

Laundry. Avoid products that contain chlorine bleach (sodium hypochlorite).

Toxic Warning

Never mix chlorine bleach with ammonia or acid products like vinegar or toilet bowl cleaners because the chemical reaction can produce poisonous gas.

Try not to use starch, presoaks, fabric softeners, or antistatic sprays. However, 20 Mule Team Borax and Wisk Free are generally safe presoaks.

Avoid dry-cleaning clothes, blankets, and curtains whenever possible, as discussed in Chapter 3.

Room Deodorizers, Air Fresheners, Perfumes, and Herbal Scents

Totally avoid all room deodorizers and air fresheners (especially the kind that plugs into an electric socket) and disinfectants (especially Lysol and the pine-scented products), because they pollute the indoor air with harmful chemicals. And forget about natural herbal scents and potpourri, because they are just as irritating to the respiratory system as the synthetic versions. Air should be fresh—it's not supposed to have any smell or scent whatsoever!

Avoid all household products in aerosol spray cans, because the propellant gases and VOCs are usually quite toxic and will get in your eyes and lungs. A hand pump spray or atomizer is a safer choice.

Avoid all perfumes, fragrances, colognes, aftershave lotions, nail polish, polish remover, and scented products such as wax candles, incense, and potpourri, because they fill the air with toxic chemicals that have the potential for causing serious respiratory and neurologic (brain) problems. The air and the human body are meant to smell clean, not artificially scented.

Newspapers and Magazines

Newspapers and magazines contain dust, lint, formaldehyde, lead, fragrances, and many other toxic substances, so always put them outdoors in a recycling bin as soon as you're finished reading, and never let your child play with them or chew on them. Magazines with scented advertisement pages and fragrance strips should never be brought inside the house.

Pesticides

Chapter 7 outlines nontoxic and least-toxic strategies for controlling insects and other pests.

Paint

There are two basic types of housepaint: oil-based (alkyd) and water-based (latex). Latex paint is the best choice because it dries fast, cleans up with plain water, and contains only a small fraction of the toxic petroleum solvents that oil-based paints do. Almost all housepaints contain VOCs that evaporate into the air as the paint dries, giving off its characteristic odor.

Most conventional paint manufacturers add biocides and fungicides to their products solely to prolong the shelf life. After application, these preservatives in the paint outgas into the room air continuously for 5–10 years. Exposure to these volatile chemical preservatives can lead to the gradual onset of fatigue, headaches, sore throats, frequent infections, and other chronic illnesses. That's why you should never settle for just a low-odor housepaint; insist that it also be low-biocide or no-biocide.

Latex housepaint is the best choice from a health standpoint as long as the brand you choose is low-odor (zero- or low-VOC), low-biocide, no-fungicide, lead-free, and mercury-free. The Glidden paint company manufactures a special "earth-friendly" line of interior latex paints called Glidden LIFEMASTER 2000 Enamel that has all of the performance characteristics of top-of-the-line conventional interior housepaints plus the following desirable properties: no petroleum-based solvents, zero VOCs, lead-free, mercury-free, and no biocides or fungicides. The Miller Paint Co. (503-233-4491) in Portland, Oregon, and Chem-Safe Products (210-657-5321) in San Antonio, Texas, also manufacture low-odor (low-VOC), low-biocide, no-fungicide house-paints for chemically sensitive people. Call for a free brochure.

Please note that many paint manufacturers used to add mercury to their latex paints, but in August 1990 the EPA banned mercury in interior latex housepaints. Apparently mercury vapors outgassed from the paint for months after application, and could, under certain conditions, cause severe mercury poisoning to the inhabitants of the house. Unfortunately, most national paint manufacturers have simply switched to other preservatives which are, in many ways, as toxic as mercury. Incidentally, it's still legal for exterior housepaints to contain mercury, but I would not use such paint under any circumstances because mercury is a very toxic heavy metal. To find out if paint used on your home in the past contains mercury, call the EPA mercury hot line at 800-858-7378.

Turpentine, which is used to thin or clean up oil-based paints, is derived from pine trees, but even a natural solvent like turpentine can be very dangerous, because many people are allergic to pine and its derivatives.

Never under any circumstances use paint strippers or varnish strippers indoors, because they contain some of the most toxic chemicals ever made, such as benzene and methylene chloride, which are notorious for causing cancer. Inhaling methylene chloride can also trigger a fatal heart attack.

Redecorating and Remodeling

Never under any circumstances redecorate or remodel your home if you're pregnant or have a child under one year of age. Chemical emissions from new paint, wallpaper, furniture, carpeting, and construction materials are extremely dangerous to breathe, especially for infants.

Whenever you are remodeling or decorating, just do one project at a time, one room at a time. Painting more than one room at a time and/or combining projects will double, triple, or even quadruple the amount of toxic indoor air pollutants. Always give new material plenty of time (preferably one month) to dry and outgas before proceeding with the next project, and don't allow children into the remodeled room if there is even the slightest hint of fresh paint or new carpet odor. Remember, if you can smell the new paint, carpet, or other new materials, you are breathing harmful VOCs.

Good ventilation is absolutely essential when remodeling and painting. You must keep as many windows open as possible to remove the toxic fumes. That's why winter is the worst time to paint or carpet your home, because the doors and windows are usually closed and the toxic fumes get trapped indoors.

Home Appliances

Electric home appliances—ranges, ovens, refrigerators, clothes dryers, hot water heaters—are much healthier for indoor air than those that burn natural gas, propane, heating oil, or wood. So if you have choice, always choose electric. Electric appliances do cost more to operate than gas appliances, but in the long run they will save you money by preventing pollution-induced illnesses and trips to the doctor.

If your home has any appliances that burn natural gas, propane, heating oil, wood, or any combustible fuel whatsoever, be absolutely sure they are properly vented to the outdoors. Gas appliances should burn efficiently with a blue flame (not a yellow-tipped flame). And I strongly recommend purchasing at least one (but preferably two or three) carbon monoxide detectors, which continuously monitor indoor air and sound an alarm if dangerous levels occur.

Television Sets, VCRs, Stereos, CDs, and Other Electronic Equipment

Electronic equipment can pollute the indoor air by giving off toxic VOCs, such as toluene, when the plastic-coated wires get hot. Ozone emissions can also be a problem. Before purchasing electronic equipment, give the prospective model a good sniff during operation on the showroom floor. Avoid models that have an obvious ozone or plastic odor.

Art and Craft Materials
(Clays, Crayons, and Markers)

Art and craft materials can expose youngsters to a wide range of toxic substances such as lead, asbestos, and VOCs. Here are some general precautions to take:

- First and foremost, use only art and craft materials that carry the AP Non-Toxic or CP Non-Toxic stamp of approval from the Art and Craft Materials Institute (ACMI, 100 Boylston Street, Suite 1050, Boston, MA 02116, 617-426-6400). For $2, ACMI will mail you its list of certified nontoxic art and craft products. This comprehensive list is a must for every parent.
- Do not allow any food or beverages around areas where art and craft materials are being used. Never apply any product—paint, ink, or stamps, for instance—to the skin unless the label specifically states the product is designed to be used that way. Discourage children from getting art materials, pens, or pencils near their eyes or mouths. Always wash up immediately after using the materials.
- Do not store or use art materials near sources of heat, sparks, or flame.
- Avoid permanent felt-tip pens and permanent markers because they emit chemicals that irritate the eyes, nose, and throat. Instead, use washable nontoxic markers (such as Crayola Washable Markers and Crayola Washable Highlighter), nontoxic pencils (Crayola Colored Pencils, for example), and nontoxic crayons (such as Crayola Crayons).
- Avoid papier-mâché, dry clays, and modeling or sculpting powders because inhaling the dust particles during the mixing and cleanup can be hazardous, especially if they contain silica, talc, or asbestos. Better choices would be dustless chalk (such as

Crayola Anti-Dust) and premixed, ready-to-use clay (such as Clayola or Crayola Claytime) and modeling dough (such as Crayola Dough) approved for use by children.
- Avoid petroleum-solvent-based inks, dyes, and paints. Water-based products are preferred, such as Crayola Washable Finger Paint, Crayola Poster Paints, Crayola Water Colors, and water-based plant and vegetable inks and dyes (soy or canola ink, for example).
- Avoid professional artist paints and supplies, because they often contain hazardous substances such as lead.
- Some petroleum-solvent-based glues and cements (epoxy glue, super glue, airplane glue, and the like). Many of the Elmer's Glue products (such as Elmer's School Glue and Elmer's Glue-All) are acceptable choices.
- Avoid all aerosol spray cans, because the toxic solvents and propellants they spew into the air will linger for hours.

ELECTROMAGNETIC FIELDS

Anything that transmits or runs on electricity generates an electromagnetic field (EMF). EMFs contain both electric energy fields and magnetic energy fields. Electric and magnetic energy fields in the very low frequency (VLF) and extremely low frequency (ELF) range have recently been shown to produce detrimental effects on the health of all living creatures, including humans. This electronic pollution in the home can and should be minimized. Please note, however, that even though electric appliances generate EMFs, they're still much safer by far than natural gas and other combustion appliances.

The most common household sources of electromagnetic fields (EMFs) include electric power lines and transformers in close proximity to the home, household wiring and fuse boxes or circuit breaker boxes, electrical grounds to plumbing pipes, electric motors and tools, television picture tubes, computers and other video display terminals (VDTs), photocopiers, electric ranges, conventional and microwave ovens, electric alarm clocks and radios, stereo and entertainment elec-

tronics, cordless appliance battery-charging units and plug-in transformers, electric blankets and heating pads, water bed heaters, electric
water heaters, electric space heaters, lamps, fluorescent lights, fans, hair
dryers, electric shavers, electric toothbrushes, toasters, coffee makers,
mixers, food processors, blenders, can openers, refrigerators, dishwashers, clothes washers, electric dryers, vacuum cleaners, telephone
handsets, and cellular phones.

Inside the home the largest electromagnetic fields are generated by
television and video screens, improperly grounded electrical equipment and outlets, fluorescent lights, electric motors, and appliances
that heat things.

Distance is your friend when it comes to EMF exposure. The
strength of electromagnetic fields drops as you move farther away from
the source. The strength of an electric field depends on the voltage of
the source producing it as well as how close you are to the source. It's
usually expressed in kilovolts per meter (kV/m) units. Most experts
recommend avoiding prolonged or chronic exposure to levels above 1
kV/m (1,000 volts per meter). The strength of the magnetic field depends on the flow of current in the source as well as how close you are
to the source. Therefore, the strength of the magnetic field of an electric
appliance will generally be greater on the "high" settings, which draw
more current than the "low" settings. The magnetic field strength is
usually expressed in milligauss (mG) units. Most experts recommend
avoiding prolonged or chronic exposure above 1 mG. Electric devices
must be turned on to generate a magnetic field, but they only have to be
plugged in to generate an electric field.

Electric fields can be blocked by walls, trees, and special shields,
but magnetic fields can easily pass through soil, cement, steel, lead,
copper, and aluminum. That's why you should not put a bed or chair
next to a wall that has an electronic device (such as a television set) on
the other side; the magnetic field travels right through the wall.

Exposure to electromagnetic fields produces biological and psy-
chological changes in humans. Many scientists warn that chronic exposure to electromagnetic fields at levels that exceed either 1 milligauss
(mG) or 1 kV/m can cause a wide variety of health problems, such as

allergies, immune system dysfunction, chronic fatigue, migraine headaches, miscarriages, insomnia, anxiety, and depression.

Can chronic exposure to electromagnetic fields cause cancer? Several epidemiological studies have found that, in general, chronic (eight hours per day) exposure to a 3 mG magnetic field or a 2.5 kV/m electric field is associated with a twofold increase in the risk of cancer. In fact, a recently completed study at the respected Karolinska Institute in Sweden found a definite link between childhood leukemia and living within 300 yards of high-voltage (200,000–500,000 volts) power lines, with the cancer risk growing in proportion to the closeness to the power lines and increasing strength of the electromagnetic field. Those children chronically exposed to a 2 mG field showed a threefold increase. Also, a study reported by the University of Southern California at Los Angeles in 1991 found childhood leukemia was associated with crease. Also, a study reported by the University of Southern California Los Angeles in 1991 found childhood leukemia was associated with exposure to nearby power lines, regular use of electric hair dryers and curling irons, and sitting close to television screens.

The following list will give you a rough approximation of the average magnetic field strength associated with some common household electric appliances. Of course, the actual strength of your appliances may vary considerably, so always take your own measurements to be sure (directions follow).

- Conventional electric blankets generate 70–100 mG at the surface of the blanket where it touches the body. That's almost the same magnetic field strength exposure as standing underneath a 500,000 volt power line!
- Electric digital clocks average 70–100 mG at a 3-inch-radius distance and 1 mG at a 12-inch-radius distance.
- Old-fashioned electric dial-face alarm clocks produce 5–10 mG up to 2 feet away.
- Electric razors generate approximately 200 mG at the cutting edge, 100 mG at a 2-inch-radius distance, and 2–3 mG at a 2-foot distance.

- Computers with a 9-inch monochrome diagonal screen average 7 mG at 12 inches in front of the screen and 2–3 mG at 18 inches in front of the screen.
- Television screens generate 8–10 mG at a 1-foot-radius distance, 3 mG at a 3-foot-radius distance, and 2 mG at a 5-foot-radius distance. The magnetic field from some television sets can actually extend as far as 15 feet before dropping to the 1 mG level.
- Magnetic induction battery charging stands for cordless electric appliances produce 50–100 mG at a 3-inch-radius distance and 3 mG at an 18-inch-radius distance.
- Conventional electric ovens average 2 mG at a 2-foot-radius distance.
- Microwave ovens at full power generate 70–100 mG at a 1-foot-radius distance and 2–3 mG at a 6-foot-radius distance.
- Handheld electric hair dryers emit about 100 mG near the handle and 10–15 mG at normal drying distance.
- Automatic coffee makers average 2–3 mG at a 1-foot-radius distance.

I would encourage all parents to take their own electromagnetic field (EMF) readings to be absolutely sure their home (especially the bedroom) does not have any serious "hot spots." Electromagnetic detection meters (gauss meters) range in price from $100 to $400. One of the best brands for the money is the TRI-FIELD METER, which reads electric field strength, magnetic field strength, and radio/microwave power density. You can purchase it for about $165 from Alpha Lab (800-769-3754) or Safe Technologies Corporation (800-638-9121).

It's also worth noting that some electric utility companies will send a service representative out to your home and take EMF readings for free, but remember, the utility company might downplay the significance of high readings because it's frightened by the possibility of lawsuits.

Prudent Avoidance
of Electromagnetic Fields

There are many practical, sensible, and inexpensive ways to reduce health risks from electromagnetic fields without cramping anyone's high-tech style. As the following suggestions demonstrate, the real key is prudent avoidance.

First and foremost, use a gauss meter to measure the fields inside and outside your home to accurately determine where the EMFs are coming from and how strong they are at certain distances from the source. Then maintain a safe distance from those sources. Avoid prolonged or chronic exposure to magnetic fields above 1 mG, electric fields above 1 kV/m, and radio or microwave fields above .01 milliwatts per square centimeter.

Until the safety issue of EMFs is settled once and for all, I personally would not live, sleep, work or let children play within:

- 300 yards of electric power plants and substations,
- 300 yards of very high-voltage (300,000–700,000 volts) power lines,
- 100 yards of 50,000–100,000-volt power lines,
- 30–50 feet of neighborhood primary "distribution" (4,000–15,000 volts) power lines and step-down transformers (the gray drums that look like small metal trash cans on top of power line poles), or
- 10 feet of the 115/230 volt service drop line that connects to the house fuse box or circuit breaker box.

I would also keep a half-mile radius from radar and microwave relay towers and radio and television stations and their transmitting towers.

Remember, magnetic fields travel through soil, rocks, and cement, so burying electric power lines underground may look better, but it won't block or shield their magnetic fields; it just creates a false sense of security.

Never under any circumstances use electric blankets, heating pads,

water bed heaters, or automatic adjustable/vibrator-massage beds, because as long as they're plugged in they can transfer strong electric
fields to your body all night long while you're sleeping. Conventional
electric blankets and heating pads produce a strong magnetic field that
can penetrate up to seven inches into the body. Several major manufacturers of electric blankets have come out with blankets designed to emit
no magnetic fields. The problem is that these "zero magnetic field"
blankets may still emit strong electric fields as long as they're plugged
in, so if you insist on using an electric blanket to warm the bed before
retiring, be sure to unplug it before you get in. As long as it's plugged
in, a high electric field may be transferred to your body.

Keep at least a five-foot-radius distance from any electrical device
or appliance that is plugged in or operating. This is particularly important when you're sleeping, because you don't want electromagnetic
fields from things like electric alarm clocks irradiating your body
all night. For the bedroom, use an alarm clock and radio that run
on mercury-free flashlight batteries instead of alternating-current
(A/C) electricity.

Magnetic induction battery chargers for cordless electric appliances, portable cellular phones, and similar electronic devices produce
strong magnetic fields, so keep at least a five-foot-radius distance
from them.

Arrange furniture, especially beds and cribs, a safe distance from
electromagnetic hot spots in the house. For example, keep at least a 10-
foot-radius distance away from television sets and the fuse box or
circuit breaker box where the electric power cable enters the house.
And do not put a bed, crib, or chair next to a wall that has an electric
appliance (such as a television set, stereo, radio, electric clock, or
cordless electric toothbrush charger) on the other side because the
magnetic field passes right through the wall. Do not run any electrical
wires underneath the bed or crib.

Television screens produce some of the highest electromagnetic
fields you'll find in your house, so at the very minimum you should
always maintain at least a 6-foot-radius distance from the television.
Sitting 10 feet away from the average 19-inch television reduces the EMF

exposure to almost negligible levels. However, some of the big screens can generate large electromagnetic fields (EMFs), so as a general rule, the larger the screen, the farther back you should sit.

Also stay at least a 30-inch-radius distance from computer screens. Three feet would be even better. If the computer has a detachable keyboard, place it at least 30 inches from the screen. And stay at least 4 feet from the back and sides of computers since the electromagnetic fields at those spots are often twice as high as at the front.

Antiglare and antistatic shields for television and computer screens do not block magnetic fields at all, so don't be lulled into a false sense of security. One alternative is to buy a computer VDT that has been designed specifically to produce almost no magnetic field. Safe Technologies Corporation (800-638-9121) advertises a computer monitor said to have the lowest electromagnetic emissions in the world, well below the most stringent Swedish "MPR2" standards. Safe Technologies also offers a retrofit service for several popular computer models that substantially lowers their electromagnetic emissions.

Liquid crystal displays (LCDs) are commonly used in laptop computers. LCDs can produce magnetic fields as high as 20 mG at a distance of 7 inches (which can be quite significant when it's placed right in a person's lap). Safe Technologies Corporation manufactures a specially shielded and wired LCD computer display with almost negligible EMFs.

I do not recommend cooking with microwave ovens at all, but if you are going to do so, stay at least 10 feet away from the microwave oven when it's in use and have a qualified repairperson check it for leakage once a year.

Avoid three-way electric switches and light dimmers, because they produce very high EMFs. And use traditional incandescent lightbulbs instead of fluorescent bulbs that require a ballast device. A typical ceiling fluorescent lighting fixture with four bulbs can produce a 15–30 mG magnetic field at a one-foot distance, a 5 mG field at two feet, and a 2 mG field at three feet. Therefore, rooms with low ceilings and fluorescent lights may have readings as high as 2 mG at head level. And in multistory homes, buildings, and schools, it's possible for magnetic fields from fluorescent lights on the ceiling to penetrate through the floor and zap the feet and legs of the people standing immediately above them. (This is another instance in which a gauss meter comes in handy for taking actual EMF readings.)

Don't use electric hair dryers or curling irons. If you do, at least keep the exposure time to less than two minutes a day.

Whenever feasible, arrange household electrical wiring and appliances in such a way as to avoid creating any unnecessary electromagnetic fields. Be sure all of the electrical equipment and outlets in the home are properly wired and grounded.

A circuit analyzer is a small device that plugs into a standard electrical outlet and instantly tests it for proper wiring and grounding. You can purchase a circuit analyzer for about $5 at most hardware stores and then test every electrical outlet in your home. Improperly wired outlets waste energy, increase the strength of EMFs, and may even cause a serious shock or fire. Have a master electrician repair any defective or improperly wired outlets. Also have an electrician check to be sure the electric wiring in your home is not grounded to the plumbing pipes. If it is, your pipes will transmit electromagnetic fields throughout the house. Under no circumstances should the neutral or ground wires be grounded to the plumbing or any other ground except at the fuse box or circuit breaker box.

Warning

Never try to disconnect home grounding systems yourself. To avoid fire hazards and the danger of electrocution, have a licensed electrician perform all electrical work.

LEAD POISONING

According to the U.S. Department of Health and Human Services, lead poisoning is the number-one environmental health threat to young children, whether they live in public housing or affluent suburban homes. Approximately one out of nine preschoolers in the United States has blood lead levels high enough to cause health problems. That's the bad news. The good news is that lead poisoning is easily preventable.

Lead is a toxic heavy metal (like mercury and arsenic) that bioaccumulates in the body. This means that every time a person swallows or inhales lead-containing substances, some of the lead remains stored inside his or her body for many years because it cannot be completely excreted. And as lead accumulates, it begins to damage vital organs, such as the brain, nerves, kidneys, and liver, as well as the digestive system, immune system, red blood cells, reproductive system, and bones. Eating, drinking, or breathing just 10 micrograms of lead (equivalent in size to about three granules of sugar) every day is enough to cause brain damage over time.

Symptoms of Lead Poisoning

Depending on how much lead is actually absorbed into the body, lead poisoning can cause any of the following symptoms either singly or in combination: developmental delay, mental retardation, lowered intelligence scores on IQ tests, autism, learning and reading disabilities, hyperactivity, attention deficit disorder, difficulty concentrating, Alzheimerlike disorientation and memory loss, tremors, clumsiness, loss of coordination, hearing loss, speech impairments, tingling sensations, paralysis, muscle aches and pains, irritability, chronic fatigue, stunted growth, weight loss, vomiting, constipation, abdominal pain, infant colic, kidney damage, anemia, high blood pressure, and cancer. High blood lead levels can cause encephalitis (inflammation and swelling of the brain), resulting in seizures, coma, or death. As you can see from this list, most of the symptoms are due to lead's devastating effect on the brain and neurologic system. *A child who shows any of these symptoms should have a blood lead test performed immediately.*

Common Sources of Lead Contamination

Lead paint chips and dust from walls, floors, woodwork, doors, window frames, furniture, and toys are the major sources of lead poisoning in preschool children. Just one chip of paint can contain enough lead to cause lead poisoning.

Almost all homes and buildings built before 1960 (and 75 percent of homes built prior to 1980) have lead-based paint at some level unless all of the earlier layers were previously removed by licensed lead-removal professionals. Lead was banned from housepaint in 1978, but lead is an element that persists indefinitely (it does not biodegrade or dissolve over time), and painting over the old paint with new lead-free paint does not eliminate the problem since paint chips still contain enough lead in the deeper layers to cause lead poisoning if swallowed.

Please note that some paints (such as professional artists' paints and paints for bridges, boats, and factories) are exempted from the 1978 ban and can still contain lead, as can some painted jewelry (especially imported pieces).

Remodeling projects in homes that contain lead paint can contaminate the entire house with a permanent layer of lead dust on floors, walls, furniture, and toys unless special precautions are taken during the renovation and proper cleanup is performed at completion. The soil outside the home can also become contaminated with lead from auto exhaust, factory emissions, or flaking of lead-based paint chips from the exterior walls, windows, and railings. The lead-tainted soil then gets tracked into the home and deposited on the floor, where preschoolers either inhale the dust or swallow it through their typical hand-to-mouth activities.

About 20 percent of a child's total lead exposure comes from lead in tap water. Lead enters tap water by way of lead water mains, service connector pipes, and household plumbing pipes, fittings, and fixtures with lead solder. Please note that water pumps used for private wells may contain brass or bronze parts that leach significant amounts of lead into the tap water, depending on the natural acidity and corrosiveness of the water.

Lead-containing glazes are often used on ceramic dishes (cups, mugs, plates, bowls), pottery, china, and porcelain to give them a shiny, smooth surface. When ceramicware is fired at a high enough temperature, the lead becomes sealed into the glaze and will not leach from the surface, but if the glaze is applied improperly or is damaged from harsh dishwasher detergents and everyday use, lead will leach from the dishes and into the food or beverage. Domestic pottery and ceramic dinnerware made in the United States are usually fired at high enough temperatures to make them safe, but foreign manufacturers often do not comply with the standard. In fact it's estimated that up to 14 percent of imported dishes exceed U.S. safety standards for lead. That's why imported lead-glazed pottery and ceramics are notorious for leaching lead into food and drinks, especially those high in acid, such as orange or grapefruit juice, apple juice, coffee or tea, cola, tomato sauce or juice, wine, and vinegar-containing foods such as salad dressings. Lead can also leach from pewter tableware or improperly fired lead crystal. One study found that brandy stored in lead crystal containers absorbed enough lead to exceed the safety limit by a factor of 400.

Certain businesses and industries such as smelters and foundries, mining, industrial incinerators, battery and ammunition factories, shooting ranges, radiator repair shops, auto body shops, stained-glass making, home remodeling, bridge repair, and building demolition release lead into the environment, where it may be inhaled directly or deposited in the soil or on the clothing.

Food from cans with lead-soldered seams may contain high levels of lead. More than one billion lead-soldered food cans are sold through U.S. food stores each year. Imported canned foods are generally the worst offenders.

Accidental ingestion of lead curtain weights, fishing sinkers, bullets, or other small lead objects can lead to lead poisoning.

Substantial amounts of lead are often found in calcium supplements derived from dolomite, bonemeal or hydroxyapatite, and natural-source calcium carbonate or oyster shells.

Newspapers, comic books, magazines, and food wrappers may be printed with dyes that contain lead, especially red, yellow, or orange ink.

Major Risk Factors for Lead Poisoning

The presence of one or more of the following conditions puts a child at high risk for lead poisoning and thus calls for blood lead testing at regular intervals for as long as the condition(s) exists:

- The child lives in (or regularly visits) a home, daycare center, preschool, or other building built before 1980 that has peeling or chipping paint or is being renovated or remodeled. Please note that a child who ever lived in (or regularly visited) any houses or buildings built before 1960 is at particularly high risk.
- The child exhibits the behavior pattern called *pica*, which consists of compulsively eating nonfood items, especially dirt and paint chips.
- The child has brothers, sisters, playmates, or housemates who have been diagnosed with lead poisoning.
- The child lives or spends a lot of time near a business or industry likely to release lead into the environment, such as a lead smelter or foundry, battery or ammunition factory, radiator repair shop, auto body shop, toxic waste dump, trash incinerator, or shooting range.
- The child lives or spends a lot of time near major highways and streets with a lot of traffic. The soil in these locations is likely to be contaminated with lead-tainted auto exhaust, accumulated over the years when leaded gasoline was routinely used.
- The home plumbing has lead pipes or lead solder joints, fittings, or fixtures.
- The child drinks or eats from imported pottery or ceramic glasses, bowls, or dishes.
- The child's parent or regular caregiver has a job or hobby considered high risk for lead contamination, such as lead smeltering, battery manufacturing or recycling, building demolition, home remodeling, housepainting, firearms instruction, ammunition manufacturing, radiator or auto body repairing, welding, soldering, printing, pottery making, fine art painting, or stained-glass work.

• The child has been given certain folk remedies, such as azarcon, greta, pay looah, or shung fa.

Prevention of Lead Poisoning

The following precautions will significantly reduce your child's risk of lead poisoning:

First and foremost, ask the doctor to perform a blood lead test on your child at 12 months of age and again at 2 years. It's the only sure way to find out if lead poisoning is present. The cost ranges from $30 to $40, but that's nothing compared to the possibility of irreversible brain damage from undetected lead poisoning.

Note: Be sure the doctor orders a blood lead test instead of the cheap and inaccurate FEP (free erythrocyte protoporphyrin). A child with a blood lead level above 10 micrograms/dL is at risk for the health problems just listed.

The American Academy of Pediatrics and the Centers for Disease Control (CDC) recommend blood lead testing for all children at risk for lead poisoning (see the preceding list), starting at six months and then every six months thereafter until the risk factor is removed. And a child who has any of the symptoms of lead poisoning should have a blood lead test performed immediately. The CDC can provide you with the latest information on the treatment of lead poisoning in children.

Because you cannot see, taste, or smell lead, your home (and school or daycare facility) should have its exterior and interior house-paint, water, and soil tested for lead by an accredited environmental testing laboratory or state-licensed lead paint inspector. Professional lead testing companies can use a portable x-ray fluorescence lead detector, which measures the amount of lead in all the layers of paint without having to remove samples, or they can scrape samples and send them to a laboratory for analysis.

Although not as accurate as a lead testing laboratory, a do-it-yourself lead testing kit, such as Lead Check Swabs from Lead Check (800-262-LEAD) or the Frandon Lead Alert Kit from Pace Environs, Inc. (800-359-9000), can give you a rough approximation of whether or not there is lead contamination in the paint, soil, pottery, glazed ceramics, crystal, tiles, toys, and soldered food cans in your home. Lead Check Swabs are available in the paint section of many hardware stores and home improvement centers. You simply rub the tip of an activated swab on the surface to be tested (ceramics, crystal, metals, paint, plumbing, painted toys, food can seams, dust, soil), and if the swab or the surface turns pink, you know that lead is present and leaching out in amounts greater than the current EPA limits.

No matter which lead detection method you decide to use, if lead is detected in or around your home, consult your local health department, the Centers for Disease Control (404-488-7330), or the EPA (800-424-LEAD) for advice on safe removal.

The American Board of Industrial Hygiene (517-321-2638) can verify whether a contractor has received the special training required to properly remove lead paint, and the American Industrial Hygiene Association (703-849-8888) can provide you with a list of certified lead assessment and abatement contractors in your area.

Before you sand, scrape, or strip, always test painted surfaces for lead in a home built before 1980. If lead is detected, under no circumstances should you attempt to remove the paint from your home. This is a job for trained professionals—not a do-it-yourselfer—because removal of lead-based paint can cause tremendous lead contamination and lead poisoning when done improperly. Never use power sanding equipment, sandblasting equipment, heat removal with a torch or high-temperature heat gun, or paint strippers that contain highly toxic methylene chloride. Never eat, drink, or smoke in the work area. All family members should have a blood lead test after the renovation or deleading project is finished.

If you have trouble locating a licensed lead removal contractor in your area, call your regional U.S. Department of Housing and Urban Development (HUD) office, the regional EPA office, or the Centers for Disease Control (404-488-7330) for recommendations.

The following steps will help reduce the amount of lead in tap water:

- The only way to tell whether or not your tap water contains dangerous amounts of lead is to have it tested as explained in the "Drinking Water" section of Chapter 1. This is especially important if your tap water comes from a private well. And if your child regularly drinks the water at day care or school, be sure it has been tested for lead and certified to be within acceptable limits.

  According to EPA guidelines for lead in public drinking water, the level should not exceed 15 micrograms per liter (15 parts per billion). Children who drink water that contains lead at a concentration of 15 parts per billion will raise their blood level an average of 1–2 micrograms/dL, and those who drink water that has a lead concentration of 100 ppb will raise their blood level an average of 4–7 micrograms/dL. For further information, the EPA has a Safe Drinking Water hot line (800-426-4791).

- As discussed in Chapter 1, water from the hot side of the tap should never be used for drinking, cooking, or preparing baby formula, because it contains much higher amounts of lead and other toxic heavy metals than does the cold side. If you need hot water, draw it from the cold side of the tap and heat it on the stove. (If you have a single-lever faucet, be sure the handle is turned all the way to the cold side so the hot water doesn't mix with it.)

- Whenever the water in a particular faucet has not been used for three hours or longer, let the water run for two minutes to flush the accumulated lead out of the pipes before collecting it for food or drinks.

- Avoid using ice from automatic ice cube makers, because the water sits in the pipes for extended periods of times and may pick up significant amounts of lead or other toxic heavy metals. Make your ice cubes the old-fashioned way.

- Try not to drink water from fountains or coolers, because they are often constructed in such a way that the water gets contaminated with lead.
- If you are moving into a newly built home, remove all the strainers or aerators from the faucets before using the tap water and let the water run for 15 minutes to flush loose lead solder and debris from the pipes.
- Instruct plumbers to use only lead-free materials when they install new plumbing or make repairs. Or better yet, use metal no-solder flare joints.

Whenever possible, replace dust-trapping wall-to-wall carpets with glazed ceramic tiles made in the United States, stone tiles, or solid hardwood flooring materials. (Imported ceramic floor tiles may contain improperly fired lead glazes that could potentially cause a problem.) On the other hand, if you're stuck with wall-to-wall carpeting, vacuum at least twice a week and discard the disposable dust bag after every vacuuming. And not just any vacuum cleaner will do; see "Indoor Air Pollutants" for advice on choosing a vacuum that will really work and not just spread contaminants all through your house.

Place doormats at the entrance of each door so everyone entering the home can wipe their feet first. Rinse off the doormats outside twice a week. Better yet, take off outdoor shoes as soon as you come indoors. Shoe removal will reduce the amount of lead dust tracked inside the house by 90 percent.

Discourage your child from eating or chewing paint chips, dust, dirt, or any other nonfood item that might be contaminated with lead paint. Make sure your children wash their hands after playing outside and before meals, naps, and bedtime to remove any lead-tainted dust and dirt. Do not let children chew on newspapers, magazines, or comics, because the ink and pigments may contain lead. And the print on plastic bags (such as bread wrappers) often contains lead, so don't store or carry food in such bags, especially if the printing on the bag is turned inside, where it would be in direct contact with the food. Never use antique or secondhand nursery furniture that might be painted with lead-based paint (many paints contained lead prior to 1980);

painting over the old paint with new lead-free paint does not solve the problem, since paint chips would still contain enough lead in the deeper layers to cause lead poisoning.

Do not burn newspapers or any painted wood boards, because the ink or paint might contain lead, which would then become an airborne hazard.

The Frandon Lead Alert Kit or Lead Check Swabs can be used to test dishes, pottery, ceramics, china, crystal, and other items you suspect may be contaminated with lead. Check areas that are cracked or chipped to see if lead is leaching from them. Lead crystal decanters, ceramicware that has a dusty or chalky gray residue, hand-crafted china, and dishes with hand-painted decorations or bright glazes on their inside surface should be considered highly suspect until they've been tested. If your home has old ceramic tile floors, you might want to consider testing a small sample with Lead Check Swabs, especially if the tiles were imported.

Never heat foods or beverages (especially coffee) in ceramicware, china, or pewter, because heat increases the likelihood of lead leaching into the food.

Never use imported, homemade, or old pottery or ceramic dinnerware for eating, drinking, or storing food or beverages. Stick with domestic ceramic products, because they are much more likely to have a glaze that has been formulated correctly and fired properly to prevent lead from leaching.

Do not prepare, serve, or store highly acidic foods and beverages (orange or grapefruit juice, apple juice, coffee or tea, cola, tomato sauce or juice, wine, vinegar-containing foods, and the like) in ceramic dinnerware, pottery, china, or pewter. For food storage, use lead-free glass, Pyrex, Corning Ware, or stainless-steel containers.

If you buy canned foods and beverages, avoid the cans with lead-solder seams. The cans with welded-steel seams are safer. A welded-steel seam is neat, flat, thin, shiny blue steel, as opposed to the lead solder side seams, which are raised, lumpy, and dull gray. Of course, to be absolutely sure you should call the manufacturer and ask if the can has lead solder or welded-steel seams, or you can test them with a Lead Check Swab. (Aluminum cans are usually one-piece construction and have no seams and therefore no solder. That's the good news. The bad news is that aluminum cans leach aluminum into the food or beverage, and until more research is done on the link between Alzheimer's disease and aluminum, I would avoid them.)

Don't bring lead dust into your home from work or from a hobby. For parents or caregivers who work at occupations or hobbies considered high risk for lead contamination, leave work clothes at the factory or job site and send them out to be laundered. Take a bath and shampoo your hair as soon as you get home from work or finish your hobby, because lead dust accumulates on clothing, skin, and hair. For hobbies, use only lead-free art and craft materials and lead-free solder.

Do not give your child calcium supplements derived from bonemeal (hydroxyapatite), oyster shells, dolomite, limestone, or chalk. These so-called natural-source calcium supplements may contain significant amounts of lead. Calcium carbonate synthesized in the laboratory (Caltrate, for example) is much safer than the natural brands. Other good calcium supplements include calcium combined with gluconate, citrate, malate, or glycinate.

THE NURSERY
Furniture

The guidelines given for furniture earlier in the chapter apply especially to nursery furniture. All furniture in the nursery should be solid hardwood—oak, maple, beechwood, birch, cherry, ash, walnut, poplar, pecan, hickory, or teak—with a nontoxic, no-wax finish. To reduce the risk of cuts and scratches, choose furniture with smooth edges and rounded corners. Furniture made of plastic, plywood, chipboard, particleboard, pressboard, or fiberboard should be avoided.

Cribs

To prevent falls, strangulation, suffocation, and other serious crib accidents, follow these safety tips:

- The crib mattress must be extrafirm—not soft or spongy—and fit snugly into the crib frame without any gaps along the sides or ends. Never use pillows, quilts, comforters, lambskin, sheepskin, mattress pads, water beds, or beanbag mattresses or cushions, because the baby's face may become wedged or embedded in the soft surface, resulting in suffocation.
- To prevent your child from getting her head caught, spaces between crib slats, bars, rods, and any other such openings must not be more than 2⅜ inches apart, and slats and bars should not be broken, loose, or missing. In addition, the headboard and footboard must not have decorative cutouts, and the corner posts should be no higher than $\frac{1}{16}$ inch above the headboard or footboard to prevent entanglement of clothing, toys, or cords that could hang onto the crib and cause accidental strangulation.
- Don't use bumper pads in the crib. They aren't necessary, they sometimes have plastic covers which emit chemical odors, they provide a step for older babies to climb up and out of the crib, and they block the baby's vision.
- Always lock the crib sides in the fully raised position when your baby is in the crib. Keep the mattress on the lowest setting. To prevent your child from climbing out of the crib, the distance from the top of the mattress to the top of the fully raised sides of the crib should always be greater than his or her height. When your child is 35 inches tall (usually around two years old) or can climb over the sides of the crib, it's usually time to move him out of the crib and into a regular bed.
- The latest safety standards for cribs went into effect in 1990, so I recommend buying a new crib rather than a hand-me-down.
- Don't put the crib next to windows, heaters, lamps, or wall decorations. And keep the crib away from draperies and window blinds so the baby won't get tangled up in the cords and strangle. In addition, to prevent entanglement, crib toys should have no strings longer than 12 inches. Crib mobiles and gyms should never be strung across the crib within the baby's reach. Remove

gyms and mobiles once your child is old enough to push up on her hands and knees (usually at about five months). Before your child can pull to a standing position (around 9–11 months), remove any objects from the crib (such as bumper pads or large toys) that could be used as steps to climb out.
- Never use pillows in a crib because of the danger of suffocation!

ACCIDENT PREVENTION AND SAFETY ISSUES

Accidental injuries are among the most common reasons for visits to the doctor's office or emergency room, so play it safe and take all the necessary precautions. Many of the safety products mentioned in this chapter can be purchased by mail order through the Perfectly Safe catalog (800-837-KIDS), or check with your local baby shop or home improvement center, such as Home Depot or Builders Square.

Smoke and Fire Detector

This is an absolute must. Unfortunately, almost all commercially available smoke detectors are the ionization type, which contain radioactive americium 241. For obvious ecological reasons I prefer the nonionizing smoke detectors, which do not contain radioactive components. However, the most important thing is to have a detector, and if the only one you can find is the ionization type, go ahead and get it and be sure to check its battery weekly.

Carbon Monoxide (CO) Detector

As discussed earlier in the chapter, all homes (especially those with natural gas or combustion appliances) should have one of these detectors, which will sound an alarm if dangerous levels of carbon monoxide gas occur.

Electricity Safety Devices

Use electric outlet covers or install special tamper-resistant sockets to prevent accidental electrocution. Another very important safety device is a ground fault circuit interrupter (GFCI), or shock resistor as it's sometimes called. GFCIs automatically shut off the power whenever ground fault conditions exist (when a child pokes an object into a live socket, for example). A single GFCI can be wired to protect all standard outlets on the same circuit, or you can wire GFCIs directly into the circuit breaker box.

Electric Cord Safety

All electric cords should be hidden behind furniture or tucked away safely into special hide-a-cord windup devices to reduce the risk of a child's tripping, being strangled, pulling the cord and toppling things over, or chewing on the cord and sustaining a severe burn or shock.

Safety Locks and Latches

Put childproof safety latches on all cabinets, drawers, and appliances within the child's reach. A childproof lid-lock device for the toilet seat cover will help prevent unwanted mishaps by curious toddlers. These locks and latches are inexpensive and easy to install.

Bumper Cushions

Until your child is about four years old and steady on her feet, you'll need bumper cushions on any sharp corners, such as sharp-edged coffee tables, that a toddler would be prone to fall against. You can buy ready-made form-fit bumper pads or make your own using folded cotton towels or receiving blankets. A low-odor foil tape can be used to hold them in place if necessary. Oh sure, it may look a little weird and tacky, but it works, and it will save you trips to the emergency room for bumps, cuts, and stitches.

Security Gates

Security gates can help keep crawling and toddling children in one room and away from hazards like stairs, but none of these products is totally reliable, so if you decide to buy a gate, follow these safety tips:

- Do not use homemade gates. Security gates manufactured after 1985 are preferred. The top edge should be straight (not V-shaped or saw-toothed), and the hardware should be mounted permanently so the gate will be sturdy enough to withstand the weight and force of a small child. Gates that mount by pressure bars alone may collapse under the child's weight, or the child may use the bar as a step to climb over the gate. Also, never use accordion-style gates with diamond-shaped openings, because your child might get her head or fingers caught. And avoid gates with wide-holed mesh.
- Gates should be used at the bottom of a stairway to keep the child from going upstairs without adult supervision. Never let a toddler wander alone upstairs (even if you have a security gate at the top of the stairway) because gates just aren't reliable enough.
- Do not rely on security gates to restrain children over two years old. Once they reach this age, many children become strong enough to overpower a security gate easily.

Infant Swings

Most babies enjoy the rhythmic to-and-fro motion of automatic swings. The battery-powered models don't work too well, so your best buy is a manual windup swing with a quiet winding mechanism and long running time.

Automatic swings are generally handy and safe to use if you follow certain precautions:

- Always use the restraining belt to prevent the baby from being thrown forward in the seat. If your infant swing comes equipped with a cradle or carrier bed attachment, do not use it, because the baby may accidentally get her face trapped against the side and suffocate while swinging.

- Be sure the baby's head is adequately supported and does not slump or flop forward or sideways.
- Never leave your baby alone while he is swinging.
- Stop using automatic swings once your baby is old enough to sit up without assistance (six to eight months) because of the danger of tipping over.

Baby Walkers

Baby walkers are extremely dangerous, so my advice is never to use them under any circumstances. They cause more than 20,000 accidental injuries every year, such as cuts, pinched fingers and toes, burns, brain concussions, skull fractures, broken bones, tooth injuries, and drownings.

And in spite of the name, baby walkers do not strengthen babies' legs or help them learn to walk unassisted. In fact studies have shown that excessive use (more than one hour a day) teaches abnormal movement patterns and actually interferes with learning how to walk properly.

Baby Jumpers/Exercisers

Another accident just waiting to happen is the baby jumper or exerciser, which consists of a seat attached to elastic or spring cords hung in a doorway. A baby jumper may come loose from the door frame when your child really starts to bounce up and down hard, or she may get carried away and ricochet into the side of the doorway. My advice is never to use them.

7
Pest Control

Pesticide is a general term for any substance that kills pests. Specifically, insecticides kill insects, termiticides kill termites, herbicides kill weeds, rodenticides kill rodents, and fungicides kill fungi. Many of the popular synthetic pesticides, which you can buy right off the shelf at the local supermarket, are actually watered down derivatives of toxic nerve gas. That's why they are so harmful to humans, mammals, birds, fish, and other wildlife that come into contact with them.

Despite clear evidence of adverse health effects and ecological devastation caused by the senseless and indiscriminant use of toxic chemical pesticides, millions of Americans continue to saturate their homes, lawns, and gardens with these deadly poisons. Part of the reason for this apparent insanity is a widely held—but grossly incorrect—belief that over-the-counter pesticides have to comply with strict government safety standards. The fact is, registration of an insecticide with the EPA is not a guarantee of its safety. Regulatory loopholes allowing companies to bypass important safety tests, trade secret status of so-called inert ingredients, fraudulent toxicological tests, and grossly inadequate testing for long-term adverse health effects are just a few of the ways in which very dangerous pesticide products are registered for use and sold throughout the United States and abroad. In fact the National Academy of Sciences estimates that over 75 percent of the ingredients found in pesticides have not been tested for their ability to cause cancer, chromosome damage, birth defects, and damage to the immune and neurologic systems.

PESTICIDES AND DISEASE—
HARVEST OF A SILENT SPRING*?*

In 1962 vanguard environmentalist and award-winning biologist Rachel Carson (1907–1964) wrote *Silent Spring* to warn Americans about the many dangers associated with toxic synthetic pesticides. Her book chronicles the massive deaths of birds and other wildlife caused by the irrational and utterly irresponsible use of DDT, heptachlor, chlordane, parathion, and other highly toxic chemical insecticides. It also describes how these pesticides accumulate in the tissues of plants and animals and alter the genetic (DNA) structures on which the entire future of our planet depends.

Even though scientific studies have repeatedly verified Rachel Carson's findings of severe ecological disruptions caused by pesticides, their sale has actually tripled—not decreased—over the last 30 years. In fact approximately 2.6 billion pounds of pesticides are now used in the United States each year on farm crops and in homes, hospitals, schools, and offices. And U.S. chemical manufacturers still export banned pesticides, such as chlordane and heptachlor, to foreign countries, which spray their crops and then ship the tainted produce right back to the United States for consumption.

What does this massive poisoning of the environment really accomplish? What is the ultimate harvest of pesticide abuse? Well, it's fairly obvious to most people that the bugs are still thriving—but the fish, birds, and other wildlife are suffering and dying at an alarming rate, and we humans aren't exactly in great shape either, with cancer rates rising significantly each year. As Rachel Carson put it, "Future historians may well be amazed by our distorted sense of proportion. How could intelligent beings seek to control a few unwanted species by a method that contaminated the entire environment and brought the threat of disease and death even to their own kind?"

SYMPTOMS OF PESTICIDE POISONING

Symptoms and health problems caused by pesticides depend on the level of exposure. An acute, high-level exposure to synthetic pesticides (such as farm workers might encounter) can cause paralysis, unconsciousness, seizures, coma, and death. An acute, moderate exposure can cause Alzheimerlike mental confusion and disorientation, hyperactivity, impaired concentration, headaches, loss of balance, dizziness, blurred vision, burning and watery eyes, sweating, increased salivation and drooling, sore throat, runny nose, coughing, shortness of breath, labored breathing or wheezing, muscle twitching or weakness, irregular heartbeat (palpitations), vomiting, diarrhea, stomach cramps, abdominal pain, and skin rashes. A chronic, low-level exposure (as might occur with the routine use of home and garden pesticides) over a long period of time may cause cancer, infertility, birth defects, allergies, multiple chemical sensitivity, chronic fatigue, immune system dysfunction, frequent infections, and autoimmune diseases (lupus, multiple sclerosis, and the like). If you suspect a family member may be a victim of pesticide poisoning, contact your doctor and the Poison Control Center immediately.

PESTICIDES IN THE HOME

The use of synthetic pesticide products in and around your home is much more hazardous to your family's health than eating food that has minuscule amounts of pesticide residues. For example, the National Cancer Institute found that children were 3.8 times more likely to develop leukemia if their parents routinely used pesticide sprays in the home, and dogs were twice as likely to develop cancer if their owners used the herbicide 2,4-D on the lawn. In addition, a study published in the January 1993 issue of Archives of Environmental Contamination and Toxicology (Vol 24, pp. 87–92) found that the risk of childhood brain cancer increased with the use of insecticides containing carbaryl (Sevin) or diazinon, termite treatments, herbicides to kill weeds in the yard, Kwell shampoo to treat head lice, flea collars for pets, "no-pest" strips for common household insects, and insect foggers or bombs.

Insecticides

Commercial pesticides contain two types of ingredients: active and inert. The active ingredients are the chemicals specifically intended to kill the bugs and usually constitute only about 1–2 percent of the product. The other 98 percent or so typically consists of so-called inert ingredients that are in many cases more toxic than the active ingredients.

A whole smorgasbord of toxic chemicals are registered as inert ingredients, including formaldehyde, surfactants, carriers, diluents, solvents, emulsifiers, stabilizers, catalysts, coating agents, buffers, preservatives, thickeners, attractants, dyes, defoamers, synergists, intensifiers, binders, sequestrants, anticaking agents, propellants, adhesives, and petroleum distallates. Many of the inerts are known carcinogens, but perhaps even more alarming is the fact that a complete toxicity profile has never been performed on the more than 1,200 chemicals used as inert ingredients in everyday consumer products. The potential health hazards are staggering.

The list of active ingredients in pesticides can be quite intimidating at first glance, but with the following insecticide chart you'll be able to decode instantly all the mumbo jumbo. For example, say you look at the list of active ingredients on an insecticide label and see the chemical tongue twister *phosphorothioic acid O,O-diethyl O-(3,5,6-trichloro-2-pyridinyl) ester*. Alongside the technical name you will usually notice an equivalent (and much simpler) generic name, *chlorpyrifos*, and/or brand name, Dursban. Then you'll quickly scan the insecticide chart and discover that it is in the high-toxicity organophosphate category, which is generally unacceptable and should be avoided in most instances. It's as simple as that.

There are 10 major insecticide chemical categories. Three of them are considered highly toxic and seven least toxic. Under each of the categories in the following chart and text, the generic names of the most frequently used chemicals are listed in alphabetical order along with their brand names in parentheses.

The organochlorine insecticides are extremely hazardous because they resist biodegradation and can persist in the ecosystem for 30 years or more after an application. In addition, there is growing scientific evidence of a strong link between breast cancer and exposure to the estrogenic organochlorine pesticides (DDT, DDE, endosulfan, heptachlor, and methoxy-chlor). The higher the amount of estrogenic organochlorine pesticides stored in a woman's fat tissue and blood, the higher is her risk of developing breast cancer.

HIGHLY TOXIC INSECTICIDES

Toxic Warning

Chemicals from the three highly toxic insecticide categories (organophosphates, carbamates, and organochlorines) are nerve poisons that kill insects by damaging their nervous systems. They can also damage human and animal nerves, resulting in a variety of neurologic symptoms, such as headaches, memory loss, disorientation, impaired concentration, dizziness, loss of balance or coordination, seizures, paralysis, muscle weakness, blurred vision, nausea, and vomiting. Therefore, never use any product that contains high-toxicity insecticides in or around your home or on your pets.

Organophosphate Insecticides

Acephate (Orthene)
Azinphos-methyl (Guthion)
Chlorpyrifos (Dursban, Lorsban)
Chlorpyrifos-methyl (Reldan)
Cythioate (Proban)
Demeton (Systox)
Diazinon (Spectracide, Knox Out)
Dichlorovinyl dimethyl phosphate
   (DDVP, Dichlorvos, Vapona)
Dimethoate (Cygon, Rogor)

Ethion (Ethanox, Ethiol,
   Rhodocide)
Isofenphos (Amaze, Pryfon 6)
Malathion (Cythion)
Methamidophos (Monitor)
Mevinphos (Phosdrin)
Parathion (Fosferno, Paraphos,
   Phoskil, Thiophos)
Phosmet (Imidan, Prolate)
Ronnel (Ectoral)

Carbamate Insecticides

Aldicarb (Temik)
Bendiocarb (Ficam)
Carbaryl (Sevin)
Carbofuran (Furadan)

Methiocarb (Draza, Mesurol)
Methomyl (Lannate)
Methyl carbamate
Propoxur (Baygon)

Organochlorine Insecticides

Aldrin
Alpha-benzene hexachloride (BHC)
Gamma-benzene hexachloride
   (Lindane, Kwell)
Chlordane (Octachlor)
DDT (Dichlorodiphenyltrichloroethane)
Dicofol (Kelthane)
Dieldrin

Endosulfan (Thiodan)
Endrin
Heptachlor
Methoxy-clor (DMDT,
   Methoxy-DDT, Marlate)
Pentachlorophenol (Dowicide G,
   PCP, Penta, Santobrite)

Least Toxic Insecticides

The least toxic insecticides include boric acid, hydramethylnon, insect growth regulators, avermectin, insecticidal soap, pyrethrins and pyrethroids, and synergists. Please note that the term least toxic means just that a chemical is less toxic when compared to the highly toxic ones, which are incredibly poisonous, so don't be lulled into thinking that these chemicals are completely safe to use. All pesticides are dangerous and must be handled with great caution. They must always be kept out of the reach of children and pets.

Boric acid. Boric acid is used primarily to control ants and roaches. Brand names include Borid, Drax, Roach Prufe, and Roach Kil.

Hydramethylnon. Hydramethylnon is used mainly to control ants and roaches. Even though it is considered a least toxic insecticide, I would use it only in the form of plastic bait disks or dry granules, such as Amdro, Combat SuperBait Advanced Formula Ant Control Bait Discs, and Combat SuperBait Advanced Formula Roach Control Bait Discs.

Insect growth regulators. Insect growth regulators (IGRs) are not poisons in the traditional sense of the word. They are chemicals that kill insects by arresting their growth at a critical stage in the egg-larva-pupa-adult life cycle. Since humans and mammals don't go through this particular maturation process, insect growth regulators are supposed to be safe for use in the home as long as they do not contain any other insecticides added to the formulation (read the list of active ingredients on the label to be sure). Keep in mind, however, that the IGRs are relatively new, and long-term effects of chronic exposure are unknown. In addition, the IGR foggers and aerosol sprays contain toxic inert ingredients that are dangerous to breathe. Follow directions closely when using any of these products, avoid unnecessary exposure, and use the granule bait form of IGRs when available. Examples of IGRs include fenoxycarb (Torus) for roaches, hydroprene (Gencor) for roaches, and methoprene for fleas (Precor, Flea Trol) or ants (Logic).

Avermectin/abamectin. Avermectin (also called *abamectin*) is a natural insecticide produced by common soil bacteria called *Streptomyces avermitilis*. It selectively kills certain undesirable insects, such as fire ants and roaches. It biodegrades rapidly when exposed to air and sunlight. Examples include Avert for roaches and Ascend for fire ants.

Insecticidal soap. Most commercial insecticidal soap sprays contain a 2 percent concentration of "potassium salts of fatty acids" as their active ingredient, and that's OK, but the other 98 percent of the product is composed of inert ingredients, some of which can be very hazardous to your health. Unfortunately, the manufacturers refuse to disclose the names of the inerts they use, so insecticidal soaps would not be my first choice for control of indoor pests. If you decide to use an insecticidal soap indoors, do not inhale the product or get it in your eyes or on your skin. Keep the room well ventilated with fresh air until the smell is gone. Better yet, make your own least toxic insecticidal soap spray, as explained later in the section on roaches and ants.

Pyrethrum, pyrethrins, pyrethroids, and permethrin. Pyrethrum is a natural insecticidal powder derived from whole chrysanthemum flowers that have been dried and crushed. *Pyrethrins* is a collective term for the six natural insecticidal substances extracted from pyrethrum powder. Pyrethroids are synthetic insecticidal chemicals whose structures closely resemble the natural pyrethrins, and permethrin is one of the major pyrethroid subgroups.

These agents are used for their quick knockdown power (almost instant paralysis of the insect). Unfortunately, pyrethrum, pyrethrins, and pyrethroids are nonselective and will kill all insects—good and bad—with which they come in contact; they are also highly toxic to fish. Natural pyrethrum and pyrethrins biodegrade rapidly in the presence of air, heat, and/or sunlight. The synthetic pyrethroids are slightly more resistant to biodegradation, but the biggest concern is that most of them are suspected carcinogens.

The following are the most frequently used synthetic pyrethroids:

- Allethrin (Pynamin, Pyresyn, and many others)
- Cyfluthrin (Baythroid and many others)
- Cypermethrin (Ammo, Barricade, Cypercare, Cyperkill, Demon)
- Deltamethrin (Butox, Decis, and many others)
- Fenvalerate (Pydrin, Tirade, and many others)
- Permethrin (Ambush, Dragnet, Permanone, Pounce, and many others)
- Phenothrin (Sumithrin and many others)

- Resmethrin (Scourge, Enforcer Wasp & Hornet Killer, and many others)
- Tetramethrin (Neo-Pynamin and many others)
- Tralomethrin (Scout, Tracker, and many others)

Trying to decipher the technical chemical names of synthetic pyrethroids is an exercise in futility. For example, the pyrethroid called *allethrin* has the following technical chemical name: (RS)-3-allyl-2-methyl-4-oxocyclopent-2-enyl (RS)-cis, trans-2,2-dimethyl-3 (2-methylprop-1-enyl) cyclopropanecarboxylate. This is why I recommend focusing on the common generic and/or brand names, and if the label doesn't provide them, don't buy the product.

Natural pyrethrins and synthetic pyrethroids are considered least toxic insectcides, but in my opinion they're too strong for trivial pests like roaches and ants, which can be controlled with less toxic products, such as boric acid or hydramethylnon bait. Therefore, I would reserve pyrethrins and synthetic pyrethroids for only the most difficult insect problems (wasps, hornets, and termites) that have not responded to less toxic remedies.

Toxic Warning

Persons who have asthma, hay fever, or allergies to chrysanthemums or ragweed should not use insecticide products that contain pyrethrum, pyrethrins, pyrethroids, or permethrin because of danger of a severe allergic reation.

Synergists. Synergists are chemicals added to insecticides (especially pyrethrin- or pyrethroid-based ones) to increase their killing power. Even though synergists are considered least toxic chemicals, they definitely increase the toxicity of the pesticides to which they are added, so I would avoid products that contain synergists whenever possible. The most frequently used synergists include N-octylbicylco-heptenedicarboximide (MGK 264, M2), petroleum distillates, and piperonyl butoxide (PBO, Methylenedioxyphenyl).

General Warnings for Insecticide Use in the Home

First and foremost: *Read the label.* Do not walk into a store and grab an insecticide off the shelf just because the front of the package has the name or picture of the insect you want to kill. Always take a minute to read carefully the common generic and brand names in the list of active ingredients and then consult the preceding insecticide chart and text to see if they're in the highly toxic or least toxic group.

When you're choosing a form of pesticide, never under any circumstances use insecticide foggers, fumigators, or bombs, because they leave toxic chemical residues on carpets, upholstery, and furniture, and the so-called inert propellants in foggers are either chlorofluorocarbons (CFCs or freon), which destroy the ozone layer, or highly flammable propane or butane, which could easily ignite a fire in the home.

Nor should you use pesticides in aerosol spray cans. The toxic ingredients stay suspended in the air for hours, resulting in dangerous inhalation exposure. When a liquid formulation is necessary, a hand pump spray bottle is a better choice, but remember that all commercial sprays contain inert ingredients that can be harmful, so be careful not to inhale the mist or get it on your skin or in your eyes.

Note that if you can smell the pesticide, it's not safe to be in the house breathing the air. Open the windows to increase the fresh air ventilation and stay out of the house until the odor is completely gone.

Professional pest control companies. I do not recommend signing contracts with conventional pest control companies for several reasons. First, no home needs to be saturated with chemical poisons every month. Second, most exterminators rely heavily on the highly toxic pesticide chemicals. Third, most professional exterminators seriously underestimate the dangers of the poisons they use. They state confidently that their chemicals are registered with the EPA and won't harm humans or pets, but as you've already discovered in the section on inert ingredients, being registered with the EPA amounts to very little when it comes to safety. Fourth, after a standard indoor pesticide application, it usually takes at least 1–3 days for the fumes to dissipate, and anyone entering the home or apartment during that period of time will be exposed to toxic VOCs. Incidentally, odor-free pesticides are more dangerous than smelly ones, because your nose no longer can sense their presence and warn you to get out of the room.

As an alternative, contact a local organic gardening center for recommendations or look in the yellow pages for the names of pest control firms in your area that practice integrated pest management.

General Nonchemical Strategies for Eliminating Insects and Rodents

To eliminate insects and rodents from your home without using chemicals, all you have to do in most instances is deny them access to food, water, and shelter by following these general strategies:

- Keep your home in good repair so that bugs and other critters can't get in. All windows and doors must have screens, and don't forget screens over the chimney and vents in the roof and attic. Keep gutters and downspouts free of leaves and other organic material. Apply metal weather stripping around entrance doors. Use silicone caulk to seal off cracks, crevices, and gaps around windows, doors, walls, and where pipes or wires enter the outside walls of the home.

- Prevent unwanted creatures from gaining access to water. Repair dripping faucets and any leaks in the plumbing, sinks, toilets, or roof. Eliminate stagnant pools of water.

- Cleanliness and proper food storage are absolutely essential. Store food in glass containers with rubber seals or plastic gaskets that can be closed tightly to lock bugs out. An equally effective choice would be plastic food containers with snap-on lids. Foods stored in paper bags and cardboard boxes are like magnets to bugs. Sweep or vacuum the kitchen floor every day to remove crumbs and other debris. Wipe up spills from the floor immediately. Keep stovetops and countertops clean. Rinse out jars, bottles, cans, dairy cartons, and meat wrappings before throwing them in the trash. Keep garbage in a tightly sealed plastic bag or container and try to take the trash out every night. Do not leave dirty dishes in the sink. Rinse them clean with water right after each meal is over. That goes for the pet's bowl too. Do not leave pet food sitting out overnight. Pick up the bowl and clean it after feeding time is over. Store dry pet food in tightly sealed glass containers.

- Whenever possible, avoid wall-to-wall carpeting, because it serves as a perfect hideout and breeding ground for a variety of bugs, especially fleas. Hardwood floors, ceramic tile, and stone tile are inhospitable to bugs.
- Vacuum carpets and upholstery at least once (but preferably twice) a week. Most people have found that frequent vacuuming by itself is all that's necessary to keep flea, moth, and carpet beetle populations down to tolerable levels. Pay particular attention to the dark, hidden areas where insects tend to deposit their eggs, such as under and between cushions, behind doors and curtains, around baseboards, and under beds, tables, and furniture. Places where your pet sleeps or spends a lot of time should also be prime targets. After you finish vacuuming, remove the disposable dust bag immediately, seal it shut in a plastic bag, and discard it outside in the trash. By throwing out the disposable dust bag every time, you'll reduce the possibility of reintroducing the insects.

    As mentioned previously, to be really effective your vacuum cleaner must have a rotating beater brush, strong suction, and a double-lined (two-ply) microfiltration disposable bag that traps dust particles down to the 0.1-micron size.

- Store freshly cleaned garments that are susceptible to insect attack inside tightly sealed plastic bags or other tightly sealed containers. Rotate clothing so that all items are worn regularly. Brushing garments periodically with a stiff brush also helps.
- Check your garage, attic, and basement for old clothes, cardboard boxes, brown paper grocery bags, magazines, and newspapers you can get rid of, since roaches use them for breeding grounds. And don't save brown grocery bags for more than a few days, because they're often contaminated with insect eggs, especially roach eggs, and storing them for weeks gives insects a good chance to set up house. Use them as trash bags right away

and then throw them out. Better yet, instead of using paper grocery bags, which waste natural resources, purchase a cotton tote bag to carry your groceries.

• Broad-leaf groundcover plants, such as ivy, and other dense vegetation should be removed from around the foundation of your home if possible. Do not stack lumber or firewood next to the house, and keep tree branches and shrubs pruned so they don't touch the house. Wood structures of the home should be at least eight inches above the soil.

• If you suspect bugs are entering your house from the sewer system, keep a plug or cover over the drain of the sink and bathtub when they are not in use.

• According to most experts, high-tech electronic and ultrasonic devices that claim to drive away insects and rodents are totally worthless, so don't waste your time or money on them.

Specific Strategies for Eliminating Common Pests

Roaches

Avoid aerosol roach sprays, because they spew enormous amounts of toxic chemicals into the air. If you spot a roach and need to kill it quickly, use a homemade insecticidal soap spray: mix 2 cups of water, 3 teaspoons of liquid dishwashing detergent (such as Ivory), and 4 teaspoons of vegetable oil (soybean, corn, or sunflower) in a hand-pump spray bottle. The spray will either kill the roach or at least stun it long enough for you to squash it.

One of the most effective and least toxic chemicals for killing roaches is technical grade (99 percent pure) boric acid powder (not medicinal boric acid). Place it in areas frequented by roaches—*but totally inaccessible to children and animals*—such as cracks and crevices along the kitchen and bathroom baseboards, wall voids, and behind plumbing openings in the wall. Roaches will carry the boric acid powder back to their nests and eventually kill all the other roaches hiding there. Boric acid powder is non-volatile, so roaches can't detect it and will not be repelled by it. And, because it doesn't evaporate or react with the air, boric acid remains active almost indefinitely as long as it stays dry—sometimes for years with one application. However, it is important to realize that boric acid takes about 5–10 days to completely eradicate an infestation, so don't expect results overnight. Using boric acid will virtually eliminate the need for professional pest control companies.

For ease of application you might want to purchase boric acid powder in a plastic squeeze bottle with a pointed applicator tip so you can place the tip directly in a crack or hole and thus avoid blowing dust into the room air. Or you can put the powder in a professional bulb duster (available at hardware stores). Whichever you choose, blow a very thin layer of boric acid powder into the target areas, because roaches avoid thick layers or piles of boric acid powder. The lighter the dusting, the more effective it will be. Never sprinkle boric acid where food is stored or where children or pets could get into it; be careful not to breathe the dust when applying it. Roach Prufe powder by Copper Brite (805-565-1566) and R Value's Roach Kil powder by Waterbury (800-845-3495) are good brands.

For drawers, cabinets, shelves, countertops, under sinks, and other places where powder would be too messy and might contaminate nearby objects, use bait stations in which the boric acid is fully contained within small plastic disks. A good brand is Roach Killing Bait Stations from Seabright Laboratories, Emeryville, CA (800-284-7363).

> **Toxic Warning**
> Boric acid powder is considered one of the least toxic roach killers, but ingesting a full tablespoon of 99 percent pure boric acid can kill a child, so follow directions on the package label, keep all insecticides out of reach of children and pets, and wear protective clothing, gloves, and a filter mask when applying it.

If you desire an alternative to boric acid, the synthetic pesticide *hydramethylnon* is very effective and relatively safe when used as directed. A good brand is Combat SuperBait Advanced Formula Roach

Control Bait Discs. (Avoid Combat Ant & Roach Killer aerosol spray and regular-strength Combat Roach Killing System Bait Discs, because they contain undesirable ingredients in their formulations.) Bait disks are good for drawers, cabinets, shelves, countertops, under sinks, and in other places where powder would be too messy. Like boric acid, hydramethylnon will kill the other roaches hiding back in the nests when they cannibalize the poisoned roach. Wear gloves when handling the bait disks.

Hydroprene (Gencor) by Zoecon (800-527-0512) and Fenoxycarb (Torus) by Maag Agrochemicals (407-778-4660) are insect growth regulators that cause young roaches to become sterile adults. The nice thing about IGRs is that, when used as directed, they do not appear harmful to humans, mammmmals, or the environment. However, as mentioned earlier, IGRs are relatively new, and the long-term effects of chronic exposure are unknown. Be sure the IGR brand you choose does not have any toxic insecticides added to the formulation and don't use IGRs that come in foggers or aerosol spray cans. The dry bait form is preferred, but if you use a pump spray bottle, make sure there is plenty of fresh air ventilation and that you don't inhale the mist or get it on your skin or in your eyes.

Another least toxic product for killing roaches is Avert by Whitmire (800-325-3668). Avert contains avermectin, a natural insecticide produced by the bacteria *Streptomyces avermitilis*. Avermectin (also called *abamectin*) takes a week or two to kill most of the roaches, so be patient. It can often be purchased at organic gardening centers.

Ants

Although they don't normally transmit diseases to humans, ants are definitely a nuisance. There are sugar-feeding ants (common household ants or pharaoh ants) and protein/fat-feeding ants (fire ants or Argentine ants). The following suggestions will help keep ant populations to a minimum, but you'll have to remain ever vigilant, because one thing's for sure: they'll be back.

At some point almost everyone has to resort to an insecticidal bait to control ants. One of the least toxic chemicals is boric acid. DRAX is a ready-to-use 5 percent boric acid ant bait manufactued by Waterbury (800-845-3495). It comes in two formulations, DRAX Ant Kil Gel for sugar-feeding ants and DRAX Ant Kil PF for protein/fat-feeding ants. Determine the preferred bait by placing a dab of each product next to the ant trail and seeing which one the ants feed on in greatest numbers. Then put a dab of the boric acid bait on several two-inch-square pieces of aluminum foil (this makes cleaning up easier after the job is finished) and place one bait station about every five feet alongside the ant trail (do not block the trail with bait) all the way to the point of entry so the foraging ants will carry the boric acid back to the nest where the queen lives and kill her. You should notice a significant reduction in the ant population within 24 hours. By taking this slow and easy approach instead of spraying them, you'll ultimately destroy the entire colony, not just the scouts and workers. Follow the directions on the package label and never place the bait where a child or an animal could gain access to it. Please note that you can also apply a light dusting of boric acid powder in hard-to-reach areas (as explained in the section on roaches).

If boric acid alone does not control the ants adequately, you may be forced to use hydramethylnon bait. The worker ants carry hydramethylnon back to the nest where the queen lives, often into places impossible to reach by conventional methods, and once the queen dies, the entire colony is destroyed. Amdro granules are preferred for outdoor fire ants, and Combat Superbait Ant Killing Bait Discs are handy for common indoor household ants. Keep the disks out of reach of children and pets.

If you spot ants inside your home, don't panic and don't start spraying insecticide everywhere. It's smarter to destroy the entire colony using boric acid or hydramethylnon bait as described here, but if there are so many ants that you feel you have to kill the bulk of them quickly, use the homemade least toxic insecticidal soap spray recommended in the section on roaches.

Fleas

Over 95 percent of the fleas in a home are located in wall-to-wall carpets, furniture upholstery, and pet bedding—less than 5 percent are on the pet. That's why treating the pet alone will hardly make a dent in the total flea population.

If you have a flea problem, do not under any circumstances use flea products that contain organophosphate, organochlorine, or carbamate insecticides, because they are quite toxic to pets and humans. Instead, the following suggestions will help you eliminate or reduce flea populations without having to use poisons that will harm your family and pets.

Your first line of defense is to keep the floors in your home clean. Solid hardwood, ceramic tile, and stone tile floors are preferred because they're inhospitable to fleas. Avoid wall-to-wall carpeting whenever possible, because it's the major breeding ground for fleas indoors. However, if you're stuck with carpeting, frequent vacuuming by itself is all that's necessary to keep flea populations down to tolerable levels. Start out by vacuuming once a day for a week and then twice a week from then on. Pay particular attention to places where your pet sleeps or spends a lot of time. Never place a flea collar or deodorizer tab or pellet in the vacuum bag, because the toxic chemicals will be dispersed into the room air.

In case of a severe flea infestation that requires immediate action, have the carpets and upholstery professionally steam-cleaned with a truck-mounted unit (not the do-it-yourself carpet cleaners you can rent at supermarkets). This will instantly kill most of the fleas deep in the weave and thus bring the flea population down to manageable levels overnight. Never let the steam-cleaning company use any perfumes, chemical treatments, or insecticides on the carpet or upholstery. Specify that all you want is the steam-cleaning—nothing else . . . period.

Most people don't realize that when they walk outside (especially on the grass), the soles of their shoes pick up fleas, which are then tracked into the house. That's why it's a good idea to take off your outdoor shoes and put on a pair of indoor shoes or slippers as soon as you walk inside the house. An outside doormat at every entrance of your home is also helpful.

Your second major line of defense is to keep the indoor relative humidity below 50 percent. Fleas grow and reproduce when the relative humidity is above 65 percent. Dryness is fatal to flea larvae. Therefore, follow the humidity-controlling measures mentioned in Chapter 6 under "Biological Inhalant Allergens" and "Humidity Control."

If frequent vacuuming and low humidity aren't providing adequate control, an insect growth regulator for fleas, such as methoprene (Precor or FleaTrol by Zoecon, 800-527-0512), might be worth considering. Methoprene kills fleas by arresting their growth at or before the pupal stage, thus preventing them from becoming adults and multiplying. However, pesticide manufacturers frequently combine methoprene with toxic insecticides, so always read the label carefully to be sure that methoprene is the only active ingredient in the product.

Never under any circumstances use foggers, fumigators, or flea bombs, because they coat the carpet, upholstery, and furniture with chemical residues that are toxic, especially for young children crawling on the floor and chewing on their hands. And never use diatomaceous earth or silica-aerogel "sorptive" powders, dusts, or sprays on carpets or pets, because inhaling the small particles can be quite irritating to the lungs. This can be especially harmful to people with chronic lung problems, such as asthma or emphysema.

Do not under any circumstances use flea and tick collars, because they outgas toxic pesticides (especially organophosphates and carbamates) continuously, exposing the pet and the family to dangerous chemicals 24 hours a day. Besides, they don't work anyway. Also avoid "herbal" collars, because they emit strong odors that can be quite irritating to the pet and the entire family. Please note that just because a product is labeled "herbal" or "natural" does not necessarily mean that it's safe. For example, the herb pennyroyal commonly causes allergic reactions, and the strong scent given off by either eucalyptus oil or cedar chips can be very irritating to the respiratory tract of pets and humans.

Scientific tests have proved beyond the shadow of a doubt that high-tech ultrasonic flea collars do not work, so don't waste your time or money on them.

If your pet sleeps indoors, establish a regular sleeping place with bedding that can be washed easily. A soft 100 percent cotton blanket or towel works well. Whenever you pick up the bedding, be sure to grasp it gently by all four corners and don't shake it out or you'll scatter flea eggs all over the house. Wash the bedding at least once a week in hot soapy water; dry on high heat in an electric clothes dryer.

Immature fleas are killed at temperatures above 95° F, so if you have flea-infested bedding, clothing, or other items that cannot be washed in a washing machine, give them a 20-minute tumble in the electric clothes dryer as long as the garment tag or cleaning instruction label says it's OK.

Groom your dog or cat daily with a flea comb. Inspect the comb after each pass through the hair and flick the fleas from the comb into a bowl or sink of soapy water, where they'll quickly drown. You can also use a dab of plain Vaseline on a cotton-tip applicator to catch a darting flea. (Do not crush fleas between your fingers, because they often carry disease-causing germs.) Keeping your pet's fur cut relatively short whenever possible will make it easier to spot fleas and use the flea comb.

Never have your pet dipped in an insecticide bath. Stop and think about it for a minute. Would you take a bath in water loaded with toxic pesticides that absorb into your body and then lodge in your fat tissue and vital organs (especially the brain), upset your immune system, cause cancer, and generally wreak havoc with your health for the next 20 years? I don't think so. A safer alternative that works in most cases is to give your dog or cat a two-minute rinse with plain water (without soap or pesticide chemicals) once or twice a week until the fleas are under control. Towel dry immediately after bathing to avoid chills. For severe flea infestations, the occasional use of a gentle, tear-free, pesticide-free, non-medicated shampoo is generally acceptable, but always rinse thoroughly with plain water and be careful not to get the suds on your pet's head or near his eyes or ears.

Do not coat your pet's fur with gobs of toxic insecticide flea powders, dusts, or sprays. These products can make your pet (and the rest of the family) very sick and will hardly phase a flea infestation. However, if you've made up your mind to use a chemical insecticide in spite of my warnings, one of the least toxic choices is pyrethrin. When selecting a pyrethrin spray for dogs and cats, be sure that the pyrethrin concentration does not exceed 0.02 percent, that it does not contain any other active ingredients (especially not organophosphates or carbamates), and that it comes in a hand-pump spray bottle (rather than an aerosol spray can). I would also avoid flea products that contain the synergist piperonyl butoxide (PBO). And please note that most commercial pyrethrin sprays contain about 98 percent inert ingredients of unknown toxicity, so apply them outdoors where the fresh air ventilation is adequate, don't use much, and be very careful that you and your pet keep your faces positioned upwind to avoid inhaling the mist or getting it in your eyes. Again, always check with your veterinarian before using any product on your pets.

Termites

If you suspect a termite infestation, take some time to explore all of the least toxic options with an exterminator who practices integrated pest management. Don't let the scare tactics and high-pressure sales techniques used by some conventional pest control companies stampede you into a high-toxic treatment plan that you will ultimately regret (and possibly have to live with for the next 5–20 years). And be sure the problem is termites, not ants. Get several opinions and written estimates.

Avoid termiticides that contain organophosphates (such as chlorpyrifos), organochlorines (such as chlordane), or carbamates, because they take many years to biodegrade (up to 30 years for chlordane), and during that entire time your home will have highly toxic pesticide fumes seeping up through the foundation and contaminating the indoor air. And if (as so often happens) the pesticide is not applied properly or there is a major accidental spill, it can be a financial and ecological disaster, especially if the pest control company is underinsured or otherwise won't help with the cleanup expenses (assuming it can be cleaned up in the first place).

If a chemical insecticide is needed, the synthetic pyrethroids, such as permethrin (Torpedo), cypermethrin (Demon T.C.), and fenvalerate (Pydrin), are very effective at killing termites, and they biodegrade more rapidly than the highly toxic termiticides.

Borax-based "disodium octaborate" products, such as Tim-Bor by U.S. Borax (800-9TIMBOR) and Bora-Care by the Nisus Corporation (800-264-0870), can be sprayed on wood to protect against termite invasion.

A biological method for killing subterranean or underground termites involves the use of microscopic worms called *beneficial predatory nematodes.* Predatory nematodes, such as Steinenema, can be purchased from many insectaries across the country, such as Saf-T-Shield from N-Viro Products Ltd. (516-567-2628) or BioFac (800-233-4914).

To kill drywood termites, carpenter ants, and other wood-nesting insects without resorting to chemicals, consider the innovative Electro-gun treatment by Etex Ltd. (800-543-5651). It zaps the insects with 90,000 volts and is so effective that many pest control operators will issue a two-year unconditional guarantee. Avoid the tent fumigation method, which relies on toxic chemicals, such as methyl bromide, sulfuryl fluoride (Vikane), or metham sodium (Vapam).

Flies

Flies can transmit a wide variety of human illnesses, but good sanitation practices around the home can usually prevent infestations. An old-fashioned flyswatter or a rolled-up newspaper is nontoxic and low-tech, but it gets the job done almost every time. Do not under any circumstances hang chemical insecticide pest strips indoors, because they emit toxic chemical pollutants continuously for months.

Clothes Moths/Carpet Beetles

Never under any circumstances use mothballs, moth cakes, moth crystals, or moth flakes, because they contain toxic chemicals, such as paradichlorbenzene (PDCB), naphthalene, and camphor.

Store freshly cleaned, susceptible garments inside tightly sealed plastic bags or other tightly sealed containers. It's the food, urine, sweat, and other organic material on clothing that primarily attracts clothes moths.

Rotate clothing so that all items are worn regularly. Brush, shake, and air out garments every month or two. This will kill the moth larvae and knock the eggs off. You can also store woolens in the attic during the summer, because temperatures above 105° F will usually kill moths within hours.

Vacuuming carpets twice a week is a very effective, nontoxic way to prevent moth or carpet beetle damage. Carpeting in dark, untrampled areas (such as closets and underneath beds and furniture) is most susceptible to attack and should not be overlooked. Steam-cleaning carpets (as explained in the section on fleas) will also kill moths.

Bees, Wasps, Hornets, Yellow Jackets

Natural pyrethrin and synthetic pyrethroid insecticides are least toxic options for killing bees, wasps, hornets, and yellow jackets. Keep in mind, however, that all pyrethrin and pyrethroid spray products contain inert ingredients of unknown toxicity, so use them only when absolutely necessary to kill stinging insects that require a quick knockdown and be careful not to inhale the mist or get it on your skin or in your eyes. There are several acceptable brands on the market, but you must read the labels very carefully to be sure they contain only synthetic pyrethroids. One of the less offensive brands is Enforcer Wasp & Hornet Killer (resmethrin), manufactured by Enforcer Products (800-241-5656). Please note that many pyrethrin and pyrethroid products contain synergists, such as piperonyl butoxide (PBO), which are added to increase their killing power. I normally suggest avoiding products that contain PBO or other synergists whenever possible because they increase the toxicity of the product, but occasionally an insect problem becomes so severe it requires such tough measures. See the toxic warning about pyrethrum, pyrethrins, pyrethoids, and permethrin earlier in this chapter.

Head Lice

Head lice are grayish white bugs, each about the size of a flea or a sesame seed. They don't jump or fly, but they can crawl very fast. Head lice lay eggs (called *nits*) that look like tiny ($\frac{1}{32}$ of an inch), white, teardrop-shaped beads. Although they resemble dandruff flakes, nits are firmly attached to the hair shaft with a strong gluelike substance that prevents them from being brushed off like dandruff.

The most common symptom of head lice is an itchy scalp. Head lice are transmitted by close personal contact with an infected human (usually a child at school or daycare) or direct contact with infested clothing, bedding, towels, brushes, combs, hats, and other personal items. Pets are never the source because animals don't carry human head lice.

To get rid of head lice safely, use a regular, nonmedicated shampoo first, followed by the application of CLEAR Lice-Egg Remover Cleansing Concentrate to remove all the nits and avoid reinfestation. CLEAR contains nontoxic vegetable-derived enzymes that unglue lice eggs in a matter of minutes. A special head lice "Nit Buster" comb is included in the CLEAR kit. You remove the lice eggs from the hair shafts by methodically combing two-inch-wide sections of hair starting as close to the scalp as possible. After you finish combing out the nits, rinse the hair well, and re-check for any you may have missed.

A few other tips for head lice: First, a short haircut makes combing out nits much easier. Second, don't let children share personal items, such as combs, brushes, barrettes, scarves, hats, headbands, helmets, or pillows. And third, wash infested bedding, towels, and clothing. Any items that cannot be washed in soap and water should be stored in an airtight, sealed plastic bag for two weeks or given a tumble in the clothes dryer for about 30 minutes on the high setting.

Although I do not recommend chemical head lice shampoos, if you are determined to use one, the natural pyrethrin RID Lice Killing Shampoo and the synthetic pyrethroid Nix (permethrin) 1% Lice Treatment are probably the least harmful.

Toxic Warning

Lindane 1% (Kwell) shampoo is often prescribed for the treatment of head lice in children even though it is an organochlorine pesticide from the highly toxic DDT/chlordane family. Lindane is carcinogenic and can also damage the neurologic system, liver, and immune system. The use of Kwell shampoo has even been linked to the development of childhood brain cancer. Lindane is absorbed through the skin and becomes lodged in the fat tissue and vital organs (like the brain), where it can wreak havoc with a person's health for 20–30 years because it biodegrades so slowly.

LAWN AND GARDEN HERBICIDES, FUNGICIDES, AND INSECTICIDES

Most commercially available lawn and garden herbicides (weed killers) and fungicides contain toxic synthetic chemicals that are harmful to humans, pets, birds, fish, bees, wildlife, and just about everything else in the environment. Fortunately, there's a better, safer way to have a beautiful lawn and garden (without poisoning your family or the ecosystem). It centers around an approach called integrated pest management (IPM), in which the use of synthetic pesticides is kept to the bare minimum by relying on special cultivation techniques, natural biological controls, and least toxic pesticides.

Try not to use synthetic herbicides, fungicides, or insecticides, because the weeds, fungi, and insects will develop resistance, and you'll find yourself having to use stronger and stronger applications to get results.

Toxic Warning

Compost piles and sewage sludge are breeding grounds for the potentially deadly mold *Aspergillus fumigatus*. For 10 percent of the general population, *Aspergillus* mold can cause severe allergic respiratory symptoms, such as asthma, runny nose, watery eyes, sore throat, and coughing. And for people with a weakened immune system, *Aspergillus* can be life-threatening. Whenever possible, keep a minimum distance of five miles from compost piles and sewage treatment plants to avoid exposure to *Aspergillus* mold spores.

Mowing your grass too short and too often is a sure way to invite pest and disease problems. Your local gardening center can advise you about the optimal mowing height for your particular type of lawn, but most kinds of grass should be left at least two or three inches high for optimal root system development.

Keep mower blades sharp and use a mulcher blade so that you

leave the clippings on the lawn to recycle and rejuvenate the soil instead of being wasted in a landfill.

A fertilizer with a slow-release form of nitrogen is preferred because quick-release forms tend to run off and pollute groundwater, lakes, and rivers. And, since fungi thrive on nitrogen, avoid fertilizers with a nitrogen content above 7 percent.

Herbicides

Herbicides are poisons designed to kill weeds, but they also kill grass, plants, and trees. They can make humans, animals, and birds sick too, not to mention the devastating effect they have on the entire ecosystem

---

Toxic Warning

The following synthetic herbicides should be avoided. The generic chemical names are listed in alphabetical order along with their brand names in parentheses. Do not assume that an herbicide is safe just because it does not appear in this list.

Acifluorfen (Blazer)
Alachlor (Lasso)
Atrazine (Aatrex, Atranex)
Chlorpropham (Furloe, Sprout-Nip)
DCPA (Dacthal)
Dicamba (Brush Buster)
2,4-dichlorophenoxyacetic acid (2,4-D, Weed-B-Gon, Weedone)
Glyphosate (Roundup, Kleenup)

Mecoprop (MCPP, CMPP, Duplosan, Mecomec, Mecopar)
Paraquat (Gramoxone)
Pendimethalin (Prowl, Stomp)
Sulfallate (Vegadex)
3,5,6-trichloropyridinyl-oxyacetic acid (Triclopyr)
Trifluralin (Triflurex)

(including the pollution of drinking water sources, lakes, and rivers). And it's estimated that over half of the synthetic chemical herbicides cause cancer in animals. Therefore, I strongly advise against using any synthetic chemical herbicides on your lawn or garden. As an alternative, organic gardeners stress the importance of testing the soil pH (acidity/ alkalinity), nitrogen (N), phosphorous (P), and potassium (K) about twice a year to maintain the optimal balance that will naturally resist most weed growth in the first place; do-it-yourself soil test kits are available at many gardening centers for about $5. And the safest way to remove the occasional weeds that do spring up is to either pull them by hand or use a weed popper.

Fungicides

Toxic Warning

The following synthetic fungicides should be avoided. The generic chemical names are listed in alphabetical order along with their brand names in parentheses. Do not assume that a fungicide is safe just because it does not appear in this list.

Benomyl (Benlate)
Captan (Merpan, Orthocide Garden Fungicide)
Chlorothalonil (Bravo, Daconil)
Dicloran (DCNA, Botran)
EBDCs (Maneb, Manzate, Mancozeb, Manzeb, and Zineb)
Enilconazole (Imazalil)

Folpet
Hexachlorobenzene (HCB)
Iprodione
PCNB
o-phenylphenol
Quintozene
Thiabendazole (Mertect, Omnizole)
Vinclozolin (Ronilan)
Ziram (Milbam, Zerlate)

The fungicides applied to agricultrual produce and lawns and gardens can cause many adverse health effects in humans, pets, birds, and wildlife. To reduce the need for fungicides, organic gardeners recommend the following:

• Choose plant and tree varieties that are naturally resistant to fungus attack. Most garden centers can provide you with that information.

• Fungi thrive in a warm, dark, moist, low-oxygen environment. Therefore, try to make conditions in your yard or garden naturally inhospitable to fungus growth. Don't water every day; frequent watering promotes fungal growth. The best time to water is early in the day so the plant can dry before nightfall; the worst times are late evening and at night. And don't use fertilizers with a nitrogen content above 7 percent, because fungi thrive on nitrogen.

RESOURCES

For detailed information on controlling insects and other pests the least-toxic way, consult the following resources:

1. *Silent Spring* by Rachel Carson, (Boston: Houghton Mifflin Company, 1962) (800-225-3362). This is *the* landmark book that launched the environmental movement in America. Its message—the senseless poisoning of the earth with chemicals —is more pertinent today than when it was first published over 30 years ago. It is must reading for all parents concerned about preserving the planet for their children and future generations.

2. *Pest Control for Home and Garden: The Safest and Most Effective Methods For You and the Environment* by Michael Hansen, PhD (Fairfield, Ohio: Consumer Reports Books, 1993) (800-272-0722). An easy-to-read book that summarizes the acute, chronic, and long-term effects of pesticides and provides readers with safety ratings and lists of product recommendations. Methods of integrated pest management are emphasized.

3. *Common-Sense Pest Control* by William & Helga Olkowski and Sheila Daar. (Newton, Connecticut: Taunton Press, 1991). The most comprehensive guide for integrated pest management and least toxic alternatives, this book is considered the gold standard in its field, but it contains a staggering amount of information, which can sometimes be overwhelming.

For telephone consultations and up-to-date, honest information on least-toxic pest management strategies, contact:

1. The National Pesticide Network (800-858-7378 or 800-858-PEST).
2. Northwest Coalition for Alternatives to Pesticides (NCAP), PO Box 1393, Eugene, OR 97440 (503-344-5044).
3. The Bio-Integral Resource Center (510-524-2567), Berkeley, California.

8
Protecting Your Child
from the
Great Outdoors

The "great outdoors" sometimes isn't so great, especially when it comes to sunburns, swimming accidents, animal bites, and insect bites. This chapter will help you choose the safest and most effective products for protecting your child from these hazards.

SOLAR SAFETY TIPS

Natural sunlight contains visible and invisible rays. The invisible infrared rays produce heat and a feeling of warmth on the skin. The visible light rays provide natural illumination for the eyes to see. The invisible ultraviolet A (UVA) and ultraviolet B (UVB) rays cause sunburns, wrinkles, and skin cancer (including malignant melanoma).

Prolonged exposure to solar rays suppresses the immune system and increases a person's susceptibility to viral infections and recurrences of fever blisters. (Overexposure to ultraviolet lights in tanning salons can do the same.)

Sun Exposure in Babies
Under Six Months of Age

There are several reasons why babies under six months old should avoid prolonged exposure to direct sunlight. First, an infant's ability to cool himself by sweating is not fully functional, and dangerous overheating from infrared rays is possible. Second, a baby's eyes are very sensitive to visible light rays, and damage to the immature retinas can occur. Third, sunburn from the ultraviolet rays occurs readily in infants, because melanin (the skin pigment that normally protects against burning) is not yet at optimal levels. Therefore, limit your baby's direct sun exposure to no more than 15 minutes a day during the summer months when the rays of the sun are strongest.

Sun Protection

When sun exposure of more than 30 minutes is anticipated, there are several "natural" ways to protect your child from the damaging solar rays:

1. Avoid the midday sun (between 10:00 A.M. and 4:00 P.M.), when the burning rays are most intense. Plan outdoor activities for the early morning or late afternoon or evening.
2. Dress the child in sun-shielding clothing, such as a hat or bonnet with a wide, circular brim (or a sun visor that shades the eyes and ears), and lightweight, cool, loose-fitting, 100 percent cotton clothing that covers as much skin as possible.
3. A beach umbrella or a stroller with a canopy can block out a great deal of sunshine, but shade devices are only partially protective because up to 50 percent of the sun's ultraviolet rays may reflect off sand, concrete, or water and zap your child's skin. And don't let a cloudy day lull you into a false sense of security either, since clouds reduce the burning ultraviolet rays by only 20–30 percent. That means 70–80 percent of the damaging UVA and UVB rays pass right through the clouds.
4. Many babies, especially those who have blue or green eyes, will squint, blink, and cry as soon as you take them outdoors, because the sun's brightness hurts their sensitive eyes. Be sure your child's eyes are adequately shaded from the sun. A hat with a wide-brimmed sun visor is very helpful. I don't normally recommend sunglasses.
5. Be sure to provide extra drinking water when you're outdoors on a warm day and don't stay outside too long, since babies are susceptible to overheating even if they aren't directly in the sun.

Sunscreen Lotions

Dermatologists correctly point out that 80 percent of the lifetime cumulative sun exposure occurs by 20 years of age, and if youngsters and teenagers routinely use a sunscreen with an SPF rating of 15, approximately 80 percent of future nonmelanoma skin cancers can be prevented.

On the other hand, the use of sunscreen lotions is not totally risk-free. Many of the synthetic sunblocking chemicals used in sunscreen lotions can cause allergic reactions and skin rashes such as dermatitis. Some may even be carcinogenic. Sunscreen products that contain more than 30 percent alcohol are also potentially flammable and might ignite when used near flames (such as outdoor barbecues or someone smoking). Alcohol-based sunscreen lotions also tend to burn and sting when applied.

A study appearing in the *Journal of the National Cancer Institute* 86: (January 1994): 99–105, indicates that using sunscreen lotions is actually *associated* with an increased risk of developing malignant melanoma skin cancer. The reason may be that sunscreen lotions allow people to remain out in the sun for much longer periods of time than they would otherwise, and this prolonged exposure to ultraviolet rays weakens the skin's immune defense system, making it more vulnerable to malignant melanoma. Until this question is resolved, my personal recommendation is to limit sun exposure to no more than 30 minutes a day.

Safe Sunscreens

I realize that not everyone is going to follow my advice about staying out of the sun, so a brief discussion of sunscreen lotions is warranted.

Most of the commercially available sunscreen lotions should be avoided because they contain potentially harmful synthetic sunblocking chemicals. Among the chemicals that block UVA rays, the benzophenones sometimes cause allergic skin reactions and rashes and may be carcinogenic. PABA (para-aminobenzoic acid), which blocks UVB rays, is notorious for causing allergic skin rashes. I would also stay away from sunscreens with an SPF rating above 20, since higher numbers require higher concentrations of sunblocking chemicals and may thus increase the toxicity of the lotion.

In contrast, menthyl anthranilate (a UVA blocker) rarely causes allergic skin reactions, and the same is true of the salicylates that block UVB rays. The very safest choices, however, are zinc oxide and titanium dioxide, natural chemicals that block both UVA and UVB rays. At the present time, the following are among the safest sunscreen products on the market:

1. Neutrogena Sunblock SPF 15: Octyl-methoxy-cinnamate, octyl salicylate, and menthyl anthranilate are the active ingredients. The preservative in this sunscreen lotion is propylparaben, which is relatively nonallergenic and does not release formaldehyde.

2. Neutrogena Chemical-Free Sunblocker SPF 17: Titanium dioxide is the active ingredient. A minor problem with this product is that it contains an undesirable formaldehyde-releasing and potentially allergenic preservative called *diazolidinyl urea*, but you have to balance this with the fact that most other sunscreen lotions have even worse ingredients.

3. Zinc oxide paste or ointment (Eckerd or Walgreens store brand) is nontoxic and works quite well in blocking out both UVA and UVB sun rays. It is most useful for select areas of the skin that burn easily, such as the nose, cheeks, and shoulders. The only problem with zinc oxide is that it's a little messy and somewhat unappealing cosmetically.

Tanning and Sunburns

There's no such thing as a healthy tan. Tanned skin is damaged skin, and every time your child gets a suntan, he accumulates more and more irreversible skin damage even though the visible effects won't become apparent until middle age. The eventual price of regular tanning is skin cancer and wrinkled skin that looks old and feels like leather.

Never let your child use sunlamps or take him to tanning parlors, because any light that tans the skin also damages the skin (in spite of claims to the contrary), and the effects are cumulative.

When Should You Call the Doctor About a Sunburn?

Have a doctor examine your child immediately if a sunburn causes any of the following danger signs:

- The child becomes weak or faints from heat exhaustion.
- The child's body temperature is higher than 101° F.
- The child's eyes are hurting.
- The child has more than just a few small blisters.
- The child vomits more than once.
- The child is very uncomfortable or acting sick.

First Aid for a Minor Sunburn

1. Do not put grease, oil, butter, Vaseline, or ointment on the burn, because it will trap heat and make the burn worse.
2. Do not use anesthetic (pain-relieving) sprays, lotions, or creams on the burn, especially products that contain active ingredients with the suffix *caine* (such as benzocaine, lidocaine, or xylocaine), because they tend to cause allergic reactions when applied to burned skin.
3. Discourage your child from scratching the burn. Keep his fingernails cut short. Some doctors recommend an oral antihistamine, such as Benadryl, to relieve the itching if necessary.
4. A cool bath or cool compress may help relieve the pain and itching. Don't use soap on burned skin. Gently blot dry with a soft towel.
5. Acetaminophen (Tylenol, Feverall, Tempra, or Panadol) is a good pain reliever.
6. Never deliberately break open blisters, because you'll increase the risk of infection.

SWIMMING POOLS

The American Academy of Pediatrics warns against swimming lessons for children under three years of age for the following reasons:

- Infants and toddlers swallow large amounts of pool water when they submerse their heads. In fact some may swallow enough water to upset the balance of salt within the body and trigger a seizure.
- Children who aren't toilet-trained contaminate the pool water with millions of contagious germs from their urine and stools and increase the risk of spreading infections. The chlorine does not kill all the bacteria and viruses. That's why swimming in the kiddie pool is one of the quickest ways to get sick.
- Babies get chilled very easily and may become dangerously cold (hypothermia) in an unheated pool.
- Teaching a young child to dog-paddle or float in a calm, controlled situation with the swimming instructor nearby gives a false sense of security to parents and may cause them to let down their guard just enough to allow a horrible accident. Unfortunately, there's no such thing as a water-safe toddler in a real-life panic situation.

Please note that spas and hot tubs are also very dangerous for a variety of reasons—overheating, drowning, and infection—and young children should not be allowed to use them either.

If your home has a swimming pool, there are several important precautions to take:

- Install a fence around the pool itself, not just the backyard. The gate should be self-closing and locked at all times.
- Never leave your child unsupervised near a swimming pool, not even for a second. It takes only a minute for a curious child to fall in and drown, even in a shallow baby pool.
- Install two floating pool alarms (in case one malfunctions).
- Take a CPR course through your local Red Cross or community hospital so that you'll know what to do in an emergency.

ANIMAL BITES

Most pet dogs and cats get along quite well with children. However, it might be wise to stay away from breeds that are notorious for unpredictable and aggressive behavior, such as Siamese cats and German shepherd, rottweiler, and pit bull dogs. Ferrets, raccoons, and skunks have also been known to inflict serious bite wounds, so don't have them as pets.

As soon as your baby learns to crawl, be sure to pick up the pet's food bowl when feeding time is over. And if you have a cat, put the litter box in a location that is completely inaccessible to the child.

Although it is unlikely to ever happen, there is the theoretical danger that a cat may snuggle up next to an infant's face during sleep and accidentally suffocate him, so never leave a sleeping infant unattended in a room with a cat.

First Aid for Animal Bites or Scratches

1. First and foremost, rinse the wound immediately with plain water for 10 full minutes.
2. As soon as the water-rinsing procedure is finished, clean the wound with an antiseptic, such as isopropyl (rubbing) alcohol, hydrogen peroxide, or Hibiclens.
3. If an animal bite causes more than just a minor wound, your child will need to see the doctor right away, because you can't stitch a wound that's more than a few hours old. And a prescription oral antibiotic may also be needed to prevent an infection.
4. If the wound is bleeding, use a clean cloth—a towel, sheet, or handkerchief—and apply firm pressure directly on top of the injured area.
5. Be sure your child's tetanus immunization is up to date.

Rabies

Exposure to the rabies virus occurs when the teeth or claws of a rabid animal break the skin or when the saliva from an infected animal contaminates an open wound or mucous membrane. Therefore, if your child is bitten by an animal, always consult the rabies control department for advice on whether the rabies vaccine injections will be needed. In general the probability that an animal has rabies is based on several factors: the species of the animal, whether it's a household pet or a wild animal, whether the animal has been vaccinated, whether the animal is healthy or sick at the time of the exposure, whether the attack was provoked or unprovoked.

A provoked attack by an apparently healthy, properly vaccinated pet dog or cat has a low probability of rabies, but the animal must be captured and quarantined for 14 days of observation. Notify your child's doctor and the rabies control department immediately if the animal gets sick or dies, because its brain must be examined for evidence of rabies.

An unprovoked attack by an apparently sick animal is highly suggestive of rabies regardless of the species of the animal, and the exposed person should receive the rabies vaccine injections as soon as possible unless the animal can be captured, tested by the state health department, and proved not to have rabies.

Wild dogs, cats, skunks, raccoons, woodchucks, foxes, coyotes, bobcats, and bats are the species of animals most often infected with rabies. A person bitten by one of these wild animals should receive the rabies vaccine injections as soon as possible unless the animal can be captured, tested by the state health department, and proved not to have rabies.

It's uncommon to find rats, mice, squirrels, chipmunks, hamsters, guinea pigs, gerbils, or rabbits infected with rabies, but a person bitten by one of these animals should always consult the doctor and the rabies control department to be on the safe side.

INSECT BITES AND STINGS

Insect bites and stings commonly occur on exposed areas of skin such as the face, neck, hands, arms, and lower legs. A typical insect bite consists of a red bump with a pinpoint blister or pimple in the center.

The skin lesions are usually itchy, and some of them may even be painful. Scabs, crusts, and sores develop when the child scratches the bites.

Mosquitoes, Fleas, and Chiggers

For mosquito, flea, and chigger bites, follow the home treatment recommendations for minor insect bites and stings later in this section. And avoid outdoor activities at dawn and dusk, when mosquitoes are most active.

Spiders

If your child is bitten by a nonpoisonous spider, follow the home treatment recommendations for minor insect bites and stings in this section. On the other hand, if your child is bitten by a black widow or brown recluse spider, call your doctor and the Poison Control Center immediately.

Ticks

Ticks can transmit several different infections to humans, but two of the most serious ones are Rocky Mountain Spotted Fever and Lyme disease. Always have a doctor examine your child immediately if any of the following symptoms develop within three weeks after a tick bite: fever, chills, a red rash all over the body, a circular or "bull's-eye" red skin rash, flulike symptoms, headache, sore throat, hoarseness, cough, fatigue, muscle aches, or joint pain or swelling.

Whenever it's tick season in your part of the country, get into the habit of carefully checking your child from head to toe (especially the scalp, ears, and neck) twice a day. If you find any attached ticks, remove them immediately using the following technique:

1. The preferred instrument for grasping a tick is a pair of curved-tip forceps, which can be purchased at most medical supply

stores. A regular pair of tweezers is also acceptable. If neither instrument is available, it's OK to use the tips of your thumb and index fingers as long as they're shielded with a tissue, paper towel, or disposable latex glove (not bare hands), because the fluid inside the tick may be contaminated with dangerous germs.

2. Grasp the tick by its head or as close as possible to where its mouth is attached to the skin. Then pull the tick straight up and away from the skin with a slow and steady motion. Avoid twisting or jerking movements that might cause the head of the tick to separate from the body and remain underneath the skin where it can become infected. Do not squeeze the tick's bloated abdomen, or you might pump harmful bacteria out of its mouth and into your child's bloodstream. Do not use heat (cigarettes or matches, for example), Vaseline, nail polish, kerosene, or alcohol in a misguided attempt to make the tick let go, because that will also stimulate the tick to regurgitate bacteria into your child's bloodstream.

3. After removing the tick, use plenty of soap and water to thoroughly wash your hands, the area of the tick bite, and the tweezers. Then use isopropyl (rubbing) alcohol to disinfect the tweezers and any areas of skin directly touched by the tick.

The safest way to prevent tickborne diseases is to avoid walking or playing in places known to be infested with ticks. In situations where avoidance is impossible, many parents feel that the risk of Lyme disease is substantial enough to warrant the use of an insect repellent called DEET. (See "Preventing Insect Bites and Stings" for more information.)

Bee, Wasp, Hornet, and Fire Ant Stings

The honey bee, bumblebee, wasp, hornet, yellow jacket, and fire ant cause painful stings by injecting venom into the skin. If an insect stinger remains in the skin, carefully scrape it out from below the tip with the edge of a plastic card or your fingernail. Don't pinch or squeeze a stinger, because you'll inject more venom into the skin.

For minor skin reactions, follow the home treatment recommendations for insect bites and stings, but for a severe allergic reaction—hives, swollen lips and eyes, breathing difficulty, tightness in the chest, vomiting, collapse—call the emergency medical services (dial 911 in most areas) or seek professional medical attention immediately.

First Aid for Minor Insect Bites and Stings

1. Gently rinse the bite or sting with cool water.
2. If the skin starts to swell, apply an ice bag (wrapped in a clean cloth) right away if your child will let you. Don't apply ice directly against the skin because it might cause frostbite. If you don't have an ice bag handy, an ice cube wrapped in a paper towel or washcloth will work.
3. An oral antihistamine, such as Benadryl, will reduce the itching, redness, and swelling.
4. Discourage your child from picking or scratching the skin lesions and keep his or her fingernails cut short.
5. Many doctors recommend applying a nonprescription hydrocortisone ointment (such as Cortizone-10 Ointment) on top of the skin lesions to relieve the itching. Please note that antihistamines tend to cause allergic reactions when applied directly to injured skin, so do not use creams, lotions, or sprays that contain antihistamines (such as diphenhydramine). And if possible, avoid calamine lotion, because it often contains added ingredients (camphor or phenol, for example) which are potentially dangerous.
6. Some doctors recommend the topical application of nonprescription Polysporin or Bacitracin ointment three times a day to prevent an infection.
7. Acetaminophen (Tylenol, etc.) is generally safe and effective for pain relief if necessary.
8. Avoid topical anesthetic creams, lotions, or sprays that contain active ingredients with the suffix *caine* (such as benzocaine, lidocaine, or xylocaine), because they tend to cause allergic reactions when applied to injured skin.

Preventing Insect Bites and Stings

The safest way to prevent insect bites outdoors is to wear lightweight, cool 100 percent cotton clothing as protection. Dress your child in socks and shoes (no going barefoot), a hat, a long-sleeved lightweight cotton shirt buttoned at the neck and wrists and tucked in at the waist, and a pair of trousers (not shorts) with the cuffs tucked into the socks or boots. Perfumes and fragrances attract insects, so try to use fragrance-free products.

There is no such thing as a nontoxic insect repellent, but sometimes the risk of catching a serious infection from an insect bite outweighs the risk of applying a synthetic chemical directly to the skin. The active ingredient in most insect repellents is the chemical N,N-diethyl toluamide, commonly referred to as *DEET.* It repels chiggers, mosquitoes, and biting flies quite well, but it's somewhat less effective for ticks. Unfortunately, most brands of DEET are absorbed by the skin and into the bloodstream so that repeated applications can bioaccumulate to toxic levels rather quickly. That's why insect repellents are generally not recommended for children under two years old.

Potential side effects and adverse reactions from overexposure to DEET include headaches, dizziness, seizures, irritability, insomnia, mental confusion, disorientation, loss of coordination, vomiting, burning sensations on the skin, blisters, hives and skin rashes. Swallowing DEET can be fatal. That's why, if you decide to use an insect repellent that contains DEET, you must be very careful to choose a brand that does not have more than a 10 percent concentration, such as Skedaddle Insect Protection for Children (LittlePoint Corporation, 800-243-2929) or Johnson Off! Skintastic Insect Repellent (Fragrance-Free). Skedaddle and Skintastic are available at most supermarkets and pharmacies.

Natrapel (a citronella-based repellent) and Avon's Skin-So-Soft (a concentrated bath oil) have recently been touted as nontoxic insect repellents, but when the Harvard School of Public Health compared Skedaddle, Avon's Skin-So-Soft, and Natrapel for their ability to repel insects, only Skedaddle was found to be effective. Skin-So-Soft and Natrapel did not provide any protection whatsoever against landing insects.

Avoid "herbal" insect repellents (especially those that contain pennyroyal), because breathing strong herbal scents can cause respiratory symptoms in some people, such as sneezing, red and watery eyes, nasal congestion, runny nose, sore throat, coughing, and asthma attacks. And accidentally swallowing an herbal repellent can cause vomiting, diarrhea, seizures, coma, and even death.

When using any insect repellent, follow these general safety precautions:

- Apply insect repellent sparingly and only to exposed skin or clothing as directed on the product label. Don't overdo it and don't apply it to skin that will be covered by clothing. And to avoid a toxic buildup of chemicals, never apply insect repellent more often than recommended. Also note that DEET may damage some synthetics, such as rayon, acetate, and spandex. It can also damage plastic, such as eyeglasses, lenses, vinyl upholstery or car seats, and the like.
- Do not let your child sleep all night wearing insect repellent. As soon as insect protection is no longer needed (especially before going to bed), wash the insect repellent off with soap and water in the shower. Do not let your child sit in a bathtub of water containing insect repellent that has rinsed off the skin.
- Do not use insect repellent spray, because the child will inhale toxic chemicals into his or her lungs. A lotion or cream is preferred.
- Do not use products that contain more than 10 percent DEET.
- Do not apply insect repellent over cuts, scratches, rashes, or sunburned skin, because more of the chemicals will be absorbed into the body. Do not apply repellent around the eyes or mouth. Do not apply repellent to the hands of young children or any child who tends to put his fingers in his mouth.
- Always keep insect repellents out of the reach of children.

Appendix

RESOURCES WITH PHONE NUMBERS

1 Feeding Your Baby

Ameda/Egnell: 800-323-8750
   (breast pump)

Environmental Protection Agency (EPA): 800-426-4791
   (Safe Drinking Water hot line)

Environmental Working Group: 202-667-6982
   (publications on pesticides in foods)

The Feingold Association of the United States (FAUS): 800-321-3287
   (listings of foods, beverages, and medications that contain no
      artificial additives)

La Leche League: 800-LA-LECHE
   (support group for breast-feeding mothers)

Magla Skin-Eez: 800-247-5281
   (powder-free disposable plastic gloves)

Medela: 800-435-8316
   (nursing stool, breast pump, breast cream, nipple shields, Kapoochi
      baby carrier)

Mountain Valley Spring Company: 800-643-1501
   (bottled spring water)

National Sanitation Foundation (NSF) International: 313-769-8010
   (testing of water filtering devices)

National Testing Laboratories: 800-458-3330
>(testing of tap water)

Pure Food Campaign: 800-253-0681 or 202-775-1132
>(list of companies that don't use rBGH dairy products)

United States Department of Agriculture (USDA) Agricultural
Marketing Service: 202-720-5231
>(publications on pesticides in foods)

USDA Meat and Poultry hot line: 800-535-4555
>(safe handling and storage of food products)

WaterTest Corporation of America: 800-426-8378
>(testing of tap water)

2   Diaper Care

Biobottoms: 800-766-1254
>(Biobottoms diaper covers and cotton diapers, baby clothing)

RMED International: 800-34IM DRY or 800-344-6379
>(Tushies—"green" disposable diapers)

Seventh Generation: 800-456-1177
>("green" cotton clothing, environmentally conscious products for
>home and family)

3   Clothing, Bedding, and Laundry

Hanna Anderson: 800-346-6040 or 800-222-0544
>(100% cotton clothing for babies and children)

Janice Corporation: 800-JANICES
>(100% cotton products)

The Vermont Country Store: 802-362-2400
>(100% cotton products)

4   Baby Bath, Shampoo, and Skin-Care Products

Heart of Vermont: 800-639-4123
   (organic and cruelty-free wool products)

Perfectly Safe: 800-837-KIDS
   (floating water thermometer and other safety devices)

5   Illnesses, Infections, and Other Medical Problems

Gerry Baby Products: 800-525-2472
   (Snugli baby carrier)

The Jeffrey Modell Foundation: 800-JEFF-844
   (hot line to answer questions about immune system disorders)

Meyenberg: 800-343-1185
   (goat's milk)

SleepTight: 800-NO-COLIC
   (car-ride simulator)

Thermoscan: 800-EAR-TEMP
   (ear thermometer)

Upsher-Smith Laboratories: 800-654-2299
   (Feverall acetaminophen products with no artificial colors or flavors)

6   The Natural and Nontoxic Home

Air Quality Research: 800-242-7472
   (PF1 Formaldehyde Monitor kit)

Alpha Lab: 800-769-3754
   (electromagnetic field detector: TRI-FIELD METER)

American Board of Industrial Hygiene: 517-321-2638
   (verification of contractor's licensing for lead paint removal)

American Industrial Hygiene Association: 703-849-8888
    (list of certified lead assessment and abatement contractors)

American Sensors Electronics: 800-387-4219 or 905-477-3320
    (detectors for carbon monoxide, propane, and natural gas)

Art and Craft Materials Institute (ACMI): 617-426-6400
    (non-toxic art and craft products)

Beam Industries: 515-832-4620
    (high-quality central vacuum systems)

Bionaire Corporation: 800-253-2764
    (relative humidity guage)

BRK Electronics: 800-323-9005
    (First Alert carbon monoxide detector)

C-Cure Chemical Company: 800-292-2874 or 713-697-2024
    (environmentally safe tile grouts and caulks)

Centers for Disease Control (CDC): 404-488-7330
    (advice on lead-detection methods, treatment for lead poisoning, safe removal, locating a licensed lead-removal contractor)

Chem-Safe Products: 210-657-5321
    (housepaints for chemically sensitive people)

EPA: 202-554-1404
    (professional testing for formaldehyde in the home, guidance for asbestos problems)

EPA: 800-424-LEAD
    (advice on safe removal of lead)

EPA: 800-858-7378
    (hot line for detection of mercury in the home)

EPA: 800-SOS-RADON
    (hot line for detecting radon in the home)

Hartex: 800-237-9640
    (Hartex Carpet Cushion)

Lead Check: 800-262-LEAD
   (Lead Check Swabs)

Miller Paint Company: 503-233-4491
   (housepaints for chemically sensitive people)

Nilfisk: 800-NILFISK
   (Nilfisk GS 90 HEPA Allergy Vacuum)

Pace Chem Industries: 805-499-2911
   (water-based acrylic wood sealer: Crystal Air Clear Finish)

Pace Environs, Inc.: 800-359-9000
   (Frandon Lead Alert Kit)

Radiant Heater Corporation: 800-331-6408
   (environmentally safe ceramic space heaters)

Safe Technologies Corporation: 800-638-9121
   (electromagnetic field detector: TRI-FIELD METER, low-EMF computer
   monitor)

Southwest Fibers: 800-880-6092
   (Permaloom Carpet Cushion)

7   Pest Control

BioFac: 800-233-4914
   (Saf-T-Shield predatory nematodes for underground termites)

The Bio-Integral Resource Center: 510-524-2567
   (least-toxic pest-management strategies)

Consumer Reports Books: 800-272-0722
   (*Pest Control for Home and Garden* by Michael Hansen, PhD)

Copper Brite: 805-565-1566
   (Roach Prufe boric acid powder)

Enforcer Products: 800-241-5656
   (Enforcer Wasp & Hornet Killer with resmethrin)

Etex Ltd.: 800-543-5651
    (chemical-free electro-gun treatment for drywood termites, carpenter ants, and other wood-nesting insects)

Houghton Mifflin Company: 800-225-3362
    (*Silent Spring* by Rachel Carson)

Maag Agrochemicals: 407-778-4660
    (insect growth regulators: Fenoxycarb [Torus] for roaches)

The National Pesticide Network: 800-858-7378 or 800-858-PEST
    (least-toxic pest-management strategies)

N-Viro Products Ltd.: 516-567-2628
    (Saf-T-Shield predatory nematodes for underground termites)

Nisus Corporation: 800-264-0870
    (Bora-Care borax-based termiticide)

Northwest Coalition for Alternatives to Pesticides (NCAP):
    503-344-5044
    (least-toxic pest-management strategies)

Seabright Laboratories: 800-284-7363
    (Roach Killing Bait Stations)

U.S. Borax: 800-9TIMBOR
    (Tim-Bor borax-based termiticide)

Waterbury: 800-845-3495
    (R Value's Roach Kil boric acid powder, DRAX ant bait)

Whitmire: 800-325-3668
    (natural insecticide for roaches: Avert)

Zoecon: 800-527-0512
    (Hydroprene [Gencor] insect growth regulators for roaches, Precor or FleaTrol for fleas)

8 Protecting Your Child from the Great Outdoors

LittlePoint Corporation: 800-243-2929
  (Skedaddle Insect Protection for Children)

The National Center for Environmental Health Strategies:
  609-429-5358
  (least-toxic pest-management strategies)

Index

pneumonia, 201, 204
respiratory, 200–12
secondary bacterial, 204–5
"sick-all-the-time" syndrome, 201–2
treatment for, 206–14
  coughs, 210–12
  nasal congestion, 208–10
  respiratory infections, 207–8
viral croup cough, 203–4
warning signs, 205–6
Insect bites/stings, 342–47
  ant, 344–45
  bee, 344–45
  chigger, 343
  flea, 343
  general first aid for, 345
  hornet, 344–45
  preventing, 346–47
  mosquito, 343
  spider, 343
  tick, 343–44
  wasp, 344–45
Insect growth regulators (IGRs), 310, 318
Insecticidal soap, 311
Insecticide baths, 322
Insecticides, 307–14
  highly toxic, 309
  least toxic, 310–12
  nonchemical, 314–16
  use of, in home, 313–14
Insect repellents, 346–47
Insulinlike growth factor-1 (IGF-1), 40–41
Intestinal gas. See Gas
Intestinal problems. See Stomach/intestinal problems
Intestinal virus infection, 223–25, 228–30
Irradiation, food, 81–82
Iron, 33

Isomil formula, 34
I-Soyalac formula, 34

Jaundice, newborn, 157–60
  eliminating, 158–59
Jumpers, 301

Kangaroo pouch infant carriers, 164, 220

Labels, deciphering, 140–47
Lactic acid, 16
Lactose intolerance, 34, 40
Lanolin, 23–24, 141
Latches, 299
Laundry, 128, 274
Lawn care, 327–31
Laxatives, 30
Lead poisoning, 271, 286–96
  and infant formula, 37
  preventing, 291–96
  risk factors for, 290–91
  sources of, 287–89
  symptoms of, 287
  and water, 293–94
Lice. See Head lice
Lights, 285–86
Light switches, 285
Lipids, 141–43
Liver, 194
Locks, 299
Lupus, 182

Magazines, 275, 289
Markers, 278–79
Massage (gums), 174
Mastitis, 25–26
Mattresses, 127, 238, 242, 297
MCAD deficiency, 241
Measles, 182
Meat, preparing, 87, 97
Meconium, 159